The Language of

Battered Women

DATE DUE

#47-0108 Peel Off Pressure Sensitive

The Language
of
Battered Women

A Rhetorical Analysis of Personal Theologies

Carol L. Winkelmann

State University of New York Press

BV
4596
.A2
W56
2004

Published by
STATE UNIVERSITY OF NEW YORK PRESS, ALBANY

© 2004 State University of New York

For information, address State University of New York Press,
90 State Street, Suite 700, Albany, N.Y., 12207

Production, Laurie Searl
Marketing, Jennifer Giovani

Library of Congress Cataloging-in-Publication Data

Winkelmann, Carol Lea.
The language of battered women : a rhetorical analysis of personal theologies / Carol L. Winkelmann.
    p. cm.
Includes bibliographical references (p.) and index.
ISBN 0-7914-5941-1 (alk. paper) — ISBN 0-7914-5942-X (pbk. : alk. paper)
    1. Abused women—Religious life—Appalachian Region, Southern.   2. Language and languages—Religious aspects—Christianity.   3. Appalachian Region, Southern—Religious life and customs.   4. Women's shelters—Appalachian Region, Southern.   I. Title.

BV4596.A2W56 2003
261.8'327'0820975—dc21

2003042562

10 9 8 7 6 5 4 3 2 1

For my mother,
Annella Joan Winkelmann,
and for my sister,
Linda Alane Gifford

The Bible says the meek shall inherit the earth

and, ladies, we know this is not true.

—a shelter woman

Contents

_____

ACKNOWLEDGMENTS

I would like to acknowledge the people who supported and inspired me as I wrote about violence against women. First of all, I wish to honor the women through the ages who have worked to end sexual discrimination and violence against women. More immediately, I acknowledge my profound debt to residents of the Women's House, a shelter for battered women in the upper South. The women spoke freely to me about painful events and emotions and their deep faith with the hope that their voices would be heard. Their participation is a testimony to their faith and to their activity for social change. In particular I thank Sharon, a young woman I met at the shelter, whose whereabouts I no longer know. The complexity of her behaviors and beliefs invited me to see survivors in more depth than the literature typically portrays them and to appreciate their struggles more acutely. She stirred my curiosity and caused me to ask more meaningful questions about the lives of victims and survivors of domestic violence.

I would like to recognize the administration and staff of the shelter for granting me research access during the course of my volunteer work. They helped me to learn about the social service aspects of the struggle against domestic violence. One former staff person, Debbie Burstion, has been a particular friend and teacher to me. She dedicates her life in service to marginalized women, first in the battered women's movement and now in women's AIDS education. Debbie has shown me angles on African American women's issues that I—as a white academician—may have never discovered by myself.

I owe much to my colleagues, Marie Giblin, a theologian and ethicist, and Kandi Stinson, a sociologist and ethnographer. Marie, Kandi, and I meet regularly to talk about our research and to encourage each other to move forward with our visions and projects. They have spoken to me for many hours about violence against women from the perspective of their own fields. I could not have wished for better readers, co-mentors, and friends. Life in the academy is a challenge for women, yet Kandi and Marie have supported and inspired me during the past ten years. I am thankful for the gift of their scholarly company and good friendship.

I celebrate the supportive climate at Xavier University, particularly in its concern for the spirituality of its professors, staff, and students. Undaunted by the delicacy of this task, my colleagues Joe Wessling and George Traub, S.J., have been key figures, indeed mentors, to me as I have tried to discern ways to use my intellectual, academic life in service to the community. Joe and George exemplify at its best the meaning of Catholic identity at the Jesuit university.

I am indebted to several organizations for support during the stages of this project. The Association for Religion and Intellectual Life granted me a summer fellowship at Yale University where I began to configure the initial stages of this project in the company of inspiring women scholars, including Annie Imbens-Fransen and Emilie M. Townes. At Calvin College, in Grand Rapids, Michigan, I participated with analytical philosophers in a Pew-supported summer colloquium on the problem of evil. I am grateful to Xavier University, in Cincinnati, Ohio, for granting me a sabbatical to finish this work.

I acknowledge my students at Xavier University, the young women and men who teach me as we explore the issues of language and gender. Jenny Chwalibog provided much cheerfully rendered library research assistance.

Finally, and most earnestly, I thank my family. My husband, John Ippoliti, and my son, Christopher R. McLaughlin, gave me endless encouragement. Personally, they embody for me the meaning of loving-kindness, and politically, they are the best of allies in the struggle for women's rights. My father, Edward R. Winkelmann, passed away as I was finishing my manuscript. He encouraged me lovingly to the end. May we all have the inspiration we need to flourish.

"I Stand All Amazed"

When my pain and troubles seem to get me down,
I stand all amazed at the love Jesus offers me.

—Hettie

Hettie was a thirty-seven-year-old white Appalachian woman when I met her in a shelter for battered women. She had married when she was nineteen, had two children, and worked as a waitress in a small town in Tennessee. Hettie was raised in the Holiness tradition and attended a local church. Her grandmother had been a pastor there many years ago though the congregation no longer supported female pastors or leaders. The church mothers who had known her grandmother, however, treated Hettie with the respect she did not get at home. Hettie "took the beatings." Evil was not a mystery to her. People who did not receive Spirit baptism, like her husband, were vulnerable. Sometimes Hettie thought she deserved the beatings because of her own sinfulness. Still Hettie trusted that God would watch over her so that the beatings did not get out of control. Toward the end, they did. Once Hettie had to go to the hospital for broken ribs. When she discovered her husband was sexually molesting her oldest daughter, she left with the children for her sister's house in Ohio. But her sister had her own problems and they could not stay long. I met Hettie at the Women's House, a shelter for battered women.

For nine years, I listened to women in the shelter tell similar stories—intense narratives of male brutality, escape, and seemingly unyielding pain and suffering. Shelter women share sometimes vividly recalled, sometimes half-forgotten memories of anguished scenes of physical, sexual, and emotional abuse. They weep, rage, and rail. The room fills with anxiety and despair. Then a woman raises up the name of Jesus, her savior, and other women begin to testify. The conversation lightens up, moods change, and friendships grow.

Like Hettie, many shelter women express their faith plainly. They turn their burdens over to Jesus and they go on trying to survive and heal. I myself "stand all amazed" at their strength. Their faith is sometimes a mystery to me. I started to meet women like Hettie in May of 1992 when I began volunteering at the Women's House, a shelter for battered women in an urban area of a midsized city in the upper South.[1] In the end, the shelter women substantially altered my sensibilities about gender and violence. The transformation was effected in sometimes brief, sometimes more prolonged encounters with the women who stay in the shelter overnight, a few days, or several months. Over the years, I have had multiple roles at the shelter: dishwasher, donation sorter, gardener, hot line counselor, office worker, caring listener, literacy worker, and always, ethnolinguist. Now, many years later, I am still drawn into their worlds of struggle, suffering, small triumphs, sometimes significant transformations.

The shelter, at its best, can become a place for transformative encounters. Women, both like and unlike Hettie—women with different stories, sorrows, and social status—meet and talk. Changes happen in brief conversations, in exchanges of gazes or embraces, in experiences of empathy and compassion. Simply listening to the sometimes seemingly unspeakable stories of shelter women can evoke shifts in outlook, priorities, principles, faith. Usually we are protected from such stories by the silence of shame, denial, discursive distance, or death. Women are, of course, sometimes battered to death. Mostly the voices of battered women are not welcome in polite conversation or other conventional social genres, that is, for example, in dinner table talk, school curricula, church sermons, or academic discourse. It is ironic because the distance between battered women and the rest of womankind is, in reality, so slim.

At the same time, many battered women in shelters are isolated in numerous ways: geographically, educationally, economically, and perhaps even religiously. The Women's House is in an economically depressed area and it draws most of its clientele from local neighborhoods. Some women, like Hettie, do come from afar. The women are nearly all desperately poor. Domestic violence may cut across race and class lines, but resources to escape it often do not. In general, women with no or few other resources come to the shelter: typically under/unemployed, underclass or working-class African American and white Appalachian women. They are mostly from the fundamentalist/evangelical or Holiness/Sanctified traditions. Many are the same age as my university students—early to mid-twenties, but most shelter women tote babies on their hips, not to mention bruises on their bodies and other visible and invisible wounds from abusive partners. The shelter is a loud and noisy place, oftentimes with babies crying, children shouting, and mothers yelling. The women spend their days not poring over books, but poring over classified ads in the newspaper, much of the time for jobs they will not get and apartments they cannot afford. Unless there is significant intervention, there will be no university degrees.

There may not always be emotional healing either. Many shelter women are very fragile from years of physical and emotional abuse. They are frequently coping with their own drug and alcohol dependencies. At the same time, they can be emotionally shut off from having struggled for years with racism, classism, and sexism. There are sometimes barely concealed tensions between white and black residents. There are also not-so-hidden hierarchies of worth and self-esteem based on the availability or potential for material resources and emotional support, thus independence and a better future. Most times, however, the generosity of spirit between women of different subcultures, race, ethnicity, class, education, age, sexual orientation, and other life states is utterly heartrending, tremendously moving. A last dollar is lent. Bus tokens, cigarettes, and laundry soap are shared. An encouraging smile or a silent embrace is offered. An exhausted woman watches over a more exhausted woman's child. Suggestions are extended and subtle support given. The shelter is a place of both terrible suffering and strong hope.

In 1994 I began a literacy or storytelling circle in the shelter. In previous years, as funding dropped in a changing sociopolitical climate, fewer services were offered to residents.[2] So I volunteered once a week as a literacy worker in an effort to engage women who otherwise may have had little to do in the evening. In exchange, I was able to learn from shelter women by listening to their stories. On any evening, I may work with one to a dozen women. We sit around a table, choose a topic by consensus—any topic, although the women mostly write about their shattered lives. Then we write, we read aloud what we've written, and we talk. The moods of the story sessions shift drastically, often within a session itself, as the women explore their lives, their loves, their longings. The moods swing from jubilation at having escaped a knife-wielding spouse (to name just one all-too-frequent scenario), to anger about the second-class status of women, to desolation about leaving behind a marriage, a life, a dream.

The literacy levels vary amongst the women. Most often they write their own stories, poems, essays, recipes, jokes, prayers. On occasion, because many women want to have their words in my writing or to see their own stories in a book meant for display at the shelter, I sometimes record their words myself. I may handwrite their stories as we talk, or I tape, and later I transcribe. Sometimes I bring my laptop computer, we talk, and I record the conversations. This particular activity—"talking into the computer," as we have sometimes called it, or "telling stories to the computer"—is a favorite activity. I bring copies of the conversation the next week. The women take pleasure in seeing their words in print, their stories in writing. They want to share what they know about life and loss, anguish and abuse, hope, desire, and joy. Often they laugh nervously at what is captured in ink—embarrassed by the starkness of their words, the absolute clarity of their anger or laments, their outbursts, their sufferings or sorrows. Sometimes they ask me to change words to clarify or alter their meanings. I do.

During our many conversations, I began to consider the language of shelter women in new ways. Although the women's language in the Women's House does not represent the language practices of battered women in every place or in every time, their language practices can help us to understand how some women experience and recover from partner violence. In this study, one basic contention is that many battered women attempt to survive and resist abuse, and to heal themselves and their children, by engaging in some similar linguistic strategies and communicative practices. These practices—which collectively I name the genres of "healing"—involve three stages: silence and isolation; lamentation; and solidarity and action. The movement through these stages is motivated by the intermingling of the diverse languages of battered women as they speak out of their own background, their own experience, and their own social location. As the Russian language scholar M. M. Bakhtin writes:

> The living utterance, having taken meaning and shape at a particular historical moment in a socially specific environment, cannot fail to brush up against thousands of living dialogic threads, woven by socio-ideological consciousness around the given object of an utterance; it cannot fail to become an active participant in social dialogue.[3]

The language of shelter women is not excluded from this language dynamic. As Bakhtin has it:

> The dialogic orientation of language is a phenomenon that is, of course, a property of *any* discourse. It is the natural orientation of any living discourse. On all its various routes toward the object, in all its directions, the word encounters an alien word and cannot help encountering it in a living, tension-filled interaction. Only the mythical Adam, who approached a virginal and as yet verbally unqualified world with the first word, could really have escaped from start to finish this dialogic inter-orientation with the alien word that occurs in the object.[4]

The mythic reference aside (though only momentarily since the story of the garden, as I will show in subsequent chapters, often surfaces in the terror-filled memories of women's assaults), the dialogic quality of language is fundamental. In terms of shelter talk, the "living threads" of the women's discourse intertwine to create new ways to looking at the world and at their immediate environment. On a microlevel, meaning shifts occur as words are transferred from one context to the next, thus thrusting language into new forms and functions and the shelter speakers into new linguistic territory. Bakhtin puts the process elegantly:

> But any utterance, when it is studied in great depth under the concrete conditions of speech communication, reveals to us many half-concealed or completely concealed words of others with various degrees of foreignness. [. . .] The utterance proves to be a very complex and multiplanar phenomenon if considered not in isolation and with respect to its author (the speaker) only, but as a link in the chain of speech communication and with respect to other, related utterances. . . .[5]

Like other language users, then, shelter women speak in interconnected chains of meaning. They influence one another linguistically and, thus, accompany one another to greater levels of self-consciousness and social awareness. To put it more simply: Battered women who have the opportunity to talk to other women can help each other to move to more conscious awareness of their oppression as women in intimate relationships and in society. They may begin to understand the importance of social solidarity for social change. Interestingly, one common link is religion. Women in this shelter in the upper South are Christian and their faith figures prominently in their stories.

Of course, the idea of helping one another through talk is a truism to longtime proponents of feminism or consciousness-raising groups. People do learn by listening to one another. This study, however, raises up important issues about the process of dialogic transformation. First of all, I am interested in how shelter talk reflects Bakhtin's observations:

> . . . at any given moment, languages of various epochs and periods of social-ideological life cohabit one another. Even languages of the day exist: one could say that today's and yesterday's socioideological and political "day" do not, in a certain sense, share the same language; every day represents another socio-ideological semantic "state of affairs," another vocabulary, another accentual system, with its own slogans, its own ways of assigning blame and praise. [. . .] Thus at any given moment of its historical existence, language is heteroglot from top to bottom: it

represents the co-existence of socio-ideological contradictions between the present and the past, between differing epochs of the
past, between different socio-ideological groups in the present,
between tendencies, schools, circles and so forth, all given a bodily
form. These "languages" of heteroglossia intersect each other in a
variety of ways, forming new socially typifying "languages."[6]

These are tremendous insights that, for me, offer clarity particularly to the
theological reasoning and the healing processes of survivors of domestic violence. Translated to a simplified local level, the implications of Bakhtin's
words to me are that women learn by talking to diverse others. Their talk
teaches because their various languages, theological and secular, intermix
and create new meanings.

For feminist readers, an integral related issue is this: Although the
literature on battered women largely neglects or simply critiques it, religion
is very significant in the process. The healing process of female victims of
violence sometimes involve a component—the religious component—with
which the battered women's movement would often rather not deal. Yet, a
battered woman's concept of God, religion, and suffering enters into the
process of making sense of her situation in very complex and sometimes
contradictory ways. Philosophers and theologians have long debated the
problem of suffering and evil. They call this the study of "theodicy." The
main query of theodicy is this: In traditional Christian thought, an omniscient, omnipotent, and perfectly good God created the world; yet, why
would such a God allow the evil that causes the vast amount of profound
suffering among humankind? Even in the postmodern technological age, the
issue perplexes. Volumes have been written on this subject.

Yet philosophers and theologians rarely consider theodicy from the
point of view of victims and survivors. Typically they neglect the role that
their own social institutions have played in the perpetuation of suffering and
evil. Traditional beliefs, as feminists of both secular and religious persuasion
have taught us, are very problematic—injurious even—for all women struggling to achieve social and economic equality. The teachings of the Christian church on women and their roles hurt women because they limit women's
participation in church and society and they rationalize the limitations as
divinely mandated. Sandra M. Schneiders makes this disturbing historical
fact clear: "Not only were women excluded, marginalized, and degraded in
the church, but they were also directly oppressed by church authorities, and
the church legitimated and supported their oppression by men in family and
society." The church, Schneiders continues, is "a prime legitimator of patriarchal marriage and its attendant abuses."[7] One of those abuses is called
domestic violence—the most pressing social issue of our time.

From my own standpoint as a woman raised in the Catholic faith, I do believe that the traditional religious beliefs that many battered women evoke to make sense of their situations and suffering can be problematic. As a language researcher, however, I study the function of the language of battered women in the healing process. Interestingly, their religious faith serves not only to sustain them through profound suffering, but to develop solidarity with sometimes culturally different women. In the shelter, the women's language is layered with traces of mostly fundamentalist/evangelical and Holiness/Sanctified backgrounds. It can be helpful or harmful. But no sociological study can be complete without recognizing the significant, if complicated or paradoxical, role that this Christian heritage plays in their language and lives.

This study concerns these complex aspects of the language of survivors. I first offer an overview of the pervasiveness of violence against women. Our social practices and procedures, our cultural rules and regulations, and our basic institutions (including, for example, our religious institutions) have rendered the actualities of the problem either invisible or greatly diminished in our society. The actualities are staggering. I review the frequency and kinds of domestic violence—that is, physical, sexual, psychological, emotional, and economic. The causes of intimate violence are complex and contested, but they can be categorized as sociological and nonsociological theories. The sociological theories include both feminist and family systems theories. Among the nonsociological are biological or neurophysiological theories. In chapter 1, I review the statistical, sociological, and fiercely ideological terrain on which partner violence is constructed. As a participant-observer motivated by social and feminist theories of language practice, I offer the voices of shelter women to bring to life the facts and figures.

In chapter 2, I consider the Women's House as both a material location and as a culture or social order. What does it mean for battered women to live in the shelter? The discussion begins with a historical look at the YWCA, the national nonprofit organization of which the Women's House is a part. Its mission is "the empowerment of women and the elimination of racism." Yet the shelter is based on self-help philosophies that call for women in crisis to demonstrate their willingness and ability to pull themselves up despite many social and psychological obstacles. In effect, the Women's House is a set of roles, routines, rules, regulations, and relationships that call forth an ambiguous, sometimes contradiction-laden, response from residents. Tensions arise between residents and staff, and between residents, as they try to navigate differences in race/ethnicity, age, maternal status, religion, and so forth. I consider these conditions through an exploration of the material location, the shelter participants, and the delivery of services. The shelter is a system of surveillance (via cameras, fences, locks, rules, regulations, curfews, et cetera.)

against which many residents more or less successfully resist. Interestingly, one way they resist is to create their own language of faith in God and in one another to assuage their suffering and to recreate meaning in their lives. When family, friends, faith communities, police, and the judicial systems fail to provide for their safety and well-being, this faith is sometimes battered women's only comfort.

In chapter 3, I consider the experiential or phenomenological meaning of suffering for battered women. Battered women constitute an "identity" group whose very existence is based on the experience of physical and psychological violence. Their flesh and bones literally bear the marks and meanings of pain and suffering. Imprinted with the signs of violation, the figures of trauma, and the struggle for self-control, their bodies are living testimony of the forceful infliction of patriarchal control and order. Their skin is the interface between submission or subjection and resistance and opposition. Thus, although pain and suffering are ultimately inextricable phenomena, I draw a distinction between them to explore, first of all, the fundamental meanings of *physical pain* to women. This discussion is informed by insights of researchers such as Elaine Scarry, Eric Cassell, David Morris, and others who tend to the meanings of physical pain; yet, the actual words of battered women quicken these scholarly discussions. For example, battered women tend to metaphorize the experience of pain and violence away from their bodies and onto matters of agency, weapons, or wounds. The ethnographic evidence yields reasons why women deflect attention from their corporeal experience, reasons extending from shelter culture and the broader cultural terrain, particularly matters related to gender and religious socialization. Trauma scholars, including Judith Lewis Herman, offer another source of insight, psychological or clinical insight, into the translation of violence away from battered women's corporeal experience. Secondly, I turn my attention to the fundamental meanings of *suffering* to shelter women. Contrary to the beliefs of the condescending social worker or volunteer, battered women have good senses of how and why they suffer. They speak of suffering in physical, mental or emotional, and social terms. Finally, I reintegrate the totality of battered women's experience of pain and suffering by offering seven themes yielded forth by their words. These themes cover a range of feeling from senses of emptiness to senses of the loss of human integrity. Interestingly and ironically, though shelter women's words may sometimes lack a fully sentient dimension, their words do not lack a social dimension. Indeed theologian Dorothee Soelle lucidly notes that all suffering is finally a social experience.

In chapter 4 I consider a spectrum of theological explanations for suffering and evil—known as theodicies. Why do innocent women and girl children suffer violence inflicted by the ones who claim to love them? Philosophers, theologians, and others have long debated the "problem of evil." Unmerited suffering is considered an evil. As I noted earlier, in traditional Christianity, an omniscient, omnipotent, and perfectly good God created the world. Why would such a God allow the evil that causes so much suffering? Augustine, Aquinas, Hume, Kant, and many others have contributed to the discussion. The scriptural treatments of suffering, such as the Book of Job, and the literary treatments of suffering, such as the writings of Fyodor Dostoevsky, Albert Camus, and Elie Wiesel, have also animated our attention. In this chapter I touch, first of all, upon *classical* views of suffering. I then move to the other end of the theological spectrum to introduce more contemporary views of suffering. I explore European and European American *feminist* views, including those of theologians Dorothee Soelle and Elizabeth A. Johnson and minister, pastoral care provider, and domestic violence scholar Marie M. Fortune. These writers have been influential in middle-class, feminist, Christian-based organizations. White middle-class feminist scholars, however, have a tendency to homogenize women's suffering. For example, Fortune ascribes anger against God to battered women. Blaming God may describe the reaction of some women, but it does not describe the fundamental reaction of the mostly underclass African American and white Appalachian women in the Women's House. Thus, in this chapter, I consider how the intersection of race/ethnicity and religious affiliation affects battered women's ideas about suffering. I provide a discussion of some of the theological principles of the traditional black churches offered by womanist theologians, followed by a discussion of some of the theological principles of the Holiness/Sanctified and fundamentalist/evangelical churches. These are the churches to which most of the shelter women belong. Some voices of insight include womanist theologian Emilie Townes and evangelical theologian Nancy Hardesty. Grounded in the words of shelter women, I discuss key ideas of these two denominational groupings related to language genres and worship styles, concepts about salvation and redemption, images of the divine, and gender roles. Ultimately, shelter women are not guided solely by church doctrine; more frequently, they are grounded by their lived experience and their social negotiation with other survivors.

Chapter 5 is an extended and systematic discussion of theodicy. It is concerned, however, with the meaning of suffering as battered women articulate it. I situate the words of residents within, first, a general and traditional theodicy framework. Then I situate the suffering of battered women within an elaborate ten-category typology of both traditional and alternative theodicies.[8] I use this typology to determine a fuller range of explanations to which battered women subscribe. I then identify several theodicies accepted, at least initially, by most battered women in this particular cultural context—a shelter in an urban area in the northern ridge of the Bible Belt, that is, the upper South. Specifically, Women's House residents often speak or write about suffering either as an experience of atonement or redemption or as an experience of shared suffering with God. In an Atonement/Redemption model, suffering is conceived as part of God's plan for human salvation. Suffering is endured in expiation for the sake of others or out of obedience to God. In a Suffering God model, suffering is conceived as a shared experience involving both God and the victim of violence: When battered women suffer, God suffers. And ultimately, divine and human solidarity strengthens battered women. Sometimes residents are able to move toward a more liberatory theodicy, that is, religious explanations of suffering based on lived and shared social experience. In a Liberatory model, unjust suffering is understood to be caused by the oppression of others. Even if residents do not arrive at fully integrated liberatory theodicies, their shared language about God and suffering has more or less potential to assist them in the healing process. Interestingly, the women's theodicies are less traditional or conservative than their reports of their partners' theodicies. In women's words, their abusive partners subscribe to traditional theodicies involving dualisms of good and evil or themes of punishment and retribution. In a Dualistic model, the devil schemes for control over human souls in a universe constituted of absolutes of good and evil; in a Punishment/Retribution model, a powerful God keeps track of human sin, including individual or collective sin, and punishes it. Naturally, battered women do not fair well in situations in which such values and beliefs are sustained. These traditional explanations may lead to violence against women by creating a climate in which violence becomes thinkable, even justifiable or necessary, in order to control women. Such logic frequently appears in women's reports of the speech of their abusive partners.

In chapter 6 I refocus my attention to consider what battered women have to say more generally about religion. Women's spirituality involves more than thoughts about suffering though, to be sure, such thoughts are never completely submerged or distant. In my view, domestic violence discussions would benefit from being situated within a broader discussion of religious perspectives because the control of women is effected through more than physical and psychological pain and suffering. The social control of women is effected through many interlocking cultural meanings, made through both discursive and other semiotic or symbolic means, within which religion in general and specific ideas about suffering are both significant factors. In conversation women in the shelter frequently talk about God, scripture, and their church and its traditions. Some of their talk is helpful and some harmful, some resistant to traditional gender socialization and some reinterpretive of it. In this chapter I consider the religious interpretations or hermeneutics of three themes: women's identity and relationship with God, women's suffering, and women's healing.

Within these three basic categories, a range of meanings is made by survivors that filters into shelter conversation. A spectrum of such ideas spurs women to reconsider their religious beliefs in the light of their lived experience of gender discrimination and domestic violence.

In chapter 7 I consider more carefully the language of suffering. In the midst of staggering human suffering, battered women are sometimes capable of moving from states of deathlike alienation to stances of life-filled autonomy. For my theoretical framework I make use of the scholarship in psychology and theology on trauma and recovery, including the work of Judith Herman, Dorothee Soelle, Marie Fortune, and others. In *Suffering* Soelle develops a tripartite schema for the phases of human suffering: silence and isolation, lamentation, and senses of solidarity with other survivors.[9] I use, critique, and supplement this schema by tracing battered women's evolving concepts of suffering-in-context. One important point is this: Because of the dialogic nature of language, a unilinear, monodimensional healing process cannot occur. Women's language during trauma recovery reveals the fluctuations of not only internal or psychological factors, but social and environmental factors as well, including dialogic influence from face-to-face talk. Language changes when the rhetorical context changes; that is, when women meet others who have different stories to share. Healing is a social process.

Chapter 8 considers the dynamics of language change as women talk. I consider some of the strategies used by shelter women to survive suffering and to heal themselves, that is, to cominister as together they struggle to cope with their pain. The women may move from personal autonomy to social solidarity by way of shared stories. In this chapter I illustrate the webbing or weaving, the knitting, the intertextualizing or hybridization, of personal stories. As narratives are webbed, slight meaning shifts may occur, movements of mind, stirrings in the moral imagination, that signal new ways of being in the world. The effect is sometimes a transformation of consciousness and a move toward social action—for survivors and those of us who have been challenged and graced enough to learn from them.

For social change, new stories must be told. Survivors sometimes create stories about their relationships with their partners, families, communities, and God. Indeed, this is the best hope for those who accompany survivors: new and healthier stories are told. Survivors may critique and remap power relations. They create new meanings based on their lived and shared shelter experience and, in so doing, reinflect or reimagine their world. Language about God—theology—is integral to this process. Some women reexamine what they have learned about the status and roles of women in church and community. They devise new stories about the call of women to teach and testify, to prophesy. In chapter 9 I consider this reappropriation of religious language, sometimes in acts of creative storytelling and testimony, sometimes in protest and condemnation, sometimes in celebration of women's spiritual gifts and talents. These creative linguistic acts are the basis of their local theologies, that is, their theological responses to the problems of their everyday lives. Quite apart from church doctrine or dogma, battered women—like all ordinary people in all walks of life—have their own theological understandings, religious views and visions, spiritual yearnings. They have their own organic intellectualizations and their own deeply felt cosmologies. Local theologies can function to preserve women's dignity, create community, and generate social change.[10]

For evidence, across the various sections of this study, I web and weave the scholarly language of linguists and theologians, the personal language of my own experience, and the social language excerpted from story sessions and in-depth interviews between shelter women and myself and sometimes my students who go to the shelter during a course I teach on women and violence. My students listen to women, take care of children, and assist the staff. At school, they sometimes engage online with shelter women who are often inclined to talk further.

About methodology: This project is ethnolinguistic, that is, it is an ethnography of language practices. Ethnography is qualitative social research that seeks to describe the lived experience of a group or subculture. Its methods include participant observation in an actual field site, ethnographic notetaking, and group and in-depth interviewing. It depends on multiple and recursive analysis; that is, through a longitudinal investigation of the many facets of a culture or subculture, the ethnographer interprets patterns of thought and action that define the domain. Spindler and Spindler put it this way: "Ethnographers attempt to record, in an orderly manner, how natives behave and how they explain their behavior. And ethnography, strictly speaking, is an orderly report of this recording."[11] One studies the organization of a group, their behavior, emotions, artifacts, space, language—that is, their meaning-making system or what one has to know, believe in, or communicate, in order to function in a manner acceptable to its members. In short, ethnography is the complex study of culture—the entire semiotic or meaning-making system of culture or subculture.[12] Clifford Geertz simply put it: "Believing, with Max Weber, that man is an animal suspended in webs of significance he himself has spun, I take culture to be those webs . . .".[13]

Initially at the shelter I studied general language practices. I collected and analyzed language for themes of significance arising in largely naturalistic situations or linguistic routines. Shortly, I became acutely aware of how significant religion is to victims of violence as they become "survivors" of domestic violence. So I began to focus on the meaning of their faith to them and the way statements related to it functioned in their talk. In this study I present my findings and I use the women's language to illustrate the themes

I have discovered. The analysis of the study is largely thematic and rhetorical, that is, accessible to general readers.

Finally, this study is interdisciplinary and, like all feminist scholarship, it is critical, interested, and praxis-oriented. By weaving together the speech and stories of shelter women with analysis and argument, I hope readers gain a deeper sense of the theological struggles faced by female victims of violence as they struggle to become "survivors." I wish to invite social change educators from our many professions and positions to listen more deeply to battered women when we consider how to talk, to teach, to theorize, and to theologize.

In her work Kathleen M. Sands quotes Asian theologian Chung Hyun Kyung who says, "making meaning out of suffering is dangerous business." Then Sands writes, "I would add that it is a business that women do everyday, and the closer theologians stay to those complex, organic processes, the more modes of meaning we uncover for dealing with evil and suffering."[14] I would amend: Even as we consider the literatures of our various fields, we all need to stay close to the meaning-making processes of ordinary women, violated women, battered women. We must invite survivors into the conversation when we strategize for social change. The battered women's movement would benefit from more thoughtful consideration of the faith lives of the women it seeks to serve. It has begun to teach clergy about domestic violence but has more to learn from battered women about the effects of faith on surviving the violence against them. To do less is to alienate further women who are already socially isolated. To ignore or degrade their faith is to lose an opportunity for more profound personal and social change. Traditional religion is patriarchal, perhaps beyond repair, and it has contributed greatly to the oppression of women and girl children. Yet battered women's faith is an exceptionally significant aspect of their lives. Reflecting on it, women sometimes subvert tradition and reconceive their roles and relationships in family, church, and society.

ONE

"I'll Be Scared for Everyone in the World"

THE PERVASIVENESS OF DOMESTIC VIOLENCE

———————————————

Don't trust. Men kill. The police don't help us and, if the judges
don't do it, we're lost. I'll be scared for everyone in the world.

—Josephine

INTRODUCTION

In ways nearly beyond belief, a woman's body in the world is frequently a
body in pain. Women suffer extensively from violence directed at them by
their most intimate partners. Some women suffer in silence. Other women,
like Josephine, escape to safety and speak out. Some women's bodies alone
tell the story. They suffer and die, many times without redress. Overwhelm-
ingly, domestic violence is violence directed by men at women. Women
initiate violence as often as men do, but research makes apparent the gender
disproportion of seriously injurious intimate violence.[1] Ninety-five percent of
serious assaults are acts perpetrated by men against women who are several
times more likely than men to need medical care and to experience psychological injuries after an assault.[2]

The acts of violence against women are many, the list long. Most
commonly, women's spouses or partners throw objects at them. They shove,
grab, and slap. They kick, bite, or hit women with their fists. They beat
women up. They rape them. They threaten women with guns and knives.

15

The list of violent acts does not always convey the grievous reality, or frightening extent, of male brutality or women's suffering, but women often are violated in appalling ways and means. A blow to the head is followed by another, and another, and another. A pregnant woman is kicked in her stomach. A girlfriend is hit by a car or pushed from a moving one. Eyes are blackened, limbs broken. Women from the Women's House depict the violence starkly:

— You would think that the times I was choked to the point that I lose consciousness would be enough!

— I was pregnant with my third son. My boyfriend came in angry from working. He just started yelling at me because I moved something off his desk. Somehow we ended up on the bed—him squeezing me real tight and I was scratching him in the face.

— He did stuff. Putting a gun to my head. Biting me and holding on for a long time. You know when someone bites you really hard for a long time? You can't feel it anymore. Hit me, beat me with a broom. My body is so marked up from three years, I'm afraid to show another man my body. He'd say, "What man would want you with all those bruises?" He put me in a trunk. I just couldn't stand it! I begged him to let me out. He put me in for only three minutes, but it seemed like it lasted for hours. [. . .] My son now, he was around this. [My abuser] would hit my kids, knowing it would hurt me.

Some women do not even know all the ways in which they are being injured by abusers. Lily was kicked and spat upon by her partner, but her bruised body and self-esteem were only one shard of her suffering:

My daughter, she was being molested from the time she was nine until the time she was thirteen. Her father, her natural father, was molesting her. [. . .] I could have been on death row. I could have and it wasn't that far away because my daughter was being raped by her own father. She was bleeding out of her rectum. I never knew what was wrong with my child. I could find no reason. My child was scared to death to tell it to anybody. He went to her school and kicked her and beat her like she was a dog. They called the cops. Only time my daughter had the nerve to even tell anybody that her daddy been doing that to her. The only thing I could say was, "Lord, have mercy! You've been killing my child." Then I had to look at her when she asked me, "Momma [. . .], you were my mother. Why didn't you know?"

Women suffer more subtle, less visible, forms of violence. They endure psychological, emotional, and economic abuse. They are confined or isolated. They are humiliated and degraded. Their paychecks, food, and clothing are taken away or carefully controlled. Tiffany, a twenty-five-year-old mother in the Women's House, tells her story succinctly: "He hits me with a crowbar and asks me for my money." Anything might serve as a weapon in nonphysical forms of violence, including kinship ties (especially children), jobs or coworkers, school, language, sex, and religion. Anything that can be taken away, manipulated, or suppressed serves as a weapon in the struggle for power and control. Shelter women share some stories:

— I am scared of my husband getting my kids. He wants custody. He didn't [want them] when we were there. How can he [take care of them] if he gets them? What will happen?

— [My abuser] cuts you off from your friends and family. He tells you what you can and can't wear. He has extreme jealousy. He always has to know where you are and he gets angry if he doesn't. He calls you names when he is angry. He always has to be in control of everything.

— The first signs of an abuser: He's always calling you. He wants to know your whereabouts at all times. He knows personal information about you [that you did not] give to him. He hit women in past relationships. He talks about women in a degrading manner and hates women in general. He has no respect for his mother or sisters. He makes unexpected visits. He hangs up your phone calls. He has extreme anger.

— He always told me what I was doing wrong, what I didn't do. He still tells me what I did wrong and he blames me when things go wrong. I hear it everyday. That's why I'm here. I'm tired of it—to the point I feel like I'm going to die. I admit, I don't know how to raise kids. But my husband was always sure. I never had kids! So I just raised my kids by the seat of my pants—even with all his complaints.

— I got sexual, mental, physical abuse for three years. One thing I want to say: this is the worse abuse. Not the beatings and the physical. The mental abuse was the worse, telling me I was nothing. The sexual thing too. After he beat me up, he always made me give him oral sex in front of my daughter. My son now. The thing about that was, he didn't get off. He got off on the control of making me do it when I didn't want to do it. He got off by seeing me not wanting to do it. It made me so sick when he got off. He enjoyed himself. I got so I don't even like sex anymore. Sex is like a nasty thing to me.

Obviously, domestic violence is more than bruises, black eyes, and broken bones. It involves a constellation of forms of frequently escalating violence such as physical, sexual, psychological, emotional, or economic coercion.[3] It involves intimidation of all sorts: isolation and other forms of literal or social captivity, the infliction of emotional pain and degradation, the withholding of affection or resources, the destruction of property, and the maltreatment of children or pets. This violence is used by partners in calculated ways to control women.

Perhaps because domestic violence may be the most common form of crime in the United States, many women are unsure they are suffering it or suffering it unjustly.[4] Among factors making it difficult for women to define their cases as domestic violence are these: the remorse of the batterer after the violence; the shame and guilt of the survivor who believes she triggered the violence; the infrequency or irregularity of assaults; the absence of physical assault or serious injury; and the gender of the batterer.[5] Women may believe they deserve suffering because of their own being, that is, the femaleness they embody. Everywhere, this belief garners evidence. There are many antiwoman messages in the media, in our institutions, in our social and political arrangements, rules, and regulations, and elsewhere in our world. Even our most sacred texts, such as the Bible, spread the bad news. These messages take a place in a system of oppression in which interpersonal and cultural factors are interwoven to encourage violence against women.

HOW PERVASIVE IS IT? SOME STATISTICS

The prevalence of intimate violence is simply staggering.[6] Domestic violence is the number one health threat to women. In the United States, one-third to one-half of all women will be physically assaulted in their lifetimes by partners. One woman is physically assaulted every fifteen seconds and injuries are twice as likely to occur if the attack is perpetrated by a partner rather than by a stranger. Half of all female homicide victims are killed by husbands or boyfriends while only 3 percent of male homicide victims are killed by wives or girlfriends who are often acting in self-defense. One out of every three women worldwide has been beaten, raped, or abused.[7]

Such numerical data is stunning; nonetheless, experts agree that the figures are underestimates. Most instances of violence against women are not reported. Indeed, one estimate is that only 7 to 14 percent of intimate partner assaults are reported to police.[8] In 1994, Secretary of Health and Human Services Donna Shalala called the problem domestic "terrorism," an "epidemic" in the United States.[9] The underreportage is due in part because of shame, fear, or distrust. Often women do not wish to bring their plight to the attention of their families, churches, or communities. The family is sacrosanct. Indeed, few people wish to give up notions of the family as a safe and loving haven. To make matters worse, according to shelter women, the police and justice systems are slow to intervene or they do not intervene effectively in domestic problems even in areas with mandatory or preferred arrest policies.[10] Josephine's words earlier—"The police don't help us and, if the judges don't do it, we're lost"—are a common refrain among battered women. Tiffany, the young woman whose partner hit her with a crowbar to get her paycheck, puts it this way:

> When I called up the police, they came and locked him up. Somehow he got out and now I do not know what to do. I called my mother and she told me he was out. Now I do not know what to do!

Her story is common. Battered women are bewildered when the police or the courts allow their partners to walk while they themselves are injured, homeless, and afraid for their lives. Shelter women sometimes cite harassment by police as proof that the law enforcement system is not to be trusted. One woman said: "When I was with [the police], they said all these things to me. They said, 'Let me see how you taste.' I went back to my mama. I was so scared!"

Sherri, a policeman's wife, angrily complained that the police were unwilling to intervene in the domestic affairs of one of its own—wife-beater or not. She came from a shelter nearly a thousand miles away to hide from a husband who could easily access information about her whereabouts, her legal recourse, and other self-protective measures. Now she worries about other policeman's wives: "I tell my stories of abuse for cops' wives. I want them to know there's somewhere to go. Don't take the abuse. You are going to end up dead."

In the following conversation, some shelter women share their low opinion of law enforcement to explain their unwillingness to call for help. Their words are angry, their tone of voice derisive:

PAM: Most police are bruising their own wives! It's best to get their badge numbers [when they respond to a call]. [Get their] badge number and they will face it.

TERI: I'll never forget his bad ass [that is, the police who responded to her call]!

PAM: We got a neighbor. He's a cop, and he's doing his wife the same way. I can't go to him for help. I can't call him. I'm crying with her. He's doing her the same way. The uniform is the check. The badge. They do what they want.

TERI: It's the authority they have.

PAM: Most police are doing drugs. I saw on TV. They tore up the hotel. They were shooting guns. It was in the paper and everything. Police doing what they want to do. Tore up the hotel and everything. Did you see that?

TANYA: They need more training. I was talking to the police. They were listening to me. When [my abuser] started talking to them, it changed everything! He was putting me down. They listened to him. Told me to get in the house! "Get in the house," they said. "Don't get him upset." Then they left. They separate you. I could hardly hear what he was saying, but he told them all these things about me and they said to me, "Get in the house!" I felt so stupid. He was already on probation. They let him go back to the bar. Then it all started again. [The police] need more training. [My abuser] could have stayed [that is, conned] the chief of police!

PAM: They are supposed to arrest him.

BETH: They told you to go back into the house?

DENISE: What color were they? They were white?

TANYA: They was white. And there was one, a plainclothes, following him up my street and another [plainclothesman] with two uniformed officers and they were listening to me and I was trying to explain to them and they were: "Okay, okay." And they said "You should not be hanging around with him" and "We aren't doing you any good."

These women's experience and opinions of the police are typical of shelter talk. Denise's words imply the racial conflicts, a topic to be discussed forthrightly. The women's conversation elucidates the serious underreportage of domestic violence. Of course, their perception of the unwillingness of law enforcement to effectively protect women is only one aspect of the problem. The judicial system does not usually intervene to their satisfaction either. One woman, Sasha, whose husband made the telephone call to the police though he assaulted her, was given six months of probation and a fine. She calls her piece, "The Process of Justice":

> In the courtroom, the judge stares down at you. The course of action [or lack of] taken by the law officials and the judge tells me that the victims now have something else to fear. This also tells the attacker that they now have another hold on you, another way to punish you. So what will eventually happen to the true victims if this continues?

Shasha's title is an ironic one. For her, justice was not dispensed in the courtroom. She ended up in the shelter. So did Dharma with whom I had the following exchange:

DHARMA: The courts don't care about domestic violence. This man is a drunk and two days before his first hearing he got stopped by the police again for DUI. It's escalating. I tried to talk to the prosecutor. They don't care. They won't care 'til he kills.

CAROL: You?

DHARMA: Yeah, kills me or my kids.

Unfortunately, battered women often do not receive adequate support from other institutions either, including their churches or faith communities.

WHO ARE THE VICTIMS? THE DEMOGRAPHIC DATA

The demographic data reported by the United States Department of Justice makes clear that domestic violence traverses class, race/ethnicity, and age groups.[11] Although demographic factors may vary, affecting rates of reportage and ability to escape, some of the facts often presented are these: Race or ethnicity is not associated with level of risk; women between the ages of twenty to thirty-four have the highest rates of victimization; women who graduate from college have the lowest rates compared to women who have less education; women with incomes under $10,000 are four times more likely to be victimized than women with incomes of over $50,000. The geographic location (that is, urban, suburban, rural) does not affect rates of victimization.

Clearly, the violence is not restricted to any one demographic group; yet, there are complicating factors in the data. For example, although geographical location does not affect rates, it does affect the availability of support systems or resources to escape. Rural women frequently do not have access to shelters or other social service agencies. They may be isolated from neighbors or families.[12] Rural people often hold strong notions of independence and self-sufficiency. Rural communities covering large geographical areas can be numerically small and relatively stable in population as well. People know one another. Thus, family affairs are kept quiet to avoid public attention or humiliation. Men who must depend on one another for neighborly help do not cross one another over private affairs; women are often bound to secrecy through shame. When rural folk, such as the Appalachian women in this study, come to the city, they bring such notions of silence, shame, and self-sufficiency with them.

There are also many misconceptions about domestic violence and race or ethnicity. Black, white, and Hispanic women are attacked by intimate partners at the same rate.[13] One study indicates that black women seek help from public services more frequently than white women,[14] but women of color or ethnic women may find it more difficult to escape abuse[15] because of different cultural beliefs about family and privacy. Women of color may believe race loyalty is critical in a society controlled by the white male patriarchy; thus, they sometimes hesitate to call upon the criminal or justice systems. Their partners would then be subject to discrimination. As well, women of color suffer disproportionately from poverty. The National Research Council reports that "Blacks continue to lag far behind whites on most indicators of economic and educational status."[16] Women of color often simply lack the resources to escape from intimate violence. When they do escape, they may be bound to use public resources—the shelters, for instance, rather than personal or extended family resources.

Ethnic minority women and immigrant women may experience "dual subordination" based on gender and some element of primordiality. They are discriminated against both for being nonwhite and for being female. They are marginalized for femaleness and for cultural features such as race, origin, or language. Ethnicity has a social construction dimension: that is, ethnic women experience problems with interpersonal dynamics and symbolic meaning-making in immediate settings or situational contexts. They must negotiate multiple, sometimes conflicting, identities manifested through language, history, customs, beliefs, and values in concrete and unfolding situations often unfamiliar or inhospitable to them. How does an Asian woman, for example, explain to white neighbors or social workers about the seemingly insurmountable cultural conflicts she faces when she considers leaving an abusive partner? She may not speak English fluently and she may suffer from cultural shame; meanwhile, her interlocutor may evidence prejudice, fear, or mistrust. The two dimensions—the cultural and the social—interact to create more problems for women regardless of their family incomes.[17]

Further regarding class issues and the complexities of the demographic data, there is some evidence that income disparity—rather than simply poverty or education—may be a significant factor in intimate violence.[18] Disparities in income or occupational status favoring women have been found to be related to escalating violence. Women who earn more than their partners or who enjoy more occupational prestige may suffer from the imbalance in traditional gender roles and relations. There is reason to further explore intimate violence as it relates to social class rather than simply income. Ironically, total family income may have less impact on intimate violence against women than their own economic contributions to the family. It seems that men will use violence to equalize their power in situations where women gain resources or men lose them. "When women's resources approach or exceed their partners,'" states Laura Ann McCloskey, "they are more likely to be victimized."[19] The researchers Kersti Yllo and Murray Straus find that battery is highest in states where women's status is highest.[20] Linda Gordon's research also shows that battering is a problem when the feminist movement has been strong. When women actively struggle for resources and benefits, violence arises.[21]

In truth, the demographic data are complicated and both the causes and contributing or conflicting factors need to be further explored. Yet, evidently, many men feel entitled to use physical violence to retain patriarchal control. Social institutions encourage and protect them.

THEORIES OF CAUSES OF INTIMATE VIOLENCE AGAINST WOMEN

Theories about the causes of violence against women in intimate relationships and ideas about the resolution of it through social policies and programs have been seriously conflicted areas of scholarly research. The main division in sociological approaches has been between family violence theorists (including systems theorists, exchange/social control theorists, and symbolic interaction theorists) and feminist theorists.[22] By no means exclusive, these approaches do, however, represent very different perspectives, especially as they took shape in the early years of domestic violence research.

Generally, the family violence theorists concentrate on microlevel analysis. They use survey research or study male-female or family interaction in order to explain dysfunctional communicative patterns. Typically, they attribute the causes of violence against women to individual pathology or malfunctional family communicative practices. Family interaction practices are viewed as a system. Women initiate or contribute to violence through their own aggressive language practices or physical violence; men initiate violence or respond to women's violence. Family violence theorists may advocate family therapy to change disruptive or precipitating patterns. In early family violence research, there was no or little attempt to address the social or cultural factors out of which acts of violence arise—a preoccupation of feminist researchers. More recently, family violence researchers take these factors into account. Increasingly, they recognize the social and demographic indicators of structural inequality that influence the conditions giving rise to, or propensities for, domestic violence.[23]

Feminist researchers concentrate particularly on macrolevel analysis. They view the problem as a sociocultural problem extending from the patriarchal need for power and control. Violence is a critical component of a system of coercion through which men maintain social dominance. This is the heart of the debate between family violence researchers and feminist researchers: the degree to which patriarchy figures as the source explanation in domestic violence etiology. For feminist researchers, the sources of conflict arise from "men's possessiveness and jealousy, men's expectations regarding women's domestic work, men's sense of the right to punish 'their' women for perceived wrongdoing, and the importance to men of maintaining and exercising their positions of authority."[24] Violence, argues feminist historian Linda Gordon, stems from "power struggles in which individuals are contesting for real resources and benefits."[25] For feminist researchers, the nexus of social location factors in interaction with gender are critical: income, social class, education, race/ethnicity, social status, and so forth. These factors figure importantly into the meaning of the violence. An unemployed or seasonally employed older Hispanic immigrant woman living in a rural community may be completely victimized by her batterer; a young white professional woman living within a family support network may physically suffer as much but she has resources to escape and rebuild her life.

Feminist researchers further argue that, by contributing in their own ways to the cultural fabric of the systemic oppression of women, our legal, religious, and other social and cultural institutions are complicit in the problem of domestic violence. Even when confronted with their complicity, many institutions have been unable or slow to respond; thus, relatively few men are confronted with their violent behavior. The anecdotal evidence provided by battered women about law, judicial, and (as I will discuss soon) religious institutions support this finding.

Feminist and family violence research is sociologically based research. Nonsociologically oriented researchers also offer explanations for the causes of male violence toward women. These explanations include chemical or psychological factors. Their explanations may be based on psychological or other types of intraindividual factors such as drinking or drug problems, personality disorders, or biological or neurophysiological disorders. Some nonsociological researchers, for example, may look at atypical levels of testosterone or serotonin (that is, the neurotransmitter that modulates the action of brain chemicals) in abusive men.[26] Other researchers look at depression levels. Even pediatric illness has been posited as a possible cause for domestic violence. Head injury, metabolic disorders, epilepsy, attention deficit disorder, and other neurological problems have all been posed as contributing factors.[27]

Many nonsociological researchers, however, admit to the primacy of social factors in violence against women. In fact, feminist sociological theories are a dominant influence in domestic violence research. As conceded by well-known family violence researcher Richard J. Gelles, numerous studies have all found that gender inequality explains variations in the incidence and rates of violence against women.[28] The strict delineation of camps—the feminist, the family violence, and other researchers—oversimplifies common ground. Yet the distinctions remain and the ramifications are not negligible. These camps vie for control of the field and the authority to sway policy makers as they allocate resources and make political decisions.

This study is based on the theory and principles of feminist anthropological linguistics, an interdisciplinary field that seeks to explain language in context. One basic assumption of my analyses is that there is a relationship between the language of a community and its worldviews, values, belief systems; that is, culture is socially, semiotically, and discursively constructed. The researcher can make reasonable claims about this worldview by searching for themes or patterns of language usage. Feminist linguists further assume that race/ethnicity, class, and gender are particularly cogent categories of analysis because they are used as tools in the unequal distribution of power, status, and material goods. Thus, feminist linguistics has both macrolevel and microlevel components. It is sociological, but it looks at the individual and intraindividual language in order to create knowledge and to draw conclusions. In the end, the production of knowledge for the sake of knowledge is not the goal of feminist linguistics; rather, the goal is social change. And none too soon: Linda Gordon points out that U.S. feminists have been agitating against wife-beating for at least 120 years.[29] Christine de Pisan wrote about woman battery in the early fifteenth century.[30] The struggle for social change has been going on for a long time and it is far from over.

THE AFTERMATH: SUFFERING AND SURVIVORS

Feminist research has made visible the seriousness of violence against women. With somewhat more regularity, both researchers and advocates against domestic violence are bringing the actual voices of women into our writing. Additionally, battered women frequently require medical care for serious bodily injuries. These injuries are sometimes photographed and, in publications, depicted so others may more viscerally know the horrendous truth about intimate violence against women. Perhaps such photographs are the best way to create the public outrage necessary to more adequately address violence against women. Language evades direct renderings of the actual pain and the frequently unfathomable depths of the emotional suffering. Yet battered women must be able to speak publicly—in fora that matter. This study is an attempt to give voice to battered women as they try to make sense of their suffering.

Still researchers and advocates may be ambivalent about revealing the psychological or emotional ravages of violence against women. The controversy surrounding Lenore Walker's pioneering but highly contested research on the cycle of violence and the "learned helplessness"[31] of battered women is but one example of the delicate nature of forthrightly discussing the emotive and affective components of violence against women. The notion of learned helplessness is that battered women become less able to extricate themselves from their situations because they are terrorized by males into profound levels of dependency.[32] Many researchers will not lend support to this stance because it seems to diminish the strengths of survivors. Similarly the label "victim" and the idea of "codependency" between two partners have been contested. These labels, the argument goes, add to the degradation of battered women.[33] The term "victim" makes invisible the strategies battered women devise in order to avoid or minimize male violence. It makes invisible their skills, resistance, and forbearance. The term "codependency" would seem to make women complicit in their own abuse.

Nevertheless, some staggering facts remain. Women are "significantly more likely than men to suffer psychological injuries related to their abuse."[34] Twenty-five percent of women who attempt suicide and 25 percent who seek psychiatric emergency services are battered.[35] Battered women suffer depression, fear, anxiety, shame, self-blame, low self-esteem. Their senses of self are shaken, their identities fragmented. Often they lose their families, homes, and jobs. Women suffer the violence of men against their bodies, minds, spirits, and hearts in inestimable ways. Clearly, their suffering is a social evil that remains to be fully explored and rectified. The statistics suggest a problem of enormous proportions, but the voices of battered women tell the real story. The stories are heartrending; at the same time, the strength of women comes through in stirring ways. Their strength stems from two elements in particular: the safety and support of shelter life and faith in God. Hazel says it succinctly, but her words are a common refrain:

> I felt rather confident that I was handling my departure from home in a positive way. [Then my husband] called me at work and he made me feel guilty for leaving. His call was so upsetting. I left work early and I returned to the safety of the shelter. After talking to some supportive people, I came to terms with my guilt—at least for now! Each day that I am away from home, I'm getting stronger. However, I know greater challenges are ahead. I can only take it one day at a time with the help of God.

Feminist researchers talk about shelters, but not often about the main source of strength for so many battered women like Hazel: their faith in God—with all his patriarchal trappings and interestingly, many times, without them. Shelter women depend on God to survive.

TWO

"Here We Women Support One Another"

THE WOMEN'S HOUSE AS SHELTER AND SOCIAL ORDER

I feel ashamed and angry, very angry. I want out of this shelter.

—Janelle

God shelters us women.

—Bridget

INTRODUCTION

The first shelter for battered women was opened in the United States in 1973. The first shelters were based on feminist principles of egalitarianism, mutual support, and cooperation. Residents often made the rules about childcare, curfews, and other aspects of daily life. Authority and decision making were decentralized or, at least, localized; that is, under the purview of women who controlled only their own site. Feminist shelters preferred, as Noelie Maria Rodriquez notes, "an open-door policy, set no limits on how long residents may stay, and [they encouraged] nonprofessional, egalitarian, and informal relationships within their organizations."[1] However, a growing public awareness of domestic violence as a social problem, the need for more shelters, and funding difficulties led to the institutionalization of most shelters. This "takeover" by mainstream, hierarchical, social service agencies and organizations created ideological contradictions that many times shelter women discern and contest.

In this chapter I will describe the Women's House as a location and as a culture. A social order has been established that generates senses of stability and inconsistency, relief and tension, gratitude and dissatisfaction. The tensions stem from structural and interpersonal factors regarding race, class, and religious differences between and among the nonprofit middle-class shelter organization and the under or working-class women who temporarily reside there. Yet residents' satisfaction with the shelter hinges on negotiating these tensions, building support networks, and creating a common language about their suffering, its meanings and its mitigation. Healing happens through and in spite of the bureaucratic nature of the shelter as a secular social work agency. There are many obstacles to creating this common language—the core features of which are often religious, but residents create it as they simultaneously resist and assimilate the secular language or the dominant culture of the shelter.

THE SHELTER AS PART OF A NATIONAL NONPROFIT ASSOCIATION

The Women's House is operated by the YWCA, a national nonprofit association for women and girls. The local association describes its "one imperative" in this way: to "thrust its collective power toward the empowerment of women and the elimination of racism by any means necessary."[2]

The Young Women's Christian Association has an interesting, and in view of the abundance of God-talk of its clients, somewhat ironic history. It was founded in the early 1900s by middle-class mainstream Protestant women who wanted to reach out to young, single working-class migrant or immigrant women who gravitated to urban areas without their families.[3] The middle-class association women were concerned about the moral and spiritual development of these young working-class girls who might—it was thought—turn to prostitution. In the early days, the YWCA was a Christian association that offered a slate of increasingly progressive social programs. With the support of local mainstream Protestant clergy and churches, it offered a range of services to members from affordable housing to educational, vocational, and recreational training. There were afternoon and night classes for bible study, English language and literature, beadwork, embroidery, music, and so forth, designed by middle-class women to educate and socialize young working-class women. One goal was to educate the women for marriage—that is, to be good wives and mothers according to middle-class norms of behavior. From the beginning, the working-class women resisted these efforts "to prescribe and protect an ideal of womanhood" (87). Women could be discharged from YWCA housing for rule infractions or transgressions such as smoking, drug use, insubordination, and "general undesirability of character" (93). However, the traditional Christian morals and values the association wished to promote, the models of behavior and decorum, were both actively and unconsciously challenged by women who resented the control over their sexuality and behavior. In time, the working-class clients of the YWCA effectively influenced the association. For example, some strict house rules were eased and the curricula of classes were expanded. By the 1920s, the YWCA had been transformed into a social agency with a Christian philosophy.

Today the YWCA is effectively a secular organization. The Women's House has no permanent liaisons with churches. Donations from churches are not accepted because the association does not support conservative religious tenants. Federal funding sources (34.1 percent of association revenue in 1998) preclude religious training or education.[4] But, given the YWCA's origins as moral caretaker of the lower classes, the fact that many residents desire religious programs or try to evangelize other residents is an ironic twist of social history.

THE WOMEN'S HOUSE: THE SHELTER AS A MATERIAL LOCATION

The Women's House began operating in 1978 as an emergency shelter. Its purpose, according to the Resident Agreement of Stay, is "to provide short term refuge for women and their children who are being abused in their homes. The shelter provides a safe and temporary environment while women regain the strength that will allow them to develop a course of action suitable to their needs." When I first began my participant observation, the shelter was a dilapidated three-story brick house in an underclass neighborhood of the city. The street was lined with sizeable old brick homes in various stages of urban decay—with peeling paint, broken and all-too-often boarded doors and windows, unkempt yards, battered or barely serviceable cars or trucks parked on the street side. A zoo and a hospital in the area kept a steady stream of both auto and pedestrian traffic moving along the street. The ambulance sirens were nearly constant. People congregated at a bus shelter at one end of the street. At the other end of the block, in the evening, a small group of men milled around the intersection in front of a boarded up old building. They smoked cigarettes, drank out of bottles in brown bags, and dealt illicit drugs. Once a church moved into a nearby storefront and the men moved further down the block. Later, the church moved out and the crowd came back.

A cab meets incoming women at a local hospital and drops them off at the shelter. Police sometimes bring women. Apart from this first approach, residents without vehicles are picked up and dropped off by their friends or family at a designated spot—a convenience store parking lot. In fact, security at this first shelter was minimal. The windows were barred and doors were locked and monitored with an intercom system. In a small, cluttered office by the front door, the staff kept a log of whoever entered and exited. The back door was rarely closed. The children's play area in the backyard had a standard hurricane fence but otherwise no special security. The police came if the shelter placed an emergency call—such as when abusers were spotted.

Inside the shelter, the dilapidation persisted depressingly. The furniture was nicked, scratched, and rickety. The floors were bare and scuffed hardwood, the carpet dingy and spotted. In the dining room, the heart of the house, there was a massive, round, everywhere-scratched-and-nicked wooden table. Bookshelves held old books, stacks of old *Reader's Digests* and other dated magazines—*Women's Day, Good Housekeeping, Ladies' Home Journal, Mademoiselle, Vogue,* and other white middle-to-upper-middle-class-oriented magazines. There were usually religious leaflets or tracts strewn about the tables. A worn, marked up bible or two typically sat on tables along with Bible study literature or ads for local churches. There was also literature on social ills and personal needs: domestic violence, drug abuse, welfare rights, legal assistance, and so forth. A bulletin board in the hallway was weighed down with layers of such material.

In spite of the dilapidation, the atmosphere was often upbeat or, at least, promisingly so. Empirical research on the relationship between shelter architecture and resident satisfaction indicates that neighborhood safety and children's play areas are most important, but this shelter—which boasted neither to anyone's satisfaction—had a generally positive atmosphere.[5] It was at times a lively and, if not happy, then a homey place to be. There was a sense of the residents' ownership. Children's or women's artwork decorated the walls. Home cooking was central. The kitchen was tiny, but women sat at the table, passing babies back and forth as one of the women prepared dinner for the other residents. The staff and volunteers often ate with them. In the living room, women watched television while they ate popcorn or cookies baked by residents. The dining room was a 24/7 congregating area. Women were allowed to smoke and they sat around the table in talk. The residents were responsible for cooking, cleaning, and other household duties. A chore list was hung prominently—all house duties were divided and rotated. During house meetings, they talked about these and other issues with staff. Other meetings dealt with domestic violence, drug/alcohol, and writing.

In short, the house was a shared communal space. The women were grouped together around talk and activity, particularly in the evening when they returned from court, job and apartment hunting, or other tasks. The shelter, nearly always filled to capacity, invited a material, organizational, and social "togetherness." Tempers did erupt. Emotional stress was always just under the surface; yet, shelter life facilitated conversation, thus mutual

support, through shared space and activity. At its best, it facilitated supportive alliances between residents or community workers and residents.

In 1998, the shelter moved to a new location, a three-story Victorian
house that tripled the resident capacity to between fifty and fifty-five women
and children. It is in a quieter area of the city with little traffic. The surveillance is constant and intense. The backyard is fenced with a very high
wooden fence. Residents and workers are buzzed into the yard and then the
locked door of the shelter. All windows are barred and alarmed. The staff sits
in an office and watches screens from the sixteen security cameras that scan
the parking lot, entrances, and public spaces in the shelter. A resident can
be observed from the time she drives up to the shelter until she enters her
bedroom on the third floor. The intercom allows staff to stay in the office
while they talk with one or all residents. Otherwise, the office area is secure
and the residents talk to staff through a sliding glass partition.

The increased security stems from two sources. First of all, women are
most likely to be injured by partners when the women are attempting to leave
the relationship.[6] In addition, the success of the capital campaign for a new
shelter was a crucial component. There were finally funds to beautify and
secure the shelter. This new shelter is meticulously appointed. The walls and
curtains are beautifully rich colors—salmon, lavender, rose. There are tapestry
rugs on the wood floors. Framed floral art prints adorn the walls. Two massive
chandeliers hang majestically in the spiral staircase that leads to two floors of
bedrooms that are fully appointed with new bureaus, desks, beds with hand-
made quilts, and toy boxes. One or more families might be assigned to a room
to reduce housekeeping or make more rooms available to others.

There is a very small sitting area on the second floor. Otherwise, women
visit one another in their rooms. There is a back staircase and an elevator from
the basement to the top, or third floor. The residents are encouraged to use
these back stairs because the spiral staircase is polished and children play on
the banisters. Like the original shelter, the living room on the first floor has
a television. Two or three women might watch a program together. To me,
they always look uncomfortable on the plastic-covered furniture. No eating or
smoking is allowed. The children's play area is on the first floor, but no child
is allowed in it without supervision. At times, the area is closed as a disciplin-
ary strategy or because there is not enough staff to supervise. One children's
advocate was on sick leave for a month without a replacement. Liability concerns restrict volunteers from childcare without police checks or supervision.

There is a cafeteria in the basement with an industrial kitchen staffed
by a professional cook who prepares one main meal a day for the women.
The residents are not allowed in the cooking area. They have access to a
refrigerator in the cafeteria and a vending machine for other meals. There
are rows of tiny one- or two-person tables and high chairs. The cafeteria is

only open during specified times and no food is allowed in any other area in the shelter.

Group activities—such as the writing group—are typically held in the "conference room," a cold, dark room with a long narrow conference table. A surveillance camera gazes down at participants as they enter and exit. A computer I brought to the shelter sits in the corner mostly unused since women are forbidden to enter the conference room by themselves. Children are discouraged from ever entering. On the bookshelf there are old copies of *Reader's Digest Condensed Books*, apparently for display or decoration. There are no books available in public areas. A pamphlet available in the foyer, entitled "Domestic Violence Safety Plan," does encourage women "to read articles, books, and poetry to help [them] feel stronger." A resident told me romance novels were once made available to residents. Angrily, she empha-sized that survivors are not interested in romance. Otherwise, there are no magazines, no religious material, no artwork, and no writing displayed. One may not "post" on the walls. A well-kept (that is, monitored) bulletin board in the foyer holds fliers. In fact, this drafty foyer is a congregating area. A loveseat and two chairs often seat women who just want to be in a public space. They want to talk to each other, the staff through the glass window, or residents entering or exiting the shelter. I joke that these seats are the best ones in the house. Women agree.

In the shelter, there is no common area without security cameras and there is no public area with seating for more than a few people. The excep-tion is the living room, but the television—nearly always entertaining the children and/or their moms—restricts conversation. In other areas, chairs are grouped in twos and threes—facilitating cliques, dyads and triads. There are four-person wooden tables in the backyard where there is also a children's play area—so it is not conducive to intimate talk. There is no arrangement for large group talk.

In comparison with the original shelter, there are currently fewer sched-uled gatherings. Resources have decreased in the conservative politics of our time. There is a press for tighter accountability, leaner efficiency and, thus, local resources have been streamlined and networked. Because it is a nonprofit, funding sources are not guaranteed and funds fluctuate yearly. Revenues in 1998 came from a variety of sources, including government grants (34.1 percent), program service fees (19.3 percent), community chest allocations (16.4 percent), foundation support and contributions (16 percent), invest-ment income (6.4 percent), special events (6.6 percent) and some miscella-neous sources (1.2 percent). Half of these resources (50.5 percent) were used for the shelter, crisis hotline, et cetera.

When funds are cut, the first effects are personnel cuts and loss of pro-grams. Practically speaking, this means that residents may have an option to attend a support group; however, it may be held at a different location in the city. Realistically many women are too tired or busy to travel (often by bus if they do not have their car) to a distant site. There have been times during which my writing group—volunteer on my part—has been the only activity.

For these and other reasons, it is difficult not to feel sentimental about the old dilapidated shelter. I would not claim that either shelter is absolutely better for the welfare of the women. From a proxemics (space maintenance) perspective, however, the old shelter more easily facilitated community. The shabby but homey site provided unmonitored areas more closely resembling a family residence. Food was made and shared by residents. Children were welcomed everywhere. Women were not submitted to camera surveillance. They claimed ownership of space through cooking or the display of their art or significant items like bibles.

The new shelter is beautiful, safe, and fully institutional. There is a widespread perception that the housecleaning duties residents still perform are excessive and geared toward the board of directors, donors, and other visitors who make frequent house tours. Approximately one tour group moves through a week though there may be as many as three. Often lower-level staff and residents do not know who is touring the premises. The visitor might be a local judge, a board of directors' member, a donor. Many residents believe the staff cares more about the shelter than its residents or that the house is being maintained as a showcase for community gratification. It displays social work as a modern bureaucracy or as a civic aesthetic. It also highlights the class conflicts between senses of appropriate appearance, decorum, and behavior.

THE SHELTER PARTICIPANTS

THE WOMEN

Like most urban shelters, the Women's House operates at full capacity. In 1994, the hotline staff fielded 12,498 telephone calls, that is, an average of 1,042 calls per month.[7] In 1998, 11, 509 calls were fielded on the hotline and, in 1999, 8,851 hotline calls were fielded—a small decrease attributable to the availability of another hotline (though not another shelter) service. This is an average of 738 calls per month. Most callers want basic information. They are not sure if the particular constellation of abuses they endure—physical, sexual, psychological, or economic—constitute domestic violence. They may describe their situations, get encouragement and a list of options for leaving, and then hang up. Other women need immediate escape routes from dangerous partners. If there is room, they come to the shelter; if not, they are referred to other shelters. In 1994, the shelter accepted 516 residents, that is, 230 women with their 286 children—an average of 19 women and 24 children each month. The average length of stay was 13 days: the shortest stay was 1 day and the longest was 71 days. In 1998, 537 women and children were served at the shelter. In 1999, 424 women and 386 children were served for a total of 810 people: an average of 35 women and 32 children per month. The longest length of stay was 106 days, the shortest 1 day. Regarding marital status data: 131 women were married, 154 had been cohabiting with a companion, 116 were single and living alone, 1 was divorced from her abuser, and 1 was separated. The marital status of 21 women was categorized as "other"— a designation serving for a variety of other crisis situations.[8]

In the last chapter it was noted that women between the ages of 20 to 34 have the highest rates of victimization. In 1999 at the Women's House, 190 women were between 18 and 30 years of age; 202 women were between 31 and 45 years of age; 31 women were between 46 and 59 years of age; and 1 woman was over 60 years of age. The figures approximate national data.

Ethnically, the women reflect the lower- and working-class population of the local community. Of the 230 women who lived there in 1994, 143 women were African Americans, 84 were white women, and 3 were of other races. In 1999, 259 African American, 151 white, 7 Latinos, 2 Asian Americans, and 5 "Others" were served. Many of the white women have Appalachian heritage. Nearly all are desperately poor. In 1994, 135 women reported incomes of $0 to $4,990.00 per year. This was well below the national poverty level that the federal government defined in 1994 as $7,360 for one person and $2,480 for each additional person. In 1999, 199 women reported incomes of $0 to $4,990.00 per year; 67 women reported incomes of $5,000 to $9,999 per year; 68 women reported incomes of $10,000 to $14,999 per year; 34 women reported incomes of $15,000 to $19,999 per year; and 56 women reported incomes of $20,000 to $24,999 per year. The year 2000 U.S. Department of Health and Human Services Poverty Guidelines in the mainland United States were $8,350 for a one-person family and $11,250 for a two-person family. For each additional person, $2,900 is added.[9] Clearly, most women at the shelter are in dire financial straits—many living substantially below the national poverty level.

The stress of poverty and violence takes its toll.[10] Shelter women are coping with multiple serious stresses. Intermittently the Women's House has been financially able to deliver mental health care to its residents. A psychiatrist on staff for a time estimated that 25 percent of the women are "chemically dependent." Among the drugs most commonly used by the women are alcohol, marijuana, and crack. Women who have been abused often resort to drugs and alcohol use and other self-destructive behaviors to numb their suffering and anguish.[11] Battered women frequently require medical care for injuries; further, they are "significantly more likely than men to suffer psychological injuries related to their abuse."[12] Indeed, up to 64 percent of hospitalized women psychiatric patients have histories of being physically abused as adults. Studies have shown that 22 to 35 percent of women in emergency room visits are there because of symptoms "related to ongoing abuse, whether secondary to an injury or as a manifestation of the stress of living under abusive conditions."[13]

According to the psychiatrist, who consulted with residents once a week until federal funds were cut in 1994, nearly half of the women were treated for some form of "mental illness," mostly depression. Some research shows that battered women have substantially increased rates of depression. Sometimes they are diagnosed with PTSD (post-traumatic stress disorder). Women who have been sexually and physically abused, in fact, make up one of the largest groups of PTSD sufferers.[14] We should, however, use caution with such labels. Like the recent trend toward medicalization of violence against women (casting it as a medical health issue), the psychologizing of the problems of shelter women tends to diminish the structural origins of the violence. The health problems of low-income women are often caused by their economic situations: from the constant stresses in their lives to the lack of resources to effectively deal with them. As Belle puts it: "Women will continue to be over represented among the depressed as long as they are over represented among the poor."[15] This being said, shelter women often are fit into a therapeutic framework in which they are characterized as depressed.

Although family, mental health, and medical data are gathered by the staff for funding purposes, training personnel, or assisting women to find employment, education data are not compiled. If they were, the result would be mixed. Most women have high school diplomas, but many dropped out of school. Some have GEDs. A minority has some vocational, college, or university training. Several women I met had bachelor's degrees; one had a master's degree. Many women express interest in job training; yet, preoccupied with family crisis, few have immediate interest in school. Education is one of the paths toward resolving the problem of domestic violence, but residents are often too overwhelmed with matters of survival to pay heed to formal education. After their immediate crisis, after they are settled into the shelter and have begun to imagine new futures, survivors are more likely to consider a career or vocation. Often they express interest in the helping professions, particularly the battered women's movement.

THE CHILDREN

In 1994, 286 children resided with their mothers in the shelter. Some women, of course, do not have children and some mothers do come to the shelter without their children. They may have already lost custody of them, or—if there has been no spousal legal action—they may have left them in the present or previous crises with their extended family, usually their own mothers. Typically, however, the shelter is filled with the sounds of children laughing, playing, talking, fighting, and crying.

Over the years the shelter has been more or less able to provide for children. An advocate with a master's degree in social work transfers children to new schools if the family is relocating outside the district. She monitors children's activities throughout the day. If a child appears to have stress—aggression toward other children or their mothers, for example—the advocate intervenes. This occurs routinely. Children who witness domestic violence exhibit many behavioral and emotional problems, including more violent and antisocial behavior than other children. Such problems are exacerbated by age, gender, and relationships with mothers. Preschool children exhibit more problems than older children, and boys more problems than girls. The more maternal stress, the more problems the children experience.[16] One study found more social problems among current shelter children than former shelter children, suggesting that the turmoil and instability of the shelter and transitional times temporarily escalates problems.[17]

Although it is against shelter rules, there is a fair amount of both overt and ostensibly covert mother-toward-child violence, particularly in the form of verbal violence. Some mothers are aggressive toward their children through habit, stress, or defense against the perceived (but greatly exaggerated) power of their own children.[18] There is also a fair amount of sibling- or peer-directed physical and verbal aggression. Race/ethnicity and class differences surface, causing tension between residents who disagree over child-rearing practices.[19] Aggression in shelter children is no surprise. One study of nine hundred children in battered women's shelters found that nearly 70 percent of the children had been victims of neglect or physical abuse and nearly 50 percent had been victims of sexual abuse. Lenore Walker's 1984 study found that mothers were eight times more likely to hurt their own children when they were battered than when they were safe.[20] If violence begets violence, inter and intra family tensions in the shelter are not to be unexpected in spite of the rules.

THE STAFF AND VOLUNTEERS

Besides the shelter women and their children, other participants in the culture of the Women's House (currently) include a shelter director, a house manager, case managers, family support specialists, the children's advocate, residential aids, interns, volunteers, a cook, contract cleaners, and a handyman. Ideally, staff members would be survivors of domestic violence, so they might more easily empathize with residents. This is sometimes, but not often, the case. The pay is low and the burnout rate quite high. This is a continual problem.

There are other people who come to the shelter, including various visitors. Cabbies or police drop off incoming residents at the shelter. Sometimes police take out a woman who is charged with some crime. In general police are not welcomed by residents—many of whom view them as racially biased and as ineffectual in domestic violence situations. Women think that police do not believe their renditions of assaults and they may only briefly jail the abusers. The local "preferred arrest" policy created another problem—the police might not arrest anyone. The policy designates that when police respond to a domestic violence call they are strongly encouraged to make an arrest if violence has been committed. It replaced a mandatory arrest policy.

Also interfacing with the Women's House via cooperative activity is Women's Helper, another local provider of crisis intervention and support services for domestic abuse as well as incest and rape cases. Women's Helper provides services such as short-term crisis intervention, support groups, court advocacy, hospital accompaniment for rape and assault victims, and community education. The Women's House makes regular use of its services, particularly the court advocates who accompany domestic violence victims to court to give support.

THE IDEOLOGICAL TERRAIN

As one can ascertain from the list of shelter participants, the Women's House—as a social agency type of shelter—is staffed largely by professionals. Their qualifications are based on credentials from education and training. Residential aids may have less education, but the house director and house manager are required to have a master's degree in social work. Some staff members have had an experience of battery, but it is not a requirement (as it is in feminist shelters staffed by former residents, for example) that would help to form the basis of trust and empathy with women in crisis. This is not to say that women who have not been battered cannot empathize with or assist battered women. It does mean there may be additional layers of negotiation that must be successfully managed before genuine communication can take place. Kelly and India, shelter residents, testify to the problems in communication that occur because of educational differences:

KELLY: The director [is] an academic and she never asked my name! She stayed in the office and when she came out she goes like this: [gets up and mimics a nasal upper-midwestern standard accent]. There was this distance. There was no loving. There should be hugs. We need hugs. When you just leave your abuser, you don't need no rules and regulations. You need hugs. [The director] was a little brainiac.

INDIA: And she got a good job.

KELLY: But I know those women. I had a friend who was an academic. It took a long time to get close to her. The academics don't know about loving people. Me, I'm the girl from the hood. [. . .] Academics talk about theory, not feelings. My friend was an academic. It's all theory. It's not about the way it is. When I told the intake person my views on my husband, we had a disagreement. The intake person said: "I studied domestic violence." So I said, "Okay, now I know." I saw how it was gonna go. We had a disagreement about my husband. I don't want my husband to go to jail. I want him to go to counseling. I want my husband to say: "I was an abuser." But the intake person, an academic, is part of a scholastic movement on domestic violence that is the dividing line. I want my partner to go to counseling. I don't want him to go to prison for what he did to me. But I want him to do counseling. He has to be healthy to be with my children. I wasn't healthy in that relationship either. He came from an abusive family. His mother was abusive. He was beat for years. I didn't provoke him. It was in his nature. But he was in denial. My mother wasn't just beat, beat, beat, but it was the alcoholism. I think there's something in [about the idea of] provoking a person into anger. But the academics would try to say you can't provoke a person. I think you can provoke a person into anger even though you can't provoke a person into hitting you. I mean, I think you can provoke a person into hitting you. A person shouldn't hit you.

In this conversation, Kelly and India try to reckon with the educational (as well as class and race/ethnic) differences between themselves and the staff. With respect to race/ethnicity, most staff and volunteers are white women while at least half of house residents are women of color. There are also religious differences. As mostly middle-class members, most staff have been raised in mainstream (particularly) Protestant religions. The residents are largely nonmainstream working-class or underclass Sanctified/Holiness and fundamentalist/Evangelicals. There are ideological differences regarding family and gender. For example, most fundamentalists support traditional roles for women in family, church, and society while many mainstream members are exploring new roles for women and men. These issues will be addressed in upcoming chapters.

Both the residents and the staff acknowledge ideological conflicts in the shelter stemming, for example, from class, education, race, and religious differences. There may be political differences. One family specialist emphatically claimed that neither the shelter nor the association is feminist despite the stated mission to "empower" women and girls. The claim was based on the lack of adequate training for staff members on sexual orientation, same sex violence, and the complications of race and class. "Definitely, definitely," she says. The staff reflected middle-class social/political values that clash with the working class and pluralistic residents. For her, white middle-class women elicit the most staff sympathy.

The ideological conflict between feminist and social agency type shelters has been long noted.[21] At the most significant level, the conflict can affect residents' perceptions of their ability to recover and survive. This happens through the mundane nexus of interactions that make up everyday shelter life—including the delivery of services and the rendering of rules and regulations.

THE DELIVERY OF SERVICES

Services currently offered at the shelter include once-a-week evening programs such as groups for alcohol education, domestic violence, art and crafts, and writing. The domestic violence and alcohol education groups are facilitated by social workers; the art and writing groups are facilitated by volunteers. The domestic violence support group is mandatory, but participation in all groups is strongly encouraged. Participation is noted as evidence of a resident's motivation, cooperation, and willingness to engage in self-help activities. In reality, participation is difficult for mothers because of childcare. Childcare is frequently unavailable since a new rule forbids volunteers from attending to children without a police check. The children's advocate is typically not available in the evening. Mothers with infants are invited into the writing group, but children are not allowed because the conversation is simply too intense. Sometimes another resident will look after another resident's child, but she must sign a form to release the shelter of responsibility if there is an accident. The bureaucracy cuts into long-established friend and kinship patterns among the urban working poor, particularly among African American women.[22] Underclass women depend on one another in an exchange of resources and services, such as childcare. Shelter rules weaken these ties, at least temporarily, and make it more difficult for women to spend more than a few hours away from their children to look for housing, employment, legal aid, and so forth.

For several years, the domestic violence group was taught by the same social worker. Leigh was a white middle-class woman in her mid-twenties with a bachelor's degree from a local university. To me, she seemed always ill at ease. She hurriedly set up her presentation board, raced through her session, and left immediately afterward. She set up clear boundaries between herself and the residents. She dressed in casual suits with very short skirts and she wore heels and jewelry. Her hair was permed and she used a lot of makeup and perfume. This presentation of self was problematic. Many residents have only the clothes they wear on their backs, packed hastily in a suitcase, or clothes they rummaged from the donation closet at the shelter once they arrived. Many residents are also Sanctified or Holiness women whose religious communities teach that women should clothe and carry themselves with great modesty. To compound matters, Leigh presented herself as the authority in charge of the sessions, conducting the sessions as monologues or little lectures, and habitually asked closed-ended questions that demanded only "yes" or "no" answers or short answers taken verbatim from her presentations. The presentation closely followed the charts on the easel: One session was much the same as the next. The reception of these sessions depended upon the attendees. They could perform cooperation, overperform cooperation, or refuse to cooperate, depending on the makeup or mood of the particular group. The sessions seemed mostly ineffectual; yet, often I heard keywords from Leigh's presentations when women later participated in the writing group: They were assimilating some of her language into their own language and conceptual systems. However, I suggest that class differences were exacerbated by a pedagogy of control. When Leigh was promoted, a series of new social workers filled the vacancy to quite similar effect.

In the mid-1990s, a medical team came twice a month. Otherwise, sick women would go to a local hospital's emergency clinic. Sometimes women would go to the emergency rooms because some private doctors do not take Medicaid or Medicare patients or some doctors have a full quota of such patients. When women visit doctors who know they are in the shelter or who know they are on Medicaid, they feel they are treated "lower than [the doctors] or other patients." The doctors assume "superiority." They assume the women are "homeless," "drug abusers," "part of a plague," "helpless" or that they simply "aren't paying for this [medical care]." The doctors, however, "don't know [the women]" and are making assumptions about them. They won't give women "hard medicine" [narcotics, tranquilizers, et cetera] because they assume the women will sell it on the street. After the women come to the shelter, they have to "explain themselves" to the doctors. They don't simply get treated as anyone else would be. The fundamental issue is respect and "courtesy" and many shelter women believe they don't get it. In fact, the two most widespread complaints about the delivery of medical care is that the doctors do not give adequate medication or show courtesy. Currently, there are once-a-week morning visits by two nurses who perform health checks, refill prescriptions, make referrals, and so forth.

Psychological counseling services are offered—at least, basic services such as mental health assessments are offered. A licensed social worker makes referrals to local resources such as counselors, clinics, or other mental health care providers. Emergency referrals are sometimes made to local psychiatric facilities. (Chapter 3 concerns psychological issues and abuse.)

Finally, there are once-a-week visits by the Department of Human Services whose personnel assist women with information and applications for welfare, daycare provision, medical cards, and other services. This service is appreciated by women who are already ashamed of their circumstances, their visible bruises and blackened eyes, so they often do not wish to present themselves publicly.

After six weeks, a woman may apply and be accepted for temporary housing in one or two transitional housing units, that is, apartment buildings in two different locations in the city that are also maintained by the association. A total of twelve women along with their children may stay in these units—six in each building. One unit has a six-month program and the other has an eighteen-month program. The latter program is designated for women who are in some type of educational, professional, or vocational training such as nursing school or GED classes. Because the transitional housing only holds twelve families, it is not an option for most of the women who pass through the shelter. The staff is careful about which women it encourages to apply for transitional housing. A woman who is not considered appropriately motivated or needy is not invited to apply. This is a significant basis for social control, at least for the women who are interested in transitional shelter support. Women who do not relocate into transitional housing are not eligible for continued services through the YWCA shelter system, but they may be eligible for at least continued education on domestic violence or drug/alcohol dependency through the wider network of social services in the area.[23]

In addition to consultations held with family support specialists, these services comprise the slate of services offered to battered women within the shelter. There are interactions with other community workers, the volunteers, and the other residents. Yet, upon these services and interactions, so much depends. In order to begin to heal herself and have a chance at a life without male violence, a battered woman must learn from staff and other residents new ways to think and to speak about herself, her life, and her current crisis. Of course, she may interact with others of significance in the community—including the police, the judicial system, other social service agency workers, her church, her family, and her friends. But much depends on these services and the manner in which they are delivered. Are these social supports enough?

Many residents would like to have other services available to them. For example, many women talk about problems with childcare—a perennial problem for mothers generally. But when a battered woman comes to the shelter, she may have to find new housing and a new job. She may be looking for transportation, furniture, clothes, and schools for her children. She may be dealing with human service agencies and the judicial system. It is difficult under the best of circumstances to deal with such responsibilities by oneself. To deal with these issues while toting children from office to office or apartment to apartment may be nearly more than a woman under stress can handle. A battered woman may be experiencing post traumatic stress disorder or she is at least emotionally drained and uncertain about her future. To have more help with childcare seems reasonable and appropriate.

Battered women talk about space maintenance issues such as freer access to the kitchen and/or food services. At the Women's House, food is not allowed outside the cafeteria and it is distributed within limited time slots around the traditional meal times. As any mother knows, often children do not eat three regular meals a day and small children, in particular, cannot eat on demand. When people are under stress, irregular eating habits may be exacerbated. In addition, some women miss food preparation and family-style meal serving. These may have been main or significant activities in their lives and they may miss their roles in the kitchen. Other women, of course, do not miss such activities. Most women do miss the opportunity to just hang out together in the kitchen—the proverbial heart of the home—together with other women as they perhaps did with their mothers and grandmothers in their own homes.

There are a host of other issues. Smokers wish they did not have to go outside in inclement weather to smoke cigarettes. Women without children wish one of the floors of the shelter could house women who were not mothers or who did not have their children with them. Women who take medications wish they could keep their medications with them instead of having to turn over drugs to the office and then report there to have their medications doled out. Privacy issues may stem from the shelter practice of rooming residents together even when there are vacant rooms. This practice may be well-intended: It invites women to relate with one another, thus removing them from the psychological and physical isolation to which they have become accustomed in their relationships with abusers. The practice saves housecleaning labor and it assures free space for other women who will undoubtedly call for shelter. Yet it may feel like an invasion of privacy to some women who would rather room alone.

Some women at the shelter have mentioned of their own volition that they would like to have better access to a religious community. This desire has a variety of meanings. Some women wish religious or spiritual guidance counselors would visit them at the shelter, perhaps interdenominational counselors with whom they could discuss their lives and problems. Some women wish there were an opportunity for residents to worship together in the shelter, an activity that sometimes happens adventitiously as a few women spontaneously and collectively begin to witness to spiritual matters such as divine intervention in their lives or the flow of grace and strength to women in need. Other women wish for more structured opportunities for prayer and witness. They would like easier access to local church services or bible study groups. However, the churches (particularly the conservative churches) and the battered women's movement have historically not had an easy relationship. Some church communities withhold support from shelters because they believe the feminist movement undermines traditional family values; many feminists reject mainstream or, more especially, conservative churches, because they believe their patriarchal principles and views promote violence against women. More recently feminists have begun to imagine the positive impact the churches could have on shelters.[24]

Finally, many residents speak about the need for more choices or options for general mentoring or women's advocacy. When a woman enters the shelter she is assigned a family support specialist with whom she is supposed to have a special advocacy liaison. Not infrequently, the relationship is not a close one and many women feel dissatisfied with the relationships and their outcomes. Given the shortage of funds and personnel, and given the play of personalities, the dissatisfaction seems understandable—if not predictable. One resident referred to "peer advocacy" as the supportive relations battered women create with one another in lieu of more helpful relations with the staff. From the perspective of the staff, this is not an undesirable outcome by any means. But, as the resident also noted, the information shared between residents may not always be correct or it may not lead to effective and efficient action.

In any event, the desire for a closer and freely chosen relationship with a mentor reflects a wider issue in the delivery of services at the shelter. The services rendered and how they are rendered are evidence that the shelter is organized primarily along the lines of a "self-help" rather than a "therapeutic" model of crisis intervention. The staff vouches for the day-to-day practice of this organizational philosophy and its ensuing service delivery structures. (I myself regard the shelter as having merged the two models because it provides some psychological services and, contrary to stated goals, the staff seems often to operate out of a therapeutic framework.) However, the self-help model is the chosen philosophical or theoretical model and the goal of the association and the shelter administrators. In a shelter based on the self-help model, battered women themselves are basically responsible for accessing services, finding employment and housing, and otherwise conducting the business of relocating their families and perhaps pursuing legal cases against partners. Women basically must conduct their sometimes complicated business by themselves. The assumption is that it empowers women to fend for themselves. In a therapeutic model, the resident is treated as if she needs assistance. It is a deficit model in which the battered woman is considered socially or emotionally unable to fend entirely for herself. Instead, a social worker manages her case and the social worker calls in other professional or social service assistance as she deems necessary. The self-help model would appear to be much more empowering—at least from the perspective of middle-class association members and its employees. Still many residents simply are not satisfied with the self-help model or its method of delivery of services. Alisha, says: "About the shelter, I feel like I need a one-on-one thing with someone. I can't do everything by myself. If I had a worker with me all the time! Like a mentor to say this is how you do things. To show me the way."

Alisha's words belie the ambivalence women experience about the philosophy of the shelter and the role of the staff. While many women understand the need to fend for themselves and wish not to be treated as deficient, they also are unaccustomed to fending for themselves in the public realm or they know the problems they are likely to encounter as poor, maybe black or ethnic, and female. The women are stressed and many are uncertain and afraid.

Clearly, for all the problems of the therapeutic model, the self-help model has its own. The self-help model of organization has been criticized for various reasons.[25] First of all, self-help philosophies can easily translate into "victim-blaming" ones. If the solution to a problem is one that a battered woman can effect by herself, then maybe she got herself into the problem in the first place. This possibility is an ironic one, given that the domestic violence movement has struggled so much to avoid it. The sensitivity about language and labels (discussed earlier) is evidence of the movement's concern not to impugn or blame survivors of violence.

Second, there may be built-in racial and/or social class discrimination. What resources are actually available for battered women to access once they leave the security of the shelter? A " 'survivor' of domestic violence" may have to survive on precious few resources. What resources are there for a separated or divorced mother or a single middle-aged woman on her own for the first time? What resources will the low-income neighborhood into which they must move have? The charge of the racism of the self-help philosophy is extraordinary, given that the mission of the YWCA is the "elimination of racism by any means necessary."

Last, too much self-help ideology may mean too little social responsibility. If a battered woman can help herself and her children, then maybe our cities, states, country, our society should not be required to do so. If a battered woman can help herself, then why delve into the social inequalities and sexism that created the situation in the first place? Ironically, for the self-help philosophy, the solution does not stem from the problem.

No wonder Alisha feels something is missing or wrong with her shelter experience. Such ambivalent feelings about self-help are easily translated into antagonism toward staff members. Residents feel monitored for house rules rather than mentored for "self-help." Their overwhelming sense is that they are under constant surveillance, yet—at least in some areas of their lives—they wish there were even more oversight or intervention into their domestic affairs. Alisha, however, is not so much interested in further monitoring as she is interested in better quality mentoring.

The sense of being monitored, of being under surveillance, is very strong and very widespread among residents. They feel undue attention is given to adherence to house rules and regulations. A resident may stay at the Women's House with her children for a six-week period unless she causes undue problems for herself or others. A woman who does not follow house rules or who is perceived as a slacker, malingerer, or troublemaker or a woman who is perceived as insubordinate or self-injurious is made to leave the shelter. In such a case the woman, in the language of the staff, has "been departed." Otherwise, a woman may take advantage of the shelter and its services for at least the six-week period and, in some instances—that is, if she is perceived as motivated, cooperative, and honestly in need of an extension—a few more days or weeks. However, according to staff estimates, nearly one woman a week is asked to leave the shelter before the six-week limit. Apparently, it is not difficult to be departed.

THE SHELTER AS SURVEILLANCE: RULES AND REGULATIONS

During initial (called "intake") interviews, the staff reviews intake documents and information with incoming residents. They cover issues such as the "client" and family health and abuse history, the children's program, grievance procedures, liability releases, house orientation, transportation options, the house safety plan, fire and tornado procedures, and groups and services (such as the writing group, medical team, et cetera). One handout is given on the "cycle of violence"—Lenore Walker's now disputed schema for the cyclical nature of domestic violence (see chapter 1). The family support specialists also inform the incoming residents of case management issues such as the availability of legal services, children's services (schools, childcare, et cetera), financial assistance, job training and employment opportunities, counseling, housing, and medical services.

This is a lot of information to assimilate. There are approximately twenty-eight pages of information or documentation in the intake packet. Of these pages, thirteen pages present rules, policies, and procedures regarding a host of events or issues: meals, children, confidentiality, appropriate language, and so forth. Two pages concern domestic violence. Seven pages elicit client and family information for administrative purposes. Other items include a house event calendar, a list of physical signs of communicable diseases, and a statement of resident rights. These rights include the right to receive all services without discrimination, to receive respectful treatment, and to file a grievance for the denial of rights.

Residents must sign agreements regarding the rules and regulations of the shelter. These agreements include keeping the location of the shelter confidential, refraining from physically and verbally abusive behaviors, refraining from the use of alcohol or drugs in the shelter, doing house chores, supervising their children, keeping the house schedule regarding meals and getting up and out of bed, and so forth. There are three condensed pages of rules to which an incoming resident must vouch agreement by signing. If they violate rules, then consequences are threatened. The house manager may dismiss a woman for rule infractions. In the summer of 2000, the staff estimated that at least one woman a week is dismissed from the shelter for infractions such as breaking the confidentiality agreement by having friends or family drop her off too close to the shelter or for not returning by curfew time.

The most controversial rule is the house curfew: 5:30 P.M., Sunday to Thursday and by 11 P.M. on Friday and Saturday. Winona, a forty-five-year-old resident, says: "I am not a child. I'm an adult. I should be able to decide when to come and go from this place. I'm not a baby. I'm a grown woman." Most women disclose more ambivalence. They understand the safety issues: An abuser might follow them and endanger everyone at the shelter; yet, the same situation could happen when residents are attending to business before curfew. In fact, the intake literature does not cite safety as the reason for the curfew: It is necessary "to retain an adequate house count of available beds."[26] Most women believe the curfew and other rules (for example, residents must relinquish their room keys when they come and go from the shelter) mirror the authoritarianism of their abusers. Their abusers forbid them to come and go freely; now, the women should determine their own comings and goings. Curfew and other screening mechanisms, such as phone screening and logs kept of the woman's daily progress, are perceived, at worst, as unnecessary surveillance and, at best, as perhaps useful but unwelcome. The rules are tolerated by most and violated by some who may find themselves later on the street.

Other rules contribute to this sense of unsought surveillance. One unpopular house rule regards child discipline. Residents agree not to spank or hit their children. Many mothers disagree with the rule as interference in their parental rights to discipline as they see fit. Contrary to what middle-class child rearing experts say, some mothers see a distinction between spanking to discipline children and the battery of domestic violence. In the resident intake folder, one document enjoins women to develop good communication with their children. A series of bulleted commands delineates how to do this: teach, speak, look, practice, respect, catch, use, praise, give, and so forth. For example, the first command is: "Teach your children to listen . . . gently touch a child before you talk . . . say his/her name." Another stipulates: "Give your undivided attention when your children want to talk to you. Don't read, watch television, fall asleep, or make yourself busy with other tasks."[27] On one level these suggestions seem commonsensical and well intentioned; on another level—delivered on a handout and enjoined as a house rule, these "communication tips" may seem patronizing at best and interfering at worst to women, some of whom have already struggled for years to raise their children in adverse circumstances. Another handout—written in the language of clinical social work or psychology—prescribes women to "develop a positive affective approach to managing [their] child's behavior."[28] It suggests a "time out" to interrupt children's unacceptable behavior. This is perhaps the preferred practice of the middle class, not the under or working class. Four of the twenty-eight pages of documentation make stipulations about childcare. Mothers who "disregard these policies" are cited and "any infraction can result in dismissal from the shelter."[29] Residents are annoyed particularly because many staff members are not mothers. How would they know? Residents speak forthrightly:

CHARLENE: I hate it when someone tells you how to raise your child, say little things pertaining to what the mom should be doing!

YVETTE: Cuz if you don't know the real deal, don't say nothing! I'm not gonna tell her [Charlene] how to raise her child. No one should intervene. Like someone with no kids.

Other shelter rules annoy residents to varying degrees. Residents may provide childcare for other residents for a maximum of two hours—hardly enough time to navigate on public transportation to and from an appointment on the other side of the city with a social service or mental health provider. Earlier, Kelly was expelled from another shelter:

My arm hurt. I went to [the hospital] and they put on a half cast and I went to a place where I was getting counseling. They said: "Go to sleep, we'll call the shelter." And they didn't. I came back to the shelter late and I couldn't stay because I missed my appointment [with a social worker]. You can't dogmatically enforce rules. We've been victims. It was definitely power struggles. I can see if I was drinking, but it was just power struggles. [. . .] I still feel the pull between bureaucracy and us. Rules. Infractions. They come first, and we should come first. Here [at the shelter] we women support one another, not the staff supporting us. But we can't really help each other much because we all have our burdens. I feel less comfortable with the staff. After fifteen days the focus is on when you are getting out. Intake is tricky thing. Intake is great. It's very warm. But after intake, you feel the pressure to get out.

Kelly may very likely have been dismissed from the Women's House too for missing an appointment. There are also rules about house chores, room safety, security, food, drugs and alcohol, weapons, schedules. While to my knowledge no one has ever debated the weapons rule (even though women are at most risk of death at the hands of abusive spouses when they leave them and some women might wish they could carry weapons in order to defend themselves), many women do disagree with the rule that stipulates that room keys must be returned to the front desk when the women come and go from the shelter and with the rule that the staff may enter their rooms at any time. Additionally, the cumulative effect of so many pages of rules may be less than empowering to women who are leaving relationships characterized by many rules.

Some shelter rules or expectations never make it to the "management" (as one intake form is signed) documents; that is, they do not make it into the official rules. For example, women are strongly encouraged not to see or speak to boyfriends or spouses (unlike some shelters); rather, they are encouraged to use their shelter time to "develop a course of action suitable to their needs."[30] Consequently when shelter women do interact with their spouses—as often they must whether they decide to separate permanently or not, they speak of the interaction in furtive tones and usually only with residents they trust. Women are strongly encouraged to attend group sessions as signs of cooperation. Women are strongly encouraged not to room with one another after they leave the shelter. Women are encouraged not to show signs of recognition to one another if they meet outside the shelter and, in fact, volunteers are forbidden from developing friendships with residents or even ex-residents outside the shelter. Such rules would seem to fly in the face of the development of the feminist notion of "solidarity" at the same time as they make some degree of common sense. For example, some survivors of domestic violence are embarrassed by their circumstances and do not wish to be heralded in public as battered women. The staff still presents the last several of these unwritten rules as matters of safety. Dottie, a resident, echoes a common refrain in the shelter about rules: "I just want to get started on my new life, without restrictions, rules, curfews, the other people that I get to know and then they are out of my life usually forever. This is loss to me and I hate loss in my life. I have lost enough."

The many written and unwritten rules are part of a system of surveillance that women like Dottie do not fully appreciate. The cameras inside and outside the shelter, the high fences around the building, the locks and alarms contribute as well to the women's feeling that they are in "prison." There is a pervasive sense of irony that, in order to escape the prison created by their partners, they had to enter a prison created by society—the shelter, with all its surveillance systems. Recall Janelle's words: "I want out of this shelter." She was tired of the scrutiny. Other women agree:

LANA: We are in a shelter. [Our abusers] aren't. They have a home. They have transportation, a job.

DARCY: We are prisoners. They aren't. We have a curfew. We have rules, bars, cameras. They don't.

TINA: Our lives are disrupted. They have food, shelter. I have to get out now because the shelter says I've been here too long now. I'll be in a worse situation. You should see the apartment I went to look at today. I wouldn't send my abuser there!

RITA: For me, justice? I would kill my man. The law doesn't care about me. Who wants to keep getting beat up around your kids?

HOLLY: Who wants to keep getting beat up at all?

LANA: My kids are tired. Momma, they say, when are we getting out of here?

In this brief exchange, the theme of surveillance arises. Of course, most women try to make sense of the surveillance system as necessary for their own safety. They may feel both relief and tension with respect to rules and regulations, the cameras, fences, and locks. Linda Mills, however, offers this about shelters:

> Such a system should recognize that true empowerment for battered women is achieved not through obedience to the expectations of legal or social work advocates or models but

through acknowledgment of the woman's need to reconsider and re-evaluate the meaning of trauma in a flexible time frame and a supportive environment.

Battered women need to design their own courses of action, incrementally, at their own pace. Thus social workers should "recognize her uncertainty and emotional and cultural loyalties demand a safe and nonjudgmental space in which to explore these issues."[31] To accommodate this stance would create structural changes altering the shelter's basic identity and resources.

RESISTANCE TO SURVEILLANCE

In its early days, argues Sarah Heath, "[w]orking-class women conflicted with the YWCA on appropriate notions of womanhood precisely because the YWCA offered them a sense of community and security in which they could create new norms of behavior and conduct."[32] In some senses, a similar dynamic may be uncovered at the Women's House today. The words of Hemma suggest that the security of the shelter invites women into new behaviors:

> I could say to my husband today what I wanted to say because I knew I could come back here. I wouldn't have said half the things I said. I felt more confident. He was surprised because I talked back to him. I haven't for so long because I didn't want to aggravate the situation.

Hemma resisted her partner at the same time as she resisted an unwritten shelter expectation, that is, that she not visit with him during her stay. The shelter made Hemma's new behavior possible; even so, she would be cited if she returned past curfew. Women resist many rules as they negotiate their way through shelter life. They do this both singly and concertedly. Curfew is stretched to its limit. Food is smuggled into rooms. Children are disciplined in habitual ways in the privacy of bedrooms. Women meet their partners to consider whether they should go home. According to staff, "verbally abusive" disagreements break out between residents—acts forbidden by house rules, but considered apt linguistic self-defense by disputants.

At the same time as they resist, shelter women may perform cooperation for the staff and learn through the performance. One example concerns participation in the domestic violence group. Women may not agree with Lenore Walker's "cycle of violence" model in which abusive partners are said to go through tension building and contrite stages of behavior. Sometimes abusers are consistently violent and never make amends. But women cooperate, criticize the session privately, and develop their own ideas. Later, their language reflects participation. It is laced with key words: oppression, injustice, patriarchy, equality, solidarity, and so forth. In this way, women both resist and assimilate—often to good effect.

The women's resistance to purely secular language is worth noting straightaway. Shelter women supplement wholly secular explanations with religious ones. For example, staff emphasizes the social and economic conditions that facilitate violence against women. In patriarchal society, men have control of the family and cultural resources. Meanwhile many women explain men's violence as the consequence of personal sin and cosmic evil. In the early days of the Young Women's Christian Association, there may have been a place for such religious concepts. There is no place today. Many staff would denigrate Lettie's worldview:

> I thank God for God. He is the source of all my strength. I can go to him at anytime and he will never hurt me. He comforts me, renews my strength and carries me when I'm weak. He's closer to me than anyone and he shows me love without pain. He never hurts or demeans me and accepts me no matter what.

Lettie has been assimilating staff language about domestic violence. Implicitly, she defines a loving relationship contradistinctively to the one with her partner. Yet staff would never agree that what Lettie needs most is God. For them, she needs a job and a place to live. Such disagreements are sometimes hidden, sometimes not. Yet strict boundaries between staff and residents are often maintained by the residents with great diligence. The very act of complaining about house rules creates an "us" versus "them" mentality. The tension may be unproductive or motivational. There are some benefits. Battered women learn to resist authority—something they may not have done with their abusive partners. They cultivate their own identity vis-à-vis the authority structures. And, finally, they may affect the rules. In fact, a resident may now return after curfew if she has made a mutually satisfactory arrangement with staff before she leaves the shelter. Another example is the agreement between residents and staff to allow other residents to watch their children if they will be gone for hours. These are negotiations due to the continued harangue of shelter residents who often dispute the authority of the institution over their lives. In such ways, the residents resist the agency's notions of proper behavior for battered women and create structural change.

CONCLUSION

The Women's House is a location of multiple tensions deriving from race, class, and religious differences between the nonprofit middle-class shelter organization and the under or working-class women who temporarily reside there. The organization has developed rules and regulations in the interest of the smooth and efficient functioning of a large transient living shelter. Ironically, though well-intended, these rules and regulations contribute to the residents' sense of oppression instead of empowerment—the stated mission of the organization. Additionally, the change of location in recent years to a shelter with new architectural features has made community-building more difficult. New safety features, such as in-house cameras, contribute to the residents' overwhelming sense of being under surveillance and control.

Yet obstacles to the women's senses of community and agency are frequently resisted and the middle-class association has been changed in the process. In the end, the middle-class values of the shelter are both resisted and assimilated especially as residents come into contact with staff with whom they can relate or other residents who have been positively affected by staff. Gwen sees this: "Once I get myself together, I will turn into someone who helps women like me. It took someone to help me. Someone had to offer me a way out." Shelter women, like Gwen, learn about violence as they interact. Indeed, their ability to develop friendships is important to their senses of agency and satisfaction with the shelter. Further, their ability to create a common language about suffering, its meanings and its mitigation, is a critical aspect of the healing process. A language of transformation, composed of religious, secular, self-help, and feminist elements, develops. The religious features are deeply significant to many women. Ultimately the Women's House as a shelter and a social order facilitates this language. Given all the ambiguities, contradictions, and tensions, the women begin to heal. They heal both through and in spite of the shelter's bureaucratic nature and its status as a secular social work agency. This is not to justify the bureaucracy, but to point up the women's resilience and resourcefulness. Women resist and, through their resistance, begin to heal. Relationships are built because of and in spite of the shelter as an institution. As one resident, Lia, once said: "My best friend here is someone who is always there for me no matter what. When I'm in trouble, she's there to help me out. She doesn't care if she gets into trouble to help me. She's like a sister to me."

THREE

"Sometimes I Just Want to Give Up"

WOMEN'S ANGUISH, WOMEN'S PAIN

My name is nothing. Sometimes I just want to give up.

—Amelia

I am wiped out, crushed, nothing.

—Karyl

I add up to nothing, useless, worthless and ugly.

—Marissa

INTRODUCTION

"Pain passes much of its time in utter inhuman silence," writes David B. Morris.[1] Yet, in the shelter, the bodies of women are often the living testimonies of inflicted pain. Many women have black eyes, bruises, and broken limbs. They have knife and gun shot wounds. Their bodies carry the brutal marks of having been pushed out of moving cars, off balconies, down stairs. Sometimes the marks of pain and suffering are not visible. I met women who were chained to beds or forced to stand in corners or on chairs for long periods of time. They have been raped with bottles, sticks, and kitchen

53

implements. Sometimes their testimony to pain is revealed through absence. A miscarriage hides the history of their swollen pregnant bellies having been punched or kicked.

The bodies of shelter women bear the marks of only some of their troubles. Women often come to the shelter from the emergency room of the local hospital after their physical injuries have been treated. Their emotional or psychological problems typically have not received any attention. Many cases, however, involve overwhelming psychological violence. It is much more common than physical violence and it reportedly has the most lasting effects.[2] Many shelter women have been told by partners that they are bad wives, negligent housekeepers, and unsound mothers. They have been told they are crazy, sinful, and evil. They are stupid, ugly, and worthless.

Mostly women endure both physical and psychological violence. The beatings are accompanied with a steady stream of verbal and nonverbal abuse. Sexual assault commonly accompanies physical assault.[3] With untold terror, women watch as their children are physically, sexually, or verbally assaulted and their children watch as they are physically, sexually, or verbally assaulted. Michael P. Johnson calls this "patriarchal terrorism."[4] Of course, battered women die. For every woman in the shelter, there are at least five women who do not come to the shelter for various reasons: fear, shame, doubt. And most women who use the services of a shelter do not actually move into the shelter.[5] Many women, sheltered or not, live in a world of pain and suffering.

In this chapter, I want to prepare for a theological discussion of the suffering of battered women by distinguishing pain and suffering. I offer the voices of battered women as they reflect on their bodily experience or situations. I will emphasize the experience and consequences of pain.

Suffering extends from both physical and psychological pain; thus, at times, the distinction will be artificial. However, I persevere because I want to explore reasons why the actual pain of women is disregarded by both victims and society, including its lived experience and the nonavailability of language to describe it. As Judith Lewis Herman notes: "Traumatic memory is . . . wordless and static."[6]

THE LANGUAGE OF PAIN AND SUFFERING:
VANISHING THE FEMALE BODY

"Pain leads its existence mostly in secret, in silence, without leaving written records or eloquent testimony," writes David B. Morris.[7] Curiously enough, Morris's observation can be applied to the general literature on battered women. The literature does not deeply consider the survivor's experience of pain from actual blows or beatings.

Yet this experience is the identifying or essential experience of a "battered" woman. Indeed, in the nomenclature of domestic violence, the use of the descriptor "battered" (that is, in the terminology "battered women") suggests that aggressive, injurious physical contact has been made by the abuser, presumably an assault that leaves its dire marks. In the general literature on domestic violence, however, this basic existential fact is largely neglected or left unexplored. The current trend toward using the nomenclature "survivor of domestic violence" further hides the brutal physical facts.[8]

In the general literature, lists, charts, or wheels are used to depict the activities of the abuser: hitting, slapping, shaking, shoving, pushing, choking, punching, burning, stabbing, or shooting. In these assaults, the abuser's body is used as a weapon or the abuser uses a weapon with his body to assault the body of the victim. The bodily experience is not directly attended to because the activity is defined from the point of view of the agent or actor. The focus is on the assailant, the abuser.

After the abuser's activities are listed, other boxes, wheels, and charts are used to describe nonphysical violence. The emotional or psychological assaults are listed, nonbodily assaults such as name-calling, threatening, terrorizing, and so forth. Again, the semantic focus is on the abuser. Typically the bodily and particularly the nonbodily assaults are then explored in terms of effects on the victim or "survivor." The victim is defined as "depressed," "fearful," or "anxious." She loses self-esteem or self-confidence.

In short, when the focus finally does turn to the woman, the emphasis is on the successful uptake of the activities of the abuser: that is, on how the abuser has succeeded in his attempt to control the victim by making her depressed, anxious, fearful, and so forth. Indeed the batterer now has control of the domestic situation, and psychologically-speaking, in contrast to his partner, he may very well be "satisfied," "self-assured," or "self-confident." His self-esteem may be bolstered. Perhaps only feminist literature on domestic violence more than perfunctorily explores what the batterer gains: power and control in the relationship and, by extension, in society for all males.[9]

Beyond such treatments, there is little acknowledgment of the actual bodily experience, the literal pain, of women. Even survivors do not readily discuss their bodily pain and, when they do, they often translate it in quite the same manner as the educators translate it. They tend to shift the focus to the activities of the abuser. If you walk through the Women's House, you can see the broken and bruised bodies of battered women—vivid testimony of the infliction of bodily harm by some more powerful other—and, if you talk with battered women, you can trace their pain through the stories of their suffering. One must listen carefully because most often the narratives remove both the storyteller and the listener from the actual bodily experience of pain. In ways sometimes helpful and sometimes harmful, *the language translates the experience of pain away from the body and toward the agent and his weapon.*

Initially there may be good reasons for this shifting or "translating" process for the battered woman herself. She may be protecting herself while she learns to cope with her crisis. In the long term, however, the effect of avoiding the painful actuality of assault is good for neither the woman, nor for society. What is the nature of this physical experience that defines domestic violence yet is ultimately denied, diverted, deflected? What is the essential experience that ultimately evades or avoids language, focus, or discussion? While physical violence is not the predominant behavior in the wide array of behaviors ultimately labeled "domestic violence," it is popularly considered the one behavior in which the perpetrator "crosses the line" from the territory of domestic dispute to domestic violence. What is the experience of "I am hit"? What is the actual experience of harm from beatings that causes so much suffering during and long after its occurrence?

PAIN: A BIOPSYCHOSOCIAL EXPERIENCE

Pain and suffering, according to biomedical researcher Eric Cassell, are distinct. Pain is the entire process of sensing, interpreting, and modulating physical sensations—as well as assigning cause, anticipating course, and determining response. It is based on sensory information that involves "a cognitive effort that requires judgment," thus it is a subjective experience.

The meaning of pain is constructed as much by gender, social status, class, and other cultural or historical conditions as by the nervous system. Pain is always historical—shaped by a particular time, place, culture, and individual psyche.[10] It is reinforced by psychological and emotional states, such as guilt, fear, anger, grief, and depression. We experience pain, argues David Morris,

> not simply as private individuals but also as members of a culture or subculture. We therefore experience pain in ways shaped and reinforced by the images current around us. Family, friends, and community—in their behavior and values—supply the major representations of pain that shape our experience. Children at an early age begin to encounter images of pain in nursery rhymes, bedtime stories, and television cartoons. As we grow older, newspapers, novels, and films continue our education in pain. . . . The point to emphasize is that cultural changes in the representation of pain—from advertising to high art—both reflect and often help to create significant changes in our personal experience.[11]

In short, pain is a complex phenomenon schooled by the culture, but experienced by flesh and bones, the body.

The pain of battered women, I suggest, is augmented by our inability or unwillingness to confront it. Battered women are not the only ones to evade full descriptions of their pain. Even doctors and nurses in emergency rooms have problems seeing the nature of the women's pain. They do not detect or wish to appear to detect its causes or intervene. They can be unreceptive and, in their reports, they script the violence as if it proceeded from no agent.[12] Then they may choose to deaden the physical and psychological pain with medicines and send the woman away.[13]

The pain is rendered more problematic to battered women because it has so little social meaning. This is not to say it doesn't have a social meaning, only that its meaning is dealt with in such a way as to repress or submerge its existential meanings. Ultimately, socially, it is very meaning-invested. The meaning is this: Do not acknowledge it publicly—until, that is, it can no longer be denied or hid. Hence pain is often carried alone. It engenders shame. It is isolating. Initially, when shelter women are directly asked how and where they were hurt, they may recount the stories of painful injuries with the furtive intonations of shame or with the flat, dull tones of no interior affect. They have already distanced themselves from the physical pain and the emotional pain accompanying it. Encouraged by other shelter women or workers, they may learn to express their pain, or memories of it, with shades of anger or embarrassment. They begin to process it. Even so, the actual feeling has been transformed. Indeed it may have been transformed from the moment of its occurrence. I will address this possibility shortly. First, I would like to attend to the actual language practices of battered women in these first critical weeks after they leave their partners. How do they speak about pain?

THE LINGUISTIC PROCESS: METAPHORS OF AGENCY, WEAPONS, AND WOUNDS

The biological distress of domestic assault is not typically registered—at least, explicitly. Instead, in a process similar to the one Elaine Scarry notes in her discussion of torture in *The Body in Pain*, battered women tend to metaphorize the violence away from the body and onto matters of *agency*, *weapons*, or *wounds*.[14] They do not register the assault within a semantics of the body where it is initially felt. They register it in at least three ways (with subcategories) away from their own corporeality or flesh.

First of all, for example, shelter women tend to shift attention away from their physical experience by focusing on matters of agency. There are

several variations of this linguistic shifting of agency. Ironically, in one variation, they attribute *agency to themselves*. In some way, they incriminate themselves instead of their abusive partner.

WENDY: *I also learned how to be abused* and kept trying to cover up
            my pain.

DORIS: Sometimes *I would beg him* to beat me just to shut him up.

ANGEL: If you see his anger build up, *you want him to do it* [beat you]
            before he gets really mad.

In other cases, women refer to the violence as if it proceeded from *no agent*.
Further, no body has perceived the pain of battery and blows.

HOPE: I am thirty and *I have lived with violence* all my life.

VICTORIA: When *we find ourselves in abusive relationships*, whether it is physi-
            cally or mentally, it can sometimes destroy us mentally and can
            even kill us physically.

TAMMY: *I was abused* when I was a child and through my teenage years.

APRIL: *I was stomped* when I was pregnant.

Sometimes the violence is de-emphasized to such a degree that it is not
named. In the following examples, shelter women avoid naming the atroci-
ties they endured. Here there is *no mention of the actual violence*:

MARY: I don't want *what happened* to me to happen to my child.

DIAMOND: I don't want to take *anymore*.

TAMMY: They [the children] see how their daddy *did* their mama.

MENDY: I don't believe I'd ever be dependent on a man because of *what
            I've been through*.

Mary, Diamond, Tammy, and Mendy do not even name the intimate violence they experienced at the hands of their parents or their partners. It is
de-emphasized, nondesignated, in these utterances. It is not clear what
their children saw or what they themselves endured either as children
or adults.

In a second linguistic maneuver, the women's body as a receiver or
sensor of violence is again ignored. In these instances, the attention shifts to
weapons. In some cases, the perpetrator or agent is identified as a weapon:
The *male body is the weapon*.

HOPE: I have been *molested by my father and beaten by my mother*. I married *an abusive husband*.

TAMMY: Some of the signs are *men throwing* things at you, speaking with anger towards you, lowering your self-esteem, him not bathing well. These are a few signs I am able to recognize.

CHRISTINA: The hardest thing to forgive and forget is *my daddy* when he used to . . . *beat* us with sticks, pot, pans, and shovels.

Notice that Tammy's wounds have been abstracted into "signs." Sometimes *actual weapons* are identified as in Christina's statement, but the actual pain is not acknowledged. In the following examples, the women specify the weapons used to cause pain, but the body as a sensor of gross pain is not registered.

PAT: Men sexually abusing their own kids. Get *a red hot poker* and put it [. . .] in new born babies and stick it in there.

NIGHT: He stuck a *knife* in my face and forehead and foot and he blamed me for it. He stuck a *fork* in my foot. That ain't nothing.

NELITA: He hit me in the head with a *hammer*.

INDIA: When he did, it was really bad. I probably got a bruise for every fight we had. He used to make me take my clothes off and whoop me with a *belt* . . . because I didn't agree with him when I was around his friends

Remarkably, India, Night, and other women like them, do not relate the profundity of the physical pain they must have experienced in their bodies. Language about their bodies is not used. Contrarily, Night even suggests the physical abuse did not affect her: "That ain't nothing," she says.

Oftentimes when women narrate their stories, their affect is low and their own body language is subdued. India's narration is notable for the several strategies she uses to describe the abuse—without once referring to the horrible physical pain she experienced. She notes weaponry. She shifts agency to herself. She assumes responsibility. Listen as she continues:

He went off, beating me and hitting my son. I thought I was really sick of this! He threw us out of the house. I went to the police. I had nowhere to go. I went to the police in Cincinnati. I had a man help me call the police. But in the van, after he beat me up, he put us in the van. Then he pushed me out of the van

on the highway and took my baby down to Lexington. I called
the police in the phone booth three times and they never came.
When my baby was born I had real bad abuse. He beat me when
I was pregnant. It was the worst. . . . He beat us up to two days
before my baby was born. He threw me out of the house. This is
my apartment. I had nowhere to go when I had him [the baby],
so they took him.

India has successfully detached or disassociated the physical pain away from
her body, from her flesh or her corporeal memory, as she narrates this har-
rowing chronology of domestic violence. Instead she twists agency: "I had
real bad abuse" and "I probably got a bruise for every fight we had." She
refers to her partner's actions: *He beat me, he threw me, he pushed me.* She
never once refers to her own pain. Like Night, she seems to downplay the
corporeal significance: "I thought I was really sick of this!" It is as if she were
talking about annoying comments her partner made rather than painful—
not to mention, criminal—assaults.

A third way battered women are able to translate away from relating
the experience of actual pain in their flesh and bones is to refer to the
violence in terms of wounds, either in an abstract sense or as a specified body
part. In these instances, women do refer to their bodies; yet they manage to
translate pain away as a fully sentient experience. This strategy enables them
to restrict its effect, thus to de-emphasize it. In the next set of statements,
the women refer to their wounds or injuries in terms of specified body parts.

TAMMY: He threw me against the wall. He threw me into a corner. I
           thought *my ribs* were cracked.

NIGHT: He keeps saying, "I didn't do nothing to you." I said, "Look at *my
           face*! Look at my *body*!"

Night refers to both a specific body part and her body in general. Neither
Tammy nor Night express how the pain felt in their tissue or bones. Their
bodies seem nonsentient, certainly objectified, without feeling.

Other women use more abstract language to refer to women or to
women's bodies in general. The effect is to deflect attention from their own
bodily injuries all together:

RUTH: Some relationships would go better if the men would keep
             their *hands off of us women.*

ANGELIQUE: *You* have to be almost dead. Police: *she'll* be dead when you
             come back. In a body bag.

One might not realize from these statements that Ruth and Angelique had been in the process of narrating their own stories of physical brutality they personally endured. Ruth abstracts her own pain into the pain of all women. Angelique defers the use of first person, choosing instead to use second and third person points of view, to express her fears about her own fate. Both women have jumped over their own bodily experiences to offer abstract or social commentary. While an empathic move from personal experience to social or political understandings of the situation of other women is critical for the full healing process, it is not beneficial if a battered woman has not come to terms with her own painful experiences. Why does the process of "translating pain away from the body" happen?

"Translating Away from the Body"

In keeping with the ethnographic method of this study and my goal of focusing on the actual experience of battered women, I will now offer some observations about why women, in their use of language, deflect attention away from their corporeal experience. In a subsequent section, I will offer some relevant insights from the fields of psychology and psychiatry. First, I wish to attend to the voices, the apparent rationale, of shelter residents. I will deal with three areas of concern: the shelter culture; some cultural factors as articulated by battered women themselves; and then one particularly salient cultural factor—religious socialization. These observations do not exhaust the evidence; instead, they point to the most significant and apparent issues for the women themselves.

Shelter Culture

An integral mission of battered women's shelters is to provide a safe place for women as they sort out their various options in the aftermath of domestic violence. In some shelters, counseling and/or support groups assist women as they begin to heal from both their physical injuries and psychological pain. There is plenty of evidence that talking or writing about traumatic experiences helps victims to recover.

Ironically, however, shelter culture itself presents some obstacles to women's disclosure. First of all, as we have seen in chapter 2, the shelter is necessarily a bureaucracy. It is an institution with rules and regulations, some of which the residents may not approve. Domestic violence survivors are granted or denied assistance based first on an *adequate performance* of suffering and then on an adequate performance of self-help behaviors. The staff has and uses its power to admit or expel women based on sufficient performance. Thus many women never fully trust the shelter staff to whom they must disclose at least some information about their battery or abuse.

At the same time, the performance must not be overdone. A domestic violence survivor may have a sense of caution or fear, particularly initially, about the staff's assessment of her ability to take care of her children. If she shows too much engagement in pain, she may be sent to the local hospital and her children will be separated from her. If she demonstrates, or if someone believes that she is demonstrating, an inability to take care of her children, she may risk intervention from child protection agencies.[15]

Hence full disclosure of the extent of her injuries may jeopardize her family. I have met women who tried to de-emphasize or hide their injuries, or the limitations they cause, for fear of being written up and sent away from the shelter to the hospital where the women are by necessity separated from their children. The children would then face an increased risk of being taken by the abusive parent. In short, battered women may hide physical injury or de-emphasize physical pain in an attempt to protect their families. It is an act of family survival.

Among the residents themselves, there may also be some obstacles to women's full disclosure of physical injuries and ensuing, possibly chronic, pain. Among the women, there is a kind of "hierarchy" of assault. That is, women whose bodies show signs of severe physical assault are most stigmatized by other shelter women. Their arrival at the shelter is news that quickly spreads throughout the house. Residents and staff may stare when they see a woman who has been severely battered. They whisper about her wounds, her situation, when she passes by. Ginnie and Amanda express the two points of views: Ginnie as victim and Amanda as observer.

GINNIE: Before I knew everybody, I felt that even though we were all in the same situation, I felt uncomfortable coming downstairs. I stayed in my room, and when I came down here, I thought they was thinking, "She got her butt kicked."

AMANDA: He done beat her brains out once. No woman can beat on a man. No woman can beat on a man like that. I know what I would do if it happened to me.

Ginnie hid her pain and her wounds. Amanda implies that she herself would not tolerate severe physical abuse. Both women's words suggest that more women are injured, or women are more injured, than we might know. Severe physical injury is stigmatized even amongst battered women.

Some shelter women believe that *no one cares* about either their physical or emotional pain. Why bother expressing it? Kim and Laura both suffer from physical pain. Laura had a patch of blackened dead flesh on her leg that would have to be removed as soon as her pregnancy was over or she would loose her leg. Her husband kicked her with his steel-toed boots. Kim has multiple lacerations on her arms. She hides the painful bruises with a long-sleeved shirt. She is black and blue, she says, "in places where the sun don't shine," and it hurts her to walk. In disclosing her sexual assault, even so generally, Kim departs from many battered women in the shelter who will not discuss it except in the most secure of encounters.

Kim and Laura believe that "no one cares" about them even in the shelter. They differ in their interpretation of the collective indifference. Kim believes that other shelter women are already overwhelmed by their own pain and suffering and cannot assume any more through empathic listening. Laura believes the indifference stems from apathy; that is, there is a sense that "nothing can be done about the pain" except to medicate it. Why focus attention on it? Both women believe their interpretations apply to sexual assault—widespread as it is among the experiences of shelter residents—as well as the more general physical assault.

Another woman, Angela, will not talk about her obvious pain and suffering because, she says, she "doesn't trust anyone, even women, especially women!" Angela thinks that talking openly makes her vulnerable to other shelter women who may know her abuser and who may tell him what she said. Her abuser threatened her over and over not to talk to anyone about "their problems"—that is, his abuse. Then she was "betrayed" by a woman to whom she did talk. After the confidant told Angela's partner "everything," the woman became his lover. Angela ran for her life. She is terrified to talk and, in our session, she initially sits sullen and silent. Her *vulnerability* prevents her from exploring the painful memories.

Judith Lewis Herman notes the importance of a safe place for women survivors of trauma and the hampering effect to recovery that takes place if the environment is (or is perceived as) hostile or unprotective.[16] Trust is essential for a sense of safety, thus the possibility of healing disclosure.

Some Cultural Factors

In short, both other residents and staff members may inadvertently prevent battered women from revealing the full nature of their injuries and the extent of their physical pain. In addition, there are significant external or cultural factors that work against the disclosure of physical pain. Invited to do so, survivors of domestic violence may speak about these factors. Some survivors of domestic violence recognize *gender socialization* as a cultural factor that inhibits their perception or expression of physical pain. The male point of view is the priorital point of view.

In one storytelling session, Mary, Berta, and I were openly discussing physical pain in violent domestic relationships. Mary, a survivor, observes:

> Culturally, women are taught to think in terms of the male. The male is the reference point.[17] It's his feelings that count. Your feelings don't register. And so, Berta said—and I believe it—" I thought I could or would kill him myself! Then I saw something in his eyes that made me run. I had to get out of there as fast as I could."

She ran. She never said anything about her own pain. Everything was about him: his feelings and what he would do.

Berta had been talking to us about her life, her domestic situation, and her partner of many years who had recently turned severely physically abusive. He had already put her in the hospital once and her own feelings of pain and anger threatened to overwhelm her. She was afraid she would strike out at him—until that is, his feelings of rage were once again made focal. His body language, his eye contact, force her focus back on his body as a threatening weapon and, intuiting the depth of his deadly rage, she flees. Mary recognizes the key dynamic: men's feelings count; women's do not. Cultural factors interact with personal factors in Berta's description, or more precisely, her lack of description about the great physical pain her partner had already caused her. The pain is left out of her account; only the fear remains.

Mary is aware of the function of the psychological terror in such brutal encounters. I will revisit her story in the next section on the psychological processes involved in women's trauma. These processes also result in the physiologically based numbing and consequent linguistic "vanishing" of women's bodies.

There are other cultural factors involved in the silencing of women's voices about their bodily pain. On their own account, many shelter women identify issues such as *social disapproval* of any public discourse about family problems, personal shame extending from the social disapproval, and low self-esteem deriving from widespread *sexism* that makes women believe their own bodies simply are not important. They are often aware of the *cultural negligence* or myopia surrounding actual violence against women while cultural images of eroticized violence against women abound. They recognize the deep personal disappointment and the social humiliation extending from their disrupted lives. Their lover or husband—the one to whom they had given their hearts, their bodies, and their money—is the one who humiliates them in public and in private. Battered women may be quite recognizant of the many cultural factors at work in the deadening of women's personal expression or language of pain. Millie writes a short poem that captures the connections between her physical and emotional pain and her shame:

> I was not to blame,
> Why do I feel so ashamed?
> He hurt me bad. I don't know why.
> Alls left is for me to cry.

Millie, a Catholic woman who, when I met her, was working seriously on her own healing process with the aid of secular self-help books, had begun to recognize and articulate the memories of pain in her flesh and in her heart. She was outspoken on the role of *religious socialization* in women's (non)language of pain. Many battered women are aware of the connection of religion to their abuse—a topic that I explore thoroughly in upcoming chapters. They are accustomed to their abusive partners quoting biblical scripture to them to justify their abuse.

I would like to point here, however, to the role of religious socialization in the repression of women's language about pain. During her girlhood, Millie was well-schooled about the lives of the saints. Her role models were women martyrs who had marched silently, wordlessly, to their rapes, torture, and deaths at the hands of evil rulers, pagans, or spurned husbands-to-be. Other role models for Catholic girls and, to a lesser extent, mainstream Protestant (Episcopalian or Anglican) girls were female saints who invited or quietly endured physical pain, privation, or illness as a path to salvation, sanctity, sainthood. A litany of long-suffering female saints was well known especially to Catholic girls of the 1950s, 1960s, and earlier. Even today, St. Therese of Lisieux, St. Teresa of Avila, and other saints who devoted their lives to others are held up as models to women who then believe they should suffer silently in their physical, perhaps chronic pain.[18] Many female saints— canonized, honored, idealized—bore either imposed or self-inflicted physical pain and deprivations for the "greater glory" of God.

Many adult women like Millie—today middle aged and older—have a difficult time being fully aware, fully conscious, of their own bodies, their own sentience, without a sense of the Christian or womanly duty to silently endure pain and suffering originating in Eve's transgression and the legacy of their own originally sinful nature. The particular denomination only affects the ideology by degrees. All Christian women are expected, on some level, to incorporate suffering into their vocations. The suffering Jesus is a critical image to both black and white fundamentalist/evangelical women and Holiness/Sanctified women—the primary denominational and racial/ethnic groups in the Women's House. As Jesus suffered, his body racked with pain on the cross, as the Christian saints and martyrs suffered, any Christian woman may be called upon to suffer even physically in silence and in expiation, forgivingly, gratefully. Repentance, contrition, reparation, redemption, atonement—all these expiatory states so familiar to traditional Christian piety suggest physical deprivation or suffering to the body of the faithful, especially to girls and women who are made to know that their bodies are, in any case, sinful and shameful.[19]

Whatever their religious upbringing, many battered women agree, however, that the emotional pain of domestic violence is ultimately greater than the physical pain. This leads to a relative diminishment of an acknowledgment of traumatic physical pain's long-term psychological damages. Surely, an unending repression or translation of physical trauma precludes full healing.[20]

Many psychologists stress the importance to victims of reliving the experience of physical violence, in sentient detail, in a therapeutic process.[21] Indeed
it is a commonsensical notion, a truism, among psychologists and other mental
health care providers that talking is beneficial for survivor recovery. Reliving
trauma in a controlled situation, that is, not endlessly translating the pain
"away from the body"—in the interest of integrating the painful experience
into a new, realistic worldview—is a goal of therapeutic discourse.[22]

THE PSYCHOLOGICAL PROCESS: THE EXPERIENCE OF TRAUMA

This study is not a psychological study; however, in trying to more deeply
understand the language practices of battered women, I have found it helpful
to learn from psychologists, clinicians, and other mental health scholars
about the nature of trauma.[23] What knowledge can the field of psychology
bring to bear on the fact that so many battered women "translate away from
the body" when they recall their physical assaults? Increasingly, trauma has
become the subject matter of interdisciplinary scholarly discussion. Alongside the voices of battered women, the voices of mental health care experts
do lend explanation to the linguistic process I have just described.

In following Judith Lewis Herman, Ronnie Janoff-Bulman, and others,
I believe that domestic violence—and certainly domestic violence characterized by physical violence—can be a traumatic event for the woman who
experiences it. The American Psychiatric Association defines a traumatic
event as an unusual crisis, one that lies outside ordinary life experience.
While there is a certain degree of personal subjectivity and cultural relativity
in identifying if a crisis will create trauma, the key features are that the
precipitating event lay "outside the range of usual human experience" and
would be "markedly distressing to almost anyone."[24] As Janoff-Bulman notes,
the victim is psychologically unprepared for the event to happen.[25]

Trauma is further conceptualized as a generalized reaction to overwhelming experience. In addition to their physical injuries, women suffer
from depression, fear, anxiety, shame, self-blame, low self-esteem. Their senses
of self are disrupted. Their religious belief systems are shaken. Their identities are fragmented and aspects of their identities are even lost. As I noted
in chapter 1, women are "significantly more likely than men to suffer psychological injuries related to their abuse."[26] Tara told me:

> I had a friend who jumped out a sixth-story window because she
> didn't see a way out. . . . She even wrote a note. She couldn't see
> going through it anymore and she thought that her kids deserved
> a better way of life. So she wanted out.

It is estimated that battered women are five times more likely to attempt suicide than nonbattered.[27] Certainly these characteristics are indicative of traumatic episodes. Many professionals view the severe ongoing victimization of battered women as an out-of-the-ordinary circumstance that leaves them in various states of traumatization.[28] Indeed PTSD is a diagnostic classification admitted in 1987 to the *Diagnostic and Statistical Manual (DSM-III)* of the American Psychiatric Association and it is now applied with some regularity to battered women by professionals and by the public.[29]

Though severe ongoing victimization may be out of the ordinary, domestic violence is not. Given its widespread occurrence it is, or it is perceived as, in some sense, ordinary or normal. Our culture and, globally, other cultures tacitly prepare women and men to expect and to accept domestic violence, at minimum, by desensitizing the public to its representation and by not adequately reacting to its occurrence. Thus it seems that, on one level, domestic violence is perceived as normal—after all, men everywhere use violence to assert their power in both private and public realms; on another level of consciousness, domestic violence is rejected as a disturbance of ideal family life. At the same time, I believe an actual domestic violence event can be traumatic to the individual woman, particularly initially, because it disrupts a worldview shaped by idealistic notions of true romantic or familial love. It leaves the battered woman in a state of fear and anxiety about a relationship that should be the source of safety and comfort. Indeed, Janoff-Bulman notes that:

> The predominant emotional experience of trauma victims is intense fear and anxiety. Their psychological world is one filled with terror. Survivors are dealt a double dose of anxiety, one associated with the realization that one's survival is no longer secure, that their self-preservation can be jeopardized in a world that is frightening and unsafe. The other is associated with the survival of their conceptual system, which is in a state of upheaval and disintegration. The very assumptions that had provided psychological coherence and stability in a complex world are the very assumptions that are shattered (64).

Certainly, for many women, the physical (leaving aside, even momentarily, verbal or other kinds of) assaults—the shoves, the slaps, the kicks, the punches—are traumatic events that force them to make psychological adjustments in order to reestablish coherence in the midst of a new and unwelcome reality. For example, women blame themselves for the violence and eventually lose self-esteem; yet, they still grasp at least the idea of the (inevitably false) security of family life.

The linguistic evidence—"the translating away from the body"—finds explanation in trauma victims' methods of coping with physical pain. Psychologists note three methods among others that are of interest to us: denial/ numbing, avoidance, and interacting with others. Typically shelter women acknowledge or manifest aspects of these three coping strategies.

Denial/Numbing

Denial or numbing is a thoroughgoing negation of a traumatic problem or situation. It can involve the negation of an impulse, feeling, or thought. The victim may not be fully aware of the stressful event, that is, of all aspects of external reality because she has cognitively shut down or emotionally turned off.[30] She has no feelings about the traumatic event. She is emotionally detached. Mary went through a period of denial or numbing before she came to terms with her childhood abuse:

> At night, my father would come up to my bedroom and tell me to go down into the basement. In the basement he would beat me—with belts, sticks, and his bare hands. When I heard his footsteps on the stairs, coming up to my bedroom, I would start to shake with fear. The adrenaline would start to pump. Then, from the moment I began to descend the basement stairs, my body would start to become numb. By the time I got into the basement and even before his first hit, I felt completely numb. I couldn't feel anything. I was away, out of that place, in some other world. I don't know where I went, but I wasn't there. To this day, I am not completely sure what happened in that basement. Did he really beat me or did I imagine it? I had to talk to my siblings to confirm my memories. Yes, he really did beat me.

Mary believes the denial contributed to her decision to marry a domestically violent man. She was middle aged before she allowed herself to confront the memories of the childhood trauma. She left her abusive partner and confronted her father. Now she speaks directly about both the physical and emotional pain.

Avoidance

Avoidance behaviors are more commonly noticeable behaviors in the shelter. The survivor consciously and deliberately decides not to think or talk about a stressful event. Shelter women engaged in avoidance do not deny the traumatic nature of the physical abuse. They just do not to talk about it. It's simply too painful. Christina acknowledges her own avoidance behavior. She says, "It's just so hard to forgive him for all the bad things he done. It's easier for me to forget than forgive."

Interaction

Another method battered women use to cope with the memories or lingering of their pain is conversational interaction. They talk with other women in the shelter. Many psychologists or scholars who deal with trauma trace recovery through therapeutic or interactivity processes.[31] In this book, chapters 7, 8, and 9 will deal with the healing processes of battered women as they engage one another in talk. In battered women's shelters, there are typically support groups. Some topics for the groups may include domestic violence, codependency, parenting, and drugs/alcohol. Some shelters hire psychologists or social workers to provide therapy. At the Women's House, funding for support groups and counseling has dropped in recent years. At any given time, there may or may not be opportunities for women to talk about their situations with professional caregivers. Opportunities to speak casually to other shelter women may vary widely depending on their schedules and other situational factors.

If interactions with others are not available or helpful, the trauma victim may experience flashbacks of the violence; indeed, flashbacks may happen in any case. In the language of psychology, the flashbacks are called "intrusive reexperiencing" or "reliving" and they often involve recalling physical injury in sentient detail. Flashbacks are a way of coping with trauma in that they are limited experiences with beginnings and endings: the survivor is not completely or permanently overwhelmed. They force the survivor to reckon with her trauma. Such a coping reaction is beyond the focus of this study though it remains a threat lurking in the shadows of the silencing or repression of women's physical and, of course, psychological pain.[32]

Of these methods of coping, denial/numbing behaviors and avoidance behavior are most suggestive, of course, for the lack of sentient acknowledgment in the language of battered women. There may be other explanations for the absence or diminishment of linguistic detail, the translating or metaphorizing "away from the body," of the physical pain of battered women. Some researchers suggest that the traumatic material is not even registered. Dori Laub argues: "Massive trauma precludes its registration; the observing and recording mechanisms of the human mind are temporarily knocked out, malfunction."[33]

Some research suggests that traumatic events may be processed and stored in distinct areas of the brain—that is, areas apart or separate from those areas that process language activity. Victims may have difficulties speaking about trauma because the memories simply are beyond the ken or horizon of language or, at least, not easily accessed by it.

Bessel van der Kolk, a psychiatrist, believes that the linguistic encoding of memory is de-activated during traumatic episodes. He believes that the nervous system reverts to sensory and iconic forms of memory such as those that form during childhood.[34]

"The power of one directly experienced negative event is 'real' in a way that the written word, for example, cannot approach," argues Janoff-Bulman (55). Thus some trauma victims are invited by psychologists to draw or to dance or to engage in other nonlinguistic therapeutic activities.

In her phenomenological study, *The Body in Pain*, Elaine Scarry suggests that intense pain crushes language. In the Women's House, Scarry's observation has some merit. Battered women do not easily speak about the physical pain of domestic violence. The reasons are many and complex. The cumulative rationale may be starkly simple: it is simply too painful to do so. After a point, however, the silencing of women's language about physical pain is detrimental to their own health, both physical and mental.[35] An unending silencing leads to even further suffering. To this we will now attend.

SUFFERING

The physical pain of many battered women may not ever subside completely or it may not subside for a very long time. The pain may be ongoing or chronic. Some battered women live the rest of their lives with painful disfigurations or disabilities. They limp painfully. They have lost the use of a limb. A finger is deadened, a cheek numbed, a nerve or bone irreparably damaged. Even if and when the physical pain subsides, the suffering does not. And, by far, most survivors of domestic violence have not been subjected to recurring atrocious bodily harm. They suffer other types of terror.

Suffering, writes Cassell, is "a specific state of severe distress induced by the loss of integrity, intactness, cohesiveness, or wholeness of the person or by a threat that the person believes will result in the dissolution of his or her integrity. Suffering continues until integrity is restored or the threat is gone."[36] Pain sometimes leads to suffering and suffering can take place without pain.

But, according to Dorothee Soelle, widespread suffering—involving all aspects of a person, that is, their physical, psychological, emotional, spiritual, and social selves—is the suffering of affliction.[37] The suffering of battered women is the suffering of affliction. In its thoroughgoing multidimensionality, affliction threatens the life integrity of the woman.

As suggested by a wide diversity of scholars such as philosopher Simone Weil,[38] theologian Dorothee Soelle, and medical doctor Eric Cassell, neither pain nor suffering are constant or unalterable.[39] Instead they are alterable states precisely because they are experienced within a historical or social location. If the meaning of the pain and suffering can be reinforced by psychological and emotional states, they may be diminished by psychological and emotional caretaking. If the integrity of the suffering person can be restored, the suffering will diminish. Still it is difficult to relieve the suffering of people who are frightened without also relieving their fear.[40] The responsibility of first order (after trying to assure their safety) is to listen to what battered women are actually saying about their pain and suffering. What do they feel? What do they fear?

BATTERED WOMEN DESCRIBE SUFFERING

In forthcoming chapters I will investigate the deliberations of theologians and philosophers on suffering and the problem of evil. Here, I offer the voices of battered women as they conceptualize their own suffering. After they have begun to reckon with their new situations in the shelter, the women begin to articulate (perhaps as much to themselves as to others) their stories of pain and suffering.

In the following short excerpts, women from the shelter describe the violence in their lives. To achieve control over these women, their abusers select from a particular kind or a cluster of kinds of violence. I categorized below these types of domestic violence that have been identified by both educators and the women themselves: physical, emotional/psychological, and social. But battered women's words often reveal their deep affliction, that is, the complex integration of physical, sexual, psychological, and social suffering. Thus, in some senses, it is artificial to separate out one source of suffering from another and I will discuss this shortly. Certainly the women's words reveal the depth of their suffering.

Physical Suffering

The stories of Tiffany, Dee Ann, and Inanna are consistent with the process of metaphorizing physical pain away from their bodies. Again, sexual assault is rarely discussed except in the most private encounters. Vanessa's account, through the cumulative effect of the description of her partner's many abuses, comes very close to approximating an authentic or direct language of physical suffering:

TIFFANY: When I was with my babby's father it was good until he gets drunk and hits me. He hits me with a crowbar and ask me to give him my money and I said no and when he got mad I told him to get away from me he just hitted me some more and when I called the police they came and locked him up. Some how he got out and now I do not know what to do. But I know I want to get myself better so I can take care of my babby without him hurrting me.

DEE ANNE: I was pregnant with my third child and my ex-boyfriend came in angry from working. He just started yelling at me because I moved something off his desk. Some how we ended up on the bed with him squeezing me real tight and I was scratching him in the face.

INANNA: All the while I was left to wonder, "What have I done? What am I doing wrong?" You would think the time I was choked to the point that I lost consciousness would have been enough.

VANESSA: The bruises, the dragging down the stairs, the mental abuse, smacks in my face, pull my hair, black eyes, screams of despair—my "ideal" man.

Mental/Emotional Suffering

The psychological suffering of women is expressed as fear, numbness, silence, or a sense of loss of control. The suffering might extend from physical, verbal, or other kinds of noncontact, psychological assaults such as the death threats endured by Angie or the marital infidelity withstood by Anetta. Once again, different sorts of suffering commingle:

JULIE: I'm scared of my husband getting on my kids. He is doing crack. I wonder what will happen to my kids.

ANGIE: When I walk by the bedroom, and he is sleeping, I think about how I should kill him before he kills me. He keeps saying he is going to kill me and throw my body in the woods. So I think when I see him sleeping, I should kill him before he kills me. But then I think, if I throw the knife and miss, I'm dead.

ANETTA: I don't care if there's another woman with him when I leave. I like to go to work because, at least, there I'm safe.

ELLA: My abuser wants to know my whereabouts at all times, talks about women in a degrading manner, hates women in general, has no respect for his mother or sister, hangs up on our phone calls, has extreme anger.

BARB: Today I was thinking should I get up? Only if I have to. . . .

LILY: My daughter was being molested from the time she was nine until the time she was thirteen. Her natural father was molesting her. [. . .] I never knew what was wrong with my child. [. . .] [When I found out] the only thing I could say was, "Lord have mercy, you've been killing my child!" Then I had to look at her when she asked me, "Mamma [. . .], you were my mother. Why didn't you know?"

Julie, Angie, and Anetta express states of extreme fear. Barb experiences the depression so common to battered women. She and Lily have been numbed with anxiety. Clearly Lily's suffering will recur as she bears the guilt of not recognizing the sexual abuse of her daughter's sexual abuse. All these women endure intense emotional suffering.

Social Suffering

Social suffering involves a sense of degradation or loss of self. Because violence is essentially about an abuser's need for power over his partner at the expense of her autonomy and social network, most battered women suffer socially.

The following excerpts illustrate the social isolation of so many battered women. Disconnection from others is an assault to women's integrity and a sign of loss of control over their own lives.

CORA JOY: In the beginning things went well enough. He helped me escape from home. He protected me. Later he became possessive. I was not allowed to leave the house and my family was not welcome. He changed the telephone number and, for a while, he would not tell me the number. Later I was allowed to go to the university to work on a degree in psychology. He wanted the credit cards I could get as a student. He made me call when I got to school and call again when I was ready to leave. I just complied. I resented having to strip for him to inspect my body when I came home. He thought I might have been with someone else. He went off a lot. I never talked back or complained. I left him when he went off for nothing. I walked in the house and he kicked me in the back. I left.

POLLY: I wasn't allowed any friends. I wasn't allowed to talk to my mother. I haven't talked to my mother for a year and a half. My own mother. He'd say you can call her tomorrow and tomorrow never comes. Because we don't have a phone and he won't let me go anywhere myself.

LEE ANN: I didn't have one person to talk to. Not one person.

LOUISE: It's like being in prison. We had a patio window, he put a blanket over the window. So no one could see through. We were on the second floor. I couldn't use my peripheral vision when we were outside.

MARIE: I didn't know not one person in Columbus. He made sure I didn't know anyone. Like my father or something. He would never leave me. Never take me to see my mother. I was held hostage by a maniac. I felt like I was in prison. He would rush me into the car, hurry, hurry, hurry. He got to the point he wouldn't go to work because he was worried about what I was doing. He put a string so he could see if I crossed the door.

RONDA: My husband would say I don't want your friends here.

GEORGIA: He opened my mail. When my mother sent me a card, he opened it.

WENDY: I was taken to and from work. I couldn't take the bus.

Clearly the women's words illustrate the loss of control over their own activities, autonomy, and, finally, their social or relational selves. This is the ultimate goal of the abuser's physical and psychological attacks.

Indeed, Dorothee Soelle argues that all suffering is social. In its disruptive power, the suffering of domestic violence is total.[41]

THE TOTALITY OF SUFFERING

Survivors do not usually break down their experience into separate categories such as "pain" versus "suffering" or such as physical, sexual, psychological, emotional, and so forth. Rather, when shelter women share their stories, they express a totality of suffering through a semantics of inner or affective states.

The inner states are embodied as a corporeal sense (of fatigue, for example, or of being prostrate) or as a bodily loss of direction. More often the states are emotionally entrained as feelings of loneliness, loss, fear, estranged senses of self (no self-love, worth, esteem, integrity), or meaninglessness and despair. I offer seven thematic expressions of these states from women's words:

1. Suffering is experienced bodily.

Ironically, although there is a dearth of detailed language of physical pain, domestic violence survivors do experience the totality of suffering within their bodies. Even nonbodily domestic assaults have bodily effects.

MELANIE: [I] keep messing up my life. I hope to get back on my feet and raise my body. But even when I try, things don't get better.

KARYL: I am wiped out, crushed, nothing.

PAT: *My bodie is burning* with decisions (I have to make).

KERRI: I am very *tired*. All the time.

2. Suffering is experienced as loss.

CHARLENE: It's in the pawn shop [until] pay day or lose it. He gave that
          to me as a present. Who gives a damn anyway? I'll lose it. So
          what, *I've lost so much.*

DOTTIE: I just want to get started on my new life, without restrictions,
          rules, curfews, the other people that I get to know, and then
          they are out of my life—usually forever. This is loss to me and
          I hate loss in my life. *I have lost enough.*

3. Suffering is experienced as fear.

MARY: I'll be leaving the shelter in three days, and I'll be *very afraid*.
          Because I don't have a support system. I do have an apartment,
          but it is in the ghetto, and I'm not happy that I have to raise my
          child in so much chaos.

KARYL: I am always so *terrified*. All my life I have been *afraid*. *Afraid* of
          everything and everyone. Now I am just *scared*. Even here in the
          shelter I feel *afraid* for my life!

4. Suffering is experienced as loneliness or emptiness.

NICOLE: I can't explain the reason why I feel *so lonely*. I think maybe my
          soul is hungry for love. I want someone to love me so much that
          I believe that it will take away this *loneliness*. [. . .] I've tried to
          have men fill this *empty place inside* me, but they only make me
          feel even more unfulfilled after they are gone. [. . .] What I need
          is some serious food for my *empty soul.*

5. Suffering is experienced as a lack of direction or confusion.

GERTRUDE: *I feel lost* in my feelings today. I am being *pulled in so many
          directions.*

6. Suffering is experienced as a loss of self-love, self-worth, self-esteem.

OPAL: I feel almost like a *cootie.*

BARB: I am *ashamed and disappointed* with myself as my family is
          with me.

FARA: I can hate my feelings because it makes me hate myself. That is
          how I felt today. *Worthless, guilty, lonely,* and an *unfit* mother. My
          feelings can also make me want to hurt myself, but, I tell myself
          I brought four children in this world and I can't leave them.

*7. Suffering is experienced as senses of despair or meaninglessness or a loss of
integrity.*

MYRTIS: *I don't like anything* today. I'm tired of everything going so slow.
          I don't feel as if I'm not moving in any direction and as though
          I have four walls enclosing me. I see *no way out.* I see nothing.
          I just can't seem to focus on the environment I'm in. There's so
          much chaos—even this place disturbs me. I'm angry because I
          have no control over my life again. I feel very alone.

BARB: I have *given all* that is mine to give. I have taken all the pain
          I can.

LISA: Want love, *don't feel whole* w/out it.

HANNA: All my life I have been searching for someone to *make me whole,*
          someone who would accept me for me—faults and all.

To sum up these seven thematic expressions: Domestic violence is often
experienced by shelter women as a totality. In the educative literature, and
from the point of view of the abuser, types of abuse are typically distinguished. In the ethnographic record, however, the women themselves map
out a more unified semantics of physical, social, psychological or emotional
suffering. These types overlap. They are frequently experienced in full measure—as an entirety. The totality is expressed (though surely not exhausted)
through these seven themes regarding inner or affective states.

CONCLUSION

All suffering is finally a social experience. The language shelter women use
to describe their suffering may lack a full sentient dimension; ultimately, it
does not lack a social dimension. They may metaphorize physical suffering
away from the body; ultimately, they may make connections to the social
body. The inner state of suffering may be analyzed as an affective experience
or corporeal sense, but whether the state is one of loss, loneliness, fear, or
meaninglessness or whether the state is one of bodily fatigue, illness, or even

collapse, the underlying message is this: The battered woman has been torn away from the social fabric. Trust in self and others has been disrupted.

In their stories, shelter women offer more: evidence of hope through a theological idiom or imagination—our next focus. Arthur Kleinman, a medical doctor, describes how he invites patients to describe their experience of their physical illnesses. There are four strata to their narratives: "symptom symbols, culturally marked disorder, personal and interpersonal significance, and patient and family explanatory models." These strata are the business of a "changing system of meanings."[42]

Harold Schweizer suggests literary inquiry as a heuristic "to witness or acknowledge the pain—not to diagnose or to explain—the solitary, secret body in pain"[43]

In working with battered women, however, one learns that a most important aspect of suffering is the explanatory models used to frame it. Women in the shelter are affected by their church's explanations for suffering—that is, their theodicies. The literature on domestic violence has largely ignored this fact because educators, and rightly so, recognize the sexism fostered by religion. Yet shelter women do not frequently target their faith as a problem; more often, they clutch onto it as their hope for survival.[44] As Wanda put it: "Before you accuse God for your suffering, give him a chance! You might find he is your best friend, the best friend you could have." After listening to countless women echo Wanda's sentiments, I believe it is critical to attend to their faith lives.

Judith Lewis Herman acknowledges this much: "We do know that women who recover most successfully are those who discover some meaning in their experience which transcends the limits of personal tragedy."[45] For many battered women, this transcendent meaning derives from their faith lives. Thus, to shelter women's religious traditions, we now turn.

FOUR

"I Sit in the Lord's Way"

THEOLOGICAL CONCEPTS OF SUFFERING

My name is Lisa and I am in pain. I just want to scream. I know it's
time for me to carry my burden to God. Whatever the problem, I'll
put it in God's hands.

—Lisa

I believe in God. I sit in the Lord's way.

—India

INTRODUCTION

The Women's House is a place of intense suffering. It is often hidden be-
neath closed doors or house routines, the banter of women trying to form a
community or the sounds of children playing, but the suffering is deep and
pervasive. Indeed, suffering is the necessary and sufficient feature for community participation, the raison d'étre of the shelter. One must suffer specifically
due to domestic violence to gain entrance to the shelter.

The Women's House is nearly always filled to capacity and there is
typically a list of women waiting to enter. Consequently, a rhetoric of hope
and action is necessary to remain the allotted amount of time of six weeks;

that is, such a rhetoric is deemed necessary by the staff and administration. In secular terms, this means the women must display activity aimed at gaining independence. They are encouraged by staff to seek employment, housing, and education or domestic violence, drug and alcohol, and/or parenting counseling. They are encouraged to attend house activities and to be sociable. To staff, these are signs of hope and healing. If they do not articulate or embody in some fashion a rhetoric of hope, if they do not perform self-help behavior within some reasonable amount of time, the women will be asked to leave the shelter.

Of their own accord, however, and not under persuasion or pressure from the shelter staff, many shelter women interpret their suffering, and formulate a language of hope and action, in religious or spiritual terms rather than secular terms. They talk to, and about, God to interpret the meaning of their suffering. Many shelter women have a deep religious faith, a faith that helps them to cope with suffering. They usually have little else. They are fleeing relationships and households with little to offer in the way of material resources or emotional support. Many women have been cut off by depression or by their abusers from their extended families and friends and they may have little in the way of a support network.

So whatever their religious upbringing or current religious practice,[1] God-talk is a typical and frequent feature of the language of shelter women. As they relive their lives in the storytelling circle, rehearsing the details of their wrecked dreams and hopes and interpreting their lived experience through the shaping of narratives of violence—the stories of the physical, sexual, verbal, emotional, and economic abuse to which they and their children have been subjected—they return again and again to their faith to seek explanation for their experience of unjust violence, to soothe themselves and other suffering women, and to sustain hope for the future.

The shelter women express their faith plainly. "I believe in God," says India, "I sit in the Lord's way." India is a woman I met in the shelter who had her jaw broken by her partner as he drove furiously down the expressway toward their home in Nashville, Tennessee. They had been arguing about whether she could visit her sisters. After he smashed her face, he kicked her out of the moving van onto the side of the road. She lay there until the police happened to drive by and notice her. India, a twenty-three-year-old African American women, was raised Baptist. As we sit around the dining room table, her new friend and shelter companion, Millie, listens intently. Millie is a forty-year-old German Catholic woman whose husband habitually locked her and their child in the house when he went out at night. On the night before she came to the shelter, he tied her and tortured her with lit cigarette ends when he came home. Millie responds to India in measure, deliberately and calmly: "One day, [men] will come back to the Lord's way. In a spiritual way, God brings justice. Now or later in life."

This ethos, this worldview, this language, is typical in the Women's House. God-talk may very well be the common idiom of the many diverse languages of the shelter, that is, the variety of languages deriving from differences of race, class, ethnicity, religion, employment, age, sexual orientation, and geographical origins. Despite its problematic patriarchal features (which I will discuss at length in upcoming chapters), God-talk is a language of resistance and revitalization for many battered women, a group whose very essence and existence is defined by the experience of suffering.

In this chapter I wish to continue to set the stage for an analysis of shelter women's language of suffering and healing. In the last chapter I attempted to do so by considering psychological views of suffering. Here I will consider a spectrum of theological views of suffering known as theodicies. First of all, I touch upon *classical* views of suffering. Although regarded by some thinkers as superstitious or outdated, these views still influence to some degree both institutional and individual accounts of suffering. I then move to the other end of the theological spectrum to introduce *process* views of suffering. In particular, I am interested in European and European American *feminist* views because they have been most influential and widely published of current scholarly accounts. European and European American feminist theologies of suffering take seriously the oppression of women and violence against them. Here I look briefly at basic ideas of theologians Dorothee Soelle and Elizabeth A. Johnson and minister and pastoral care provider Marie M. Fortune. These writers have been influential in some middle-class feminist Christian-based organizations.

One problem I find in the work of white middle-class scholars, however, is a tendency to make women's suffering homogeneous. For example, Fortune ascribes anger against God to battered women. While this dynamic may describe the reaction of some women, it does not describe the reaction of the mostly underclass African American and white Appalachian women in the Women's House. Thus, I move on in this chapter to consider how the intersection of race/ethnicity and religious affiliation may affect battered women's ideas about suffering. I provide a discussion of some of the theological principles of the traditional black churches provided by womanist theologians, followed by a discussion of some of the theological principles of the Holiness/Sanctified and fundamentalist/evangelical churches to which most of the shelter women—both white and black—belong. An extended discussion of the theodicies of battered women will be the focus of chapter 5. However, in this chapter, I wish to consider what the scholars are saying about suffering in the context of church teaching.

SUFFERING: THE CLASSICAL VIEW

Suffering, according to anthropologist Clifford Geertz, is "an experiential challenge in whose face the meaningfulness of a particular pattern of life threatens to dissolve into a chaos of thingless names and nameless things."[2] In countless philosophical, theological, and popular reflections on it, a key thematic of suffering is a profound sense of a loss of control of one's own life, leading to human degradation, and finally to a loss of human meaning. What evils—natural, moral, or social—cause suffering? Why do such evils exist?

Philosophers, theologians, and others have debated the "problem of evil" for centuries. In traditional Christian thought, the world was created by an omniscient, omnipotent, and perfectly good God. Yet why would such a God allow the evil that causes so much profound suffering among humankind? Augustine, Aquinas, Hume, Kant, and many others have contributed to the discussion of logical or epistemic explanations.[3] The scriptural treatments of suffering, such as the Book of Job, and the literary treatments of suffering, such as in the writings of Fyodor Dostoevsky, Albert Camus, and Elie Wiesel, have also animated our attention. Three traditional reasons are usually given to explain suffering:

1. Suffering is a test by God of one's faith as a way of causing people to appreciate through contrast the good things in their lives, or as a hidden part of God's overall plan for the good of the world.
2. Suffering is caused by other human beings, but allowed by God because God will not intervene in human freedom.
3. Suffering is admonishment [punishment] by God for the self-centeredness of human beings.[4]

Increasingly, many ordinary people (like many philosophers and theologians) do not find these three classical theistic explanations of suffering credible. Any one of these explanations seems to lead to a God who does not care about the suffering of the innocent. Much suffering, both human and animal, seems to be innocent suffering: It does not seem to be merited or educative. It seems caused by an indifferent God. The suffering to women and children caused by domestic violence, for example, does not seem to be merited. Why would a caring God allow so many women and girl children throughout history, for example, to be beaten, raped, enslaved, and killed at the whim of lovers, spouses, slave owners, soldiers, and secular and religious leaders? Although some theists argue that God must necessarily protect human free will, and that these are examples of free will gone terribly awry, surely the preservation of male free will cannot be a satisfactory explanation for the brutality of female victimization. To even explore such an argument in logical or epistemic terms seems to some persons singularly unethical.

The problem of evil and suffering continues to challenge philosophers, theologians and, of course, ordinary flesh-and-blood suffering persons. Indeed, in the view of some theologians, salvation history itself is a narrative of the search and struggle for redemption in the face of suffering and theology is its metalanguage. Further, theological views about suffering continue to develop and change across time, especially as theologians consider the experience of human suffering from the view of the suffering, the oppressed, of the world.

Consequently, in contradistinction to classical explanations, there are more contemporary attempts to explain suffering. For example, process theology—a contemporary view (influenced by Alfred North Whitehead and formulated by Charles Hartshorne[5])—asserts that God always seeks the "highest cosmic good," but in a two-way relationship. That is, process (or relational) theology stresses the social and relational character of God. With specific regard to the problem of suffering: God does what God ought to do, but God leaves for the world the work that the world ought to do.[6] The answer to the problem of suffering involves mutual responsibility. God "cannot control finite beings but can only set them goals which this God then has to persuade them to actualize."[7] God is not coercive; God is persuasive. As one theologian puts it:

> God does not cause all the tragedies and suffering that people experience; rather, God gives people the strength and courage to survive them. Process reflection adds that God does more than that: God gives us not only the strength to survive, but also the "ingenuity" and "hope" to draw good from evil and to change the world's suffering.[8]

For process theologians, God comes to the suffering one in the guise of other people who give strength and hope. This is a fundamental shift in the way contemporary theologians have perceived the experience of suffering. The new perspective attends carefully to the significance of social contexts and social relationships. The choice between availing oneself in solidarity or distancing oneself in alienation from the one who suffers is the matter of salvation.

EUROPEAN AND EUROPEAN AMERICAN FEMINIST THEOLOGY

In philosophical accompaniment with process theologians, white feminist theologians in mainline Christian religious traditions also offer new theodicean interpretations as they shift their attention from the causes to the meaning of suffering. Women scholars such as Wendy Farley, Kristine Rankka, Emilie Townes, and Delores Williams are among those who have written about women and suffering from perspectives very distinct from classical theodicies.

Many feminist scholars have been influenced by Dorothee Soelle, a German theologian. In *Suffering*, she rejects classical theistic positions as untenable, particularly in the face of massive human suffering—for example, at Auschwitz or in the oppression of women.[9] In Soelle's view, the traditional views fail because, in conceptualizing suffering, theologians put theory before human experience or practice: they proceed abstractly and deductively. In contrast, when one's discernment begins with faith in the context of real suffering, when one begins experientially and inductively, when one begins with the human context, then there is a clearer, multi-dimensional understanding.[10] Suffering becomes felt-reality, instead of a debatable philosophical concept. In its actual contexts and felt-reality, suffering is primarily marked by the sufferer's sense of powerlessness, and of meaninglessness, a meaninglessness yielding forth because "behavior cannot determine the occurrence of the outcomes. . . ."[11] The sufferer becomes alienated from self and others, unable to achieve full personal identity, unable to exercise human freedom.

This, for Soelle, is affliction. As in the philosopher Simon Weil's view of it, true affliction can be distinguished from other types of pain and suffering.[12] Affliction involves physical, psychological, and social dimensions: The suffering is felt bodily, it is experienced as loneliness and isolation, and it involves a sense of social degradation.[13] Certainly, the women whose voices we have heard in these pages are experiencing affliction. Beatie, a bruised and battered survivor in the Women's House, gives a glimpse of the pain of true affliction. She says:

> Women take a lot of mental abuse. It almost destroys them—the women here. Here, this is really home. To me, this [shelter] is my home. I feel safe, wanted, and loved here. I hate to leave. It makes me feel like I am a person. Abused persons feel alone. You think: No one will understand me. Here, it makes me feel human again.

To Beatie, homelessness is preferable to her previous existence where she was the unwilling recipient of beatings and other cruelties. She was made to feel less than human by her abuser. She did not feel safe, wanted, or loved. She felt utterly alone. Beatie found concern and companionship in the shelter. There were other women to solace her.

Soelle notes, however, that in the face of affliction or multidimensional suffering, others who witness may be apathetic: They may be unable to feel the pain of the sufferer. They may be indifferent. Even organizations or social structures can be unresponsive. Thus social and political structures are entangled in true affliction. But the stories of suffering, the narration of suffering, may lead those who witness suffering to behave and act differently, that is, as cosufferers, ones acting in solidarity with the sufferer.

In *She Who Is*, European American feminist theologian Elizabeth A. Johnson emphasizes this notion of choice. Apart from the suffering due to natural causes, Johnson delineates two types of suffering. The first type of suffering is the suffering experienced as the consequence of freely chosen actions for justice. This type is experienced, for example, by many women activists as they struggle for human rights for girl children and women. Even in first world contexts, they are denigrated, threatened, assaulted, or actually killed for their activism. The second type of suffering, according to Johnson, is suffering as the consequence of inflicted personal degradation, that is, with no greater good at issue. An example of this type is the suffering experienced by victims of domestic violence. When men throw objects at women, threaten them with words or weapons, rape and torture them, women suffer deep personal degradation in body and spirit. When women are pushed, slapped, kicked, choked, chained, starved, or shot, surely there can be no greater good at issue. Suffering of this second sort has no intelligibility. It destroys human dignity. It causes pain and separation. It leads to silence and suppression. "I didn't have one person to talk to," says Alma, a survivor of domestic violence. She continues:

> Not one person. It was like being in prison. He put a cover over the patio window so no one could see through it. We live on the second floor! I couldn't use my peripheral vision when we were outside. He didn't want me to look at anyone. If I take a shower, I know he's gonna be right there with [me].

As the obsessive control and senseless violence escalated, Alma's experience became increasingly unintelligible. But Johnson argues that, in experiences of unintelligible suffering, humans are open to the gifts of a compassionate, companionable God. Divine power offers strength, hope, vitality, a sense of awakened freedom, a feeling of connectedness. God opens the future for the oppressed, transforms their suffering into self-affirmation, and offers new possibilities as they shape their own human response and assume their own responsibility. God accompanies the oppressed: God is a "power-with," not a "power-over," God. For Johnson, a theologian very sensitive to the connections between first and third world women, there is no once-and-for-all, final solution to the problem of violence: there is only responsive action. Together, humans hungry for justice and a compassionate God assure that, in the end, all will be well.[14] Life arises.

At the Women's House, survivors of violence may not read the work of such theologians as Elizabeth Johnson. Yet feminist theologians do think seriously about the problem of violence against women and they influence cultural workers who connect with battered women.[15] Many pastoral care providers who actually work at the grassroots have been influenced by feminist theology. Marie M. Fortune, a European American United Church of Christ minister, is one example. Through her workshops and writings on domestic violence, she has pioneered much pastoral concern for victims. The secular battered women's movement is aware of the useful connections to be forged with this Christian-based activity. Like Elizabeth Johnson, Fortune recognizes two types of suffering: involuntary and voluntary. The suffering of abused women is involuntary suffering and Fortune has been outspoken about its serious consequences.

BATTERED WOMEN AND THE PERCEPTION OF SUFFERING: SOME COMMENTS ABOUT GOD-BLAME

Concerning theodicies, Marie Fortune notes one consequence that I would like to probe. Domestic violence victims have, she argues, a "strong tendency to hold God or themselves responsible" for their abuse.[16] Or they may explain their abuse by means of "superstition," that is, they believe that a current experience of suffering is "God's punishment for a 'preceding' sin which God has judged." [17] Yet, if a woman blames God, she is driven away from God or no one is held accountable for the violence. Clearly, her abuser is held less accountable.

If God is to blame for women's suffering, one might add—however ironically, then religion and religious institutions are also held less accountable. To me, this is a critical issue. The absent referent in the equation of woman, her abuser, and God is the religious and other sociopolitical institutions or structures that contribute enormously to violence against women.

What is the problem here? I suggest we may not be listening carefully to battered women of diverse backgrounds. The discourse of lament and blame (which I will address later, especially in chapter 7) offered by battered women is far from homogenous. But, in my experience, it is not a God-blaming monologue.[18] At the shelter, I do not hear working- or under-class battered women blame God directly for their suffering. In nine years, I never heard even an angry woman direct her anger at an insensitive God though we talk and write frequently and candidly about God, suffering, and abuse. In fact women frequently laugh when I suggest God-blame might be a reasonable response. True enough: women may consider God-blame a grave offense against God; thus, they may not engage in it publicly. Still, in our conversations, women discuss many taboo topics. They discuss a variety of socially, legally, or religiously censured acts, crimes, or sins in which they have been or anticipate being involved, such as sexual promiscuity, adultery, incest, child neglect or abuse, drug or alcohol addictions, theft, violence, homicide, and civil disobedience. "Didn't you ever dream of burning his bed?" Tammy asks. Shelter women concede: "I used to dream of poisoning his food." "I wanted to kill him in his sleep." "I hated him so much I wanted to shoot him with his shotgun." In their anger, some women detail plans for violence as retaliatory "justice." However, they will not blame God for their suffering.

In an extended counseling situation, perhaps a pastoral care worker or therapist might induce an abused woman to reactivate a childhood feeling of anger at God.[19] In some clinical accounts and other in-depth rehearsals of childhood feelings, white women have apparently displayed a tendency to rhetorically cast their stories in terms of blame and anger directed at God. For example, in a moving passage in *Christianity and Incest*, Annie Imbens and Ineke Jonker offer this passage from a child incest survivor named Ellen who recounts her girl-child feelings:

> I was mad at God-the-Father because he hadn't protected me from Grampa. He had let me walk right into it. I hadn't deserved something like that. Something wasn't right. Wasn't he supposed to protect, like a father's supposed to? [. . .] I didn't understand his almightiness, because He didn't intervene and left me to fend for myself for so long [. . .]. I thought God was a very strict person, who didn't understand anything about me. Jesus was kind to children and women.[20]

When Ellen (now an adult) mentioned the abuse to her minister and her doctor, Imbens and Jonker note, they did not respond helpfully. Like the women in my field experience, Ellen might more rightfully be angry with the ministers of spiritual and physical health.

Surely, however, some survivors of violence may experience theological doubts or confusion and I do not mean to suggest that they never blame God. In any situation of suffering, God-blame is one human response, one option, certainly. In the Book of Job, the quintessential Judeo-Christian statement and study of human response to suffering, Job blames God—at least temporarily. To clarify my standpoint: While some women may blame God, the battered women in the shelter, that is, African American and white Appalachians, typically working- and underclass women, do not tend to blame God for their abuse. God-blame does not extend naturally from the lived experience of the battered women with whom I work. It is not an ordinary, everyday, felt-experience. Nor do I believe it is always or particularly helpful to induce them to express anger if it is not already a felt-experience. Not surprisingly, some battered women have expressed exasperation or amusement at me for suggesting that one might have an understandable tendency to blame God for their unhappy, unjust situations.

Clearly cultural differences have great significance. By assuming God-blame, one also makes assumptions about the critical capabilities, the theological, social, and self-understandings of all battered women. It is patronizing to proceed as if they do not have some political awareness, cannot analyze and critique power differentials to a degree, or lack theological understandings or spiritual resourcefulness. More helpfully, we might listen to what they actually do say about God, suffering, and violence. However unschooled, battered women already have theories about violence and abuse. They have their own theologies, local theologies, about God and their relationships to God. They have their own theodicies to express their understanding of the relationship between God and suffering. We need to pay heed to the diversity of response.

In my experience, I have learned that battered women may blame themselves for their victimization (particularly for not fleeing sooner), they always blame their abuser and, increasingly, battered women are blaming unresponsive institutions, such as law enforcement agencies, judicial systems, health care facilities, churches, and other seemingly or actually discriminatory or unhelpful social service agencies. They blame unjust societal structures and practices, such as racism and classism.[21] "I was talking to the police," says Tanya:

> They were listening to me. When [my abuser] started talking to them, it changed everything! "Get in the house," they said. "Don't get him upset." Then they left. They separate you. I could hardly hear what he was saying, but he told them all these things about me and they said to me, "Get in the house!" I felt so stupid! He was already on probation! They let him go back to the bar! Then it all started again. [The police] need more training. . . . [My abuser] could have stayed the chief of police!

Later, Pam comments on the story in an explanatory speech act. There is a shift of focus from the theme of "the complicity of men" to the reason or explanation of their behavior:

> They assume it was from Adam and Eve. If you are a Christian, it says in the Bible that Eve came from Adam. I've heard that from so many men. You came from me, so I don't want you to forget it. If they are poor, or rich, it's this attitude about women. They have authority. It feeds into that. Religion.

No one is blaming God here. "I am crying and I'm gonna be crying," says Pam when she reckons with the nonresponsiveness of social institutions.

Further, I would not characterize these or any woman's explanations for their abuse as "superstitious." When the workings of the religious, law and order, and judicial systems seem so discriminatory, so illogical, so unintelligible to one's sense of fairness and justice, a woman's own explanation of abuse can only (with great negative connotations toward the woman herself) be deemed superstitious. Josephine, a survivor of severe domestic violence tells me, "The police don't help us and, if the judges don't do it, we're lost." Josephine is being completely rational or logical and she is not blaming God. Her pastor counseled her to "try harder" with her marriage.

Most battered woman who go to shelters appear to be trying as much as they possibly can. They are trying to cope with homelessness, psychological upheaval, distressed children, unemployment, little or no income. If anything, the "preceding" sin for which women often blame themselves for is their naiveté, their slowness to act, in the face of the unresponsiveness of family, police, pastoral care workers, landlords, employers, and other persons who they encounter without effect in their unhappy and sometimes long journey to the shelter.

Class, Race/ethnicity, and Religious Affliation

Why do only some women appear to blame God for their suffering? In my view, the explanation lies in class, religious background, and race/ethnicity. The intersection of these factors creates vast worldview differences. Concerning *class*: the women at the shelter can hardly afford to blame God. Most often, God is all they have. Frequently, they have nothing else or next-to-nothing else in the way of material resources or family support. Nearly all are desperately poor. They left behind what little they had to flee the physical and verbal blows. Typically, even women with modest family incomes are left with nothing. Listen to Kara:

> The knife up against my throat was enough. You can take the car, the stereo, TV, my clothes, anything. I'll look raggedy. I don't care. I'm gone. I gotta go. But I gotta leave everything my babies know. I'm leaving all my family. My shoes. I'm scared if I walk out the door, I might not have my life.

The same woman says moments later: "I said to myself, I'm God's child. I don't need to have abuse. I need a ride out of here with me and my children." She left with nothing. Kara is now a new member of a growing underclass. The women in the shelter reflect the shifting and narrow mix of under-, lower-, and working-class populations of the local community. In 1999, as I mentioned earlier, 199 women reported incomes of $0 to $4,990.00 per year; sixty-seven women reported incomes of $5,000 to $9,999 per year; sixty-eight women reported incomes of $10,000 to $14,999 per year; thirty-four women reported incomes of $15,000 to $19, 999 per year; and fifty-six women reported incomes of $20,000 to $24,999 per year. Clearly, most shelter women live in poverty.

Differences in *religious backgrounds* also explain divergent points of view. Many women are deeply and outspokenly religious. They are often of fundamentalist/evangelical or Holiness/Sanctified backgrounds. In matters of religion, *race and ethnicity* intersect significantly. Recall that, of the women served at the Women's House in 1999, there were 259 African Americans, 151 whites, 7 Latinos, 2 Asian Americans, and 5 "Others." Some African Americans belong to traditionally black churches. They have backgrounds in the African Methodist Episcopal (AME), African Methodist Episcopal Zion (AMEZ), or Christian Methodist Episcopal (CME) denominations. Regional factors are important, however, and the shelter is in the upper Bible Belt. Hence, many black women were raised in or belong to Baptist or Holiness/Sanctified churches. Likewise, many white women also were raised in or belong to Southern Baptist or Holiness/Sanctified churches. It is an area of religious commonalty.

Whether black or white, their families are often Appalachian. The Women's House provides shelter for women predominantly from poorer neighborhoods in the city, that is, with traditionally large Appalachian populations. The white families relocated predominantly from eastern Kentucky and West Virginia and the black families from southern Appalachia. As Gary L. Fowler points out in a study of the city's residential distribution, most Appalachians are white, but approximately four out of every ten Appalachians living in the city's central neighborhoods are African Americans. He estimated that about 44 percent of blacks in low-status areas and 32 percent in lower-middle-class areas were black. Black and white Appalachians are concentrated in separate sections of these same areas.[22] Mainly these neighborhoods access the shelter.

Most Appalachians attend fundamentalist/evangelical churches or sectarian churches, that is, offshoots of the Holiness/Sanctified denomination. Even Appalachians currently attending more mainline urban Protestant churches recall their small Holiness churches, "spirit churches" as I have heard them called, or Bible Belt fundamentalist or evangelical churches in Kentucky or West Virginia. Thus the main denominations or orientations I will work with, after this present chapter, for both black and white women are fundamentalist/evangelical and Holiness/Sanctified. Besides domestic violence, this religious heritage is the point of commonalty in the shelter.

Yet, even when blacks and whites attend the same denominations, segregation may foster different cultural forms.[23] That is, the distinctions between women's views may not be explicitly doctrinal; they may be social. Context matters. Local context fosters local theology. Such is true in shelter women's experience even though the women often transcend the more typical racial segregation in churches by accompanying one another to local churches on Sundays.

Clearly, the intersection of class, religion, and race/ethnicity has significant import in the matter of suffering of shelter women. *Class* matters. Affiliation with organized religion generally falls out along class lines. *Religion* matters. There are fundamental differences in religious priorities, practices, and perspectives that impact the heterogeneous experiences of suffering. *Race* matters. Women of color face diverse issues. They experience multiple layers of oppression that aggravate their situations. They may respond to abuse differently because they have different resources of relationship, network, and support—both in theological and sociological terms.

Class, race, and religion matter because they create worldview differences. These differences need to be recognized and addressed when we educate persons in the community who are engaged in service-providing or in psychological or pastoral counseling of battered women. Social and doctrinal distinctions figure heavily—and in ways the domestic violence movement has not adequately addressed. Not all women experience the meaning of battery in quite the same way. The experience of white middle-class women, feminists, or theologians in mainline Protestant and Catholic churches can and does impact the ideas of underclass shelter women and vice versa (and this will be a concern of chapters 8 and 9). But variation in class, religion, and race account for the failure of some white feminist theorists to fully capture the nature of battered women's view of God and their understanding of who is responsible, thus accountable, for their suffering.

In the remainder of this chapter, I want to focus on the critical nexus of religion and race—with race at the foreground. In some ways, this is an artificial process because most shelter women—either white or black—are Holiness/Sanctified or fundamentalist/evangelical. In what follows, I separate out the black church experience from the white church experience to account for possible and real differences. In subsequent discourse analysis, I do not separate black and white experience; rather, I attempt to find coherent and meaningful form in the many mixed race conversations about God at the shelter. For, as Clifford Geertz notes, "Religious concepts spread beyond their specifically metaphysical contexts to provide a framework of general ideas in term of which a wide range of experience—intellectual, emotional, moral—can be given meaningful form."[24] As I try to make sense of some meaningful form to the plurality of lived experience, womanist theologians have been very helpful.

WOMANIST THEOLOGY, BLACK CHURCHES, AND SUFFERING

Religious feeling runs deeply and fervently in the Women's House. Whether or not they are church-goers, many women seek solace and strength in God as they navigate their way through their current life crisis. God-talk, either as a primary focus of conversation or as a discursive thread woven throughout any conversation, is a regular linguistic feature.

African American women are especially forthright in their public faith testimony. In a 1987 Gallup poll, 74 percent of blacks surveyed rated religion as "very important" to their lives in comparison with only 55 percent of whites.[25] The black experience, of course, is not homogenous. The break down of black denominational preferences, in American society at large, is this: 82–86 percent Protestant; 4–5 percent Catholic; 7–8 percent no preference; and 1–2 percent other denominations.[26] The three largest Protestant black religious bodies in the United States are Methodist (that is, AME, AMEZ, and CME), Baptist (that is, National Baptist Convention, U.S.A., the National Baptist Convention of America, and the Progressive National Baptist Convention), and Pentecostal (that is, Church of God in Christ and other denominations).[27]

The preferences and attitudes toward religion in the Women's House reflect those of American society at large. In the shelter, the most well-represented religious backgrounds of the black women I have encountered in the shelter are Baptist, Pentecostal (African Holiness or Sanctified), and Methodist (the historically black churches), white women are most often either of Baptist or Pentecostal (white Holiness or Sanctified) denominational backgrounds. Fundamentalism and evangelical activity is well-represented in both racial groups through particularly Baptist church affiliation. Situated in a historically German-Catholic urban area, the shelter appears to serve more white women of Roman Catholic than mainstream Protestant backgrounds in the shelter.[28] Of course, there is a good deal of change, that is, denominational and attendance changes, between childhood and adult church participation. Many women currently do not regularly participate in church community, although they consider themselves faithful and even deeply spiritual women.

Yet womanist theologians have pointed out differences in the way white women and black women experience religion and spirituality in their ordinary lives.[29] Among other differences, I wish, here, to touch lightly upon fundamental differences in four areas: language genres and worship styles; key concepts about salvation and redemption; divine images; and gender roles.

In matters of *language genres* (that is, forms) *and worship styles*, black churches, even relative to white evangelical churches, have strong oral traditions of testimony, lamentation, and praise. A woman of color and experience, Denia says:

> I've been to all black Baptist and all white Baptist churches. There's a difference in a predominantly white and a predominantly, mainly black church. White Baptist and black Baptist— I've been to both and they are totally different. White churches teach from the Bible and go into the songs. It's more of a schooling atmosphere, instead of a spiritual atmosphere. We [African Americans] are praising Him, sending Him all our praises, songs, testifying, until the end! We don't care, no matter how long it takes. So what if it cuts the sermon short? We praise to the end.

Praising and testifying is a linguistic genre bodily and deeply felt. African Americans, according to black shelter women, use their whole being to assert their religious faith. So it is with the genre of lamentation. Like psalmic language in general, lamentation regularizes and validates the cry and complaint against injustice. Lamentation is not God-blame. It is the sound, the sign, of the suffering one, the lamb. Denia says, "I say prayers and say, 'God, why is this so hard on me? Is there another purpose? Let me be happy. I don't want gold or riches.' We might ask what it's about—the suffering. But we never blame God."

Indeed, the sufferer cannot blame God because in addition to being a sign of the sufferer's participation in innocent suffering, lamentation is a demand for the participation of the divine in its resolution. About this mutual participation, Nikki, a shelter woman, says:

> It teaches in the Bible, the Israelites, they praised and cried and God delivered. The Israelites were like the blacks here. The exile, the suffering, that makes people more spiritual. Then there was the deliverance.

Womanist theologian Emilie M. Townes delineates further the differences in mainline white and black religiosity. *Salvation* is an uplifting, sustaining notion in black spirituality. *Redemption* is not related so much to the individual sin, or to individual sin, as it is related to the hope of the community. Nikki's reference to the Israelites illustrates Townes's point.

In my view, this is a critical point in the attribution of guilt and blame in the matter of domestic violence and in the access of support networks to counter its life-disabling effects. Rather than engaging in a discourse of God-blame, battered black women engage in a discourse of God-praise. Indeed, God enables black women "to rely on an authority beyond the world of men."[30] Thus, thoughts and ideas attributed by women to God supersede thoughts and ideas originating with abusive men. Aided by a discourse of righteousness and redemption, many black women, in contrast to many white women, seek out and use communal support networks.[31]

Religious concepts are both expressed and shaped by symbols, signs, and images. In the black experience of religion, Jesus—the innocent sufferer—is a central *divine image*. One survivor, Lavonia, recounts how a preacher rebaptized her "in Jesus" because, in her previous ceremony, she was baptized "in the name of the Father, Son, and Holy Ghost." Regarding shift of emphasis in divine images: many white women, particularly white women in mainstream churches, center on God the Father or on Jesus as Christ and King as central images of religious devotion. In contrast black women, according to theologian Jacquelyn Grant, have developed fervent feeling for Jesus as friend and cosufferer.[32] Jesus, friend and brother, has both masculine and feminine characteristics.[33] Above all, he is a cosufferer, not a regal king. Lavonia, an African American survivor of violence, says:

> We understand Jesus more because of his suffering. In the black
> church, we understand his pain and sorrow. I'm not saying white
> women can't understand. But we understand more because we are
> closer to the suffering. Some white women can, but it's stronger in
> black women. Black people are closer to God because we are
> oppressed like Jesus. And black women are closer to God than
> white women because we have been oppressed more. It's all the
> people who have been through the suffering, the hardships. Jesus
> went there. When you have been suffering, the praises go higher.

Further, in black spirituality, there is a reliance on the Holy Spirit, who is felt bodily and celebrated communally.[34] There is a *gender* component to the experience. Scholar Gloria Wade-Gayles describes how the Spirit "moves, inspires, and directs" black women in their ordinary lives, blurring the boundaries between the secular and the sacred.[35] In the shelter extraordinary stories, for example, of women miraculously healing deathbed-ridden family members by "tarrying in the spirit" (that is, calling down the Spirit, speaking in tongues in prayer gatherings for the sick) blend somewhat seamlessly with ordinary stories of calling on the Spirit for strength to cook supper after a long day's work. The Spirit is felt by women as energy, as a rushing air, as a certainty or a certain resolve. It is transmitted through the voices of other women, children, strangers, the homeless and down-and-out, cosufferers. Rhonda testifies to its inflowing:

> If I get the Spirit, I feel light in my heart. Every burden is gone.
> I feel overjoyed. [. . .] It's an overwhelming, overjoyed feeling!
> You are so relieved! The Spirit takes over your emotions. The
> tears flow. You get the chills. It's the Spirit.

The indwelling of the Spirit is socially, if not doctrinally, a gendered experience. Women are susceptible to "getting the Spirit" and, indeed, the Spirit-filled woman plays a prophetic role.

Not all roles, of course, were traditionally open to women. Yet most African American churches now sanction women's ordination and ministry. The full realization of women's gifts and talents hinges on the breakdown of the hierarchical power structure in the church; obviously, women's ordination is critical to more balanced, equitable, and egalitarian gender relations. Still, African American theologians and scholars note the lingering sexism in black churches even toward women ministers. This may be truer of fundamentalist/evangelical churches than Holiness/Sanctified churches though even the latter have become more rigidified in gender codes in recent years. Further, clerics and pastoral workers of all colors continue to resist counseling battered women to separate and/or divorce. Traditional views of gender and the sanctity of family and marriage work against women's full realization and, in fact, endanger their lives.

African American women have often risen above their traditionally limited, biblically-prescribed public roles. In the Sanctified Churches, Cheryl Townsend Gilkes notes, women of color were able to find roles as educators, founders, ministers, and prophets. The gender rigidity of new codes of conduct is meeting resistance from many Holiness/Sanctified women. "Anointing can go through anyone!" a woman told me. "Women can preach the Word of God!"

Still, the range of ways in which African American women experience spirituality, religion, or witness for the spirit are not always and everywhere synchronous or synonymous with the ways in which white women do. The influences on black battered women's lives, thus the way they understand and survive their suffering, may sometimes be quite distinct.

WHITE APPALACHIAN WOMEN, EVANGELICAL AND HOLINESS CHURCHES, AND SUFFERING

SANCTIFIED OR HOLINESS WOMEN IN THE SHELTER

Most white women at the Women's House have backgrounds in either Holiness or Evangelical churches.[36] Many of them are members of multigenerational families who—if not now, then once—belonged particularly to Holiness churches in Kentucky and West Virginia, that is, the upper South and middle-southern state Appalachia. The Holiness Churches emerged after the American Civil War as a revival movement in Methodism. Their primary doctrine is that of Sanctification: the Saints, as they call themselves, believe that after a person is "born again," the convert grows in grace and "perfect love" through the power of the Holy Spirit.

In matters of language genres and worship style, the Holiness Churches emphasize public testimony, song, and prayer. Like traditional Black churches, they have strong traditions of personal witness, that is, oral genres of thanksgiving and praise. One worship genre is "shouting" or "hollering." Shouting and/or hollering (sometimes called "tarrying in the Spirit") is ritual behavior characterized primarily by jumping up and down while spinning in a circle. Whoops, shouts, and songs of praise can accompany the body motion.[37]

As public performance, shouting is an important activity. In matters of salvation and redemption, the Holiness creed is clear. Doctrine specifies that a born-again Christian is subject through grace to the action of the Holy Spirit. To be saved, one must be baptized in the Spirit and evidence its indwelling. Sanctification, the infilling of the Spirit, often comes as the result of a personal crisis and it is usually an instantaneous experience. It is a second blessing from God.[38] If it does anything, shouting provides public proof of the presence of the Spirit.

Speaking in tongues, glossolalia, is proof of the indwelling of the Spirit. The tongues are unintelligible, heavenly languages that arise spontaneously. Interestingly, male fundamentalists say that speaking in tongues, primarily a female activity, is devil-inspired activity. Yet Holiness doctrine stipulates that one must be baptized in the Holy Spirit to go heaven. Interestingly, because men do not so often speak in tongues, heaven (by implication) is conceptualized by shelter women as a mostly feminine sacred space. This, of course, is not official doctrine.

Central divine images are distinct. Women in Holiness Churches are primarily motivated and moved by the metaphors and images of the Spirit. Being "slain in the spirit," for just one example, is for some worshipers "a dissociative experience of temporary loss of consciousness [representing] a form of ritual empowerment."[39] But the suffering Jesus is also a central image. According to doctrine, Jesus feels and suffers as a human being. By his suffering, he made full atonement for human sin. The Atonement is the only source of salvation and is "efficacious for those who reach the age of responsibility, only when they repent and believe." In my view, a difference between African American and white conceptions of redemption is the centrality of the act of belief for white women in contrast to the centrality of the experience of suffering for African American women. That is, African American women believe they are close to Jesus by virtue of similar experiences of unjust suffering; white women believe they are close to Jesus by virtue of belief. In this matter, the critical point is emphasis, not doctrinal differences.

With a somewhat different emphasis, then, the suffering Jesus is also an important image in the religiosity, the song and worship, of white Holiness

Churches. Access to divine images is mediated through scripture which is "infallibly true as originally given."[40] According to some Saints, only the preacher brings a Bible to church or uses it in his or her ordinary life. The congregation does not ordinarily use a bible. Instead, images of the suffering Jesus are sustained through song. Some popular hymns that shelter women recall are: "The River of Jordan," "It's a Grandiose Feeling To Be a Child of God," "Working on the Building of My Lord," "Amazing Grace," "In This Sweet By and By," "The Old Rugged Cross," "Calgary," and "Gather at the River." The themes of hymns are the crucifixion, the cross, the blood of Jesus, and heaven.

In many Holiness Churches, women have diverse and wide-ranging gender roles. They engage in all aspects of ministerial life.[41] Women are pastors, ministers, missionaries, ushers, revival leaders—though not always in equal numbers to men. Although male pastors outnumber women pastors, prayer meetings are more often led by women. Women's leadership roles also increase in rural areas, in revivals, and in healing sessions. Though episcopacy-organized, there are no specific gender roles based on doctrine. Women are extolled, however, not to cultivate—as one woman put it—the "Jezebel attitude," a seductive demeanor; hence, most women do not wear jewelry, makeup, short-sleeved clothing, and so forth. There are other gender distinctions, for example, the above-mentioned matter of speaking in tongues. Healings—that is, intense prayer gatherings for sick neighbors and friends— are most often carried out by women. At healings and other gatherings, women speak in tongues, shout, and holler. Women often dominate services by testifying longer and louder.[42] And women are thought to be closer to God which explains why, it is commonly believed, they speak in tongues more often than men. As one shelter woman told me: "Women is more in the Word of God and a woman does more of the right things."

EVANGELICAL OR FUNDAMENTALIST WOMEN IN SHELTER

Other shelter women are fundamentalist/evangelical, mostly of Baptist or Bible Church affiliation. The fundamentalist family of denominations emerged from the post–Civil War revivalist movement. Holiness and Pentecostals were once in alliance, but a split occurred in the early twentieth century. The core denominations are independent Baptists and Bible churches. Many shelter women were raised in Baptist churches (which originated in the seventeenth century).

In matters of language genres and worship style, these churches reject Holiness doctrinal belief in the baptism of the Holy Spirit, glossolalia or speaking in tongues, and other gifts of the Spirit, including divine healing and prophecy. Some fundamentalist, for example, Baptist doctrine, stipulates that speaking in tongues was a first century manifestation of the Spirit available to disciples at Pentecost, but no longer available to modern-day followers of Christ.[43]

Fundamentalists believe in the infallibility of scripture and some believe in its inerrancy (that is, they affirm its validity even in the face of scientific and historical contradictions). With respect to this primary feature of their orientation to and use of sacred or scriptural language: It has been suggested that fundamentalists often speak in formula, that is, in memorized bits of scriptures or religiously-inflected commonplaces; hence, the argument goes, fundamentalist battered women tend to speak uncritically about God. But, while ritualized, formulaic, and/or uncritical language about God does occur, the claim that these women always or largely resort to it patronizes and denigrates them. Fundamentalists will often quote scripture as the authoritative Word of God; yet, how biblical passages and citations are rhetorically managed and linguistically manipulated can also be considered a matter of dexterity, creativity, and proprietorship.

In addition, some Baptists have become more conservative in the last twenty years. The Southern Baptist Convention has instituted a degree of fundamentalism and hierarchy unknown in congregations that have traditionally supported democratic processes on the local level. This imposition has created deep rifts in Baptist churches and upheavals in schools and seminaries.[44]

Notwithstanding, for the Christian fundamentalists, the Bible is indisputably the "supreme standard by which all human conduct, creeds, and opinions should be tried."[45] It bespeaks the will of the Father. This patriarchal orientation rests on the primary importance of filial obedience. Thus central divine images are God, the Father, and Jesus, his obedient son. Satan is the fallen angel who would not obey the Father, who tried to usurp the power and place of the Father. Adam and Eve were expelled from Eden for disobedience. In a fundamentalist cosmology, Satan battles endlessly, if ultimately futilely, with goodness and he figures highly in both popular conception and in doctrine. Jesus is the one who deals the final defeat to Satan in full accordance and submission to the will of the Father. His acceptance of suffering and death was an act of perfect obedience and it suffices as the full Atonement of mankind. A premillennialist attitude suffuses the fundamentalist Baptist outlook: that is, a way of life governed by the belief that the end of our age is fastly approaching, Christ will return soon to reign a thousand years, and the Final Judgment may occur imminently. At the Judgment, the evil shall be relegated to eternal punishment in hell and the righteous to eternal bliss in heaven. The act of believing, made possible by grace, guarantees redemption and salvation while the Great Commission, bestowed by Christ, is to witness and proselytize.

Although egalitarian (feminist) Evangelicals question the hierarchical ordering of church and family,[46] the fundamentalist church and popular culture generally uphold restrictions on gender roles and the importance of traditional family values, citing scripture as the authoritative guide. Even if individual women interpret scripture in creative, resistant, more equitable ways, traditional gender roles and expectations are upheld in most fundamentalist churches or public space. Even in fundamentalist churches, however, women have access to subrealms in which some of women's needs for congregational power are met.[47] In these all-female enclaves, women support and assist one another in life crises and leadership development.

Whatever their current church climate and whatever their personal view about the use of scripture to sustain power imbalances within fundamentalist families, many white battered women are fervently religious. They regard Jesus as their personal savior, healer, and king. In ways sometimes contiguous, and sometimes contrasting, to the ways of women from Holiness or the historically black churches, white fundamentalist women believe in the power of the Holy Spirit. They believe the Spirit is active in their lives and available to them in their suffering.

CONCLUSION

In this chapter, I very briefly touched upon some classical and current theological views toward suffering, particularly middle-class white feminist views. I raised problems I see with these views, particularly as they come to light within the actual situations of battered women of different racial/ethnic, class, and religious backgrounds. To take just one point of entry, the mostly underclass battered black and white women in the shelter do not blame God for their troubles. On the contrary, most shelter women are deeply faithful. They look elsewhere for causes—and there are plenty of places to look in a sexist society. To seek a solution to this contradiction, I touched on some basic tenants of historical black religiosity in America with the help of womanist scholarship. Further, I examined some basic tenants of the Holiness/Sanctified and the fundamentalist/evangelical church traditions, two well-represented denominational groups of shelter women, many of whom—both black and white—are of Appalachian descent.

Certainly the theological terrain is vast and complex. For simplicity's sake, I looked at language genres and worship styles, key concepts about salvation and redemption, divine images, and gender roles. The black churches and the white Holiness/Sanctified and fundamentalist/evangelical church, it may be reasonably argued, hold somewhat different perspectives on these basic religious traditions and tenants. These different emphases, in the unfolding context of religious and ritual response, have implications for the way battered women experience and survive violence. Yet battered women do not always heed doctrine or dogma. They do not simply mimic their churches. They learn from, and even sometimes resist, the tenants of their churches.

In short, battered women have their own experience of the sacred. They have their own worldviews, including views of the causes and meaning of suffering. Their experiences of brutality and violence— social evil—form a basis for their theological concepts.

They also have their own ideas about appropriate language, worship styles, salvation, redemption, divine images, and gender. These derive from their churches, their lived experience, and their negotiation of meaning with other women in the shelter. As they talk to one another, shelter women of different persuasions influence one another in these matters. They also talk to staff and volunteers who may be more aware of womanist and feminist views on religion and violence. It is worth noting that womanists and feminists emphasize the unjust suffering of the oppressed, not simply the suffering of Jesus. Even this stance enters the dialogic mix.

At times, even battered women themselves disregard or de-emphasize their race/ethnicity-based religious differences as they seek community. As one African American woman put it: "We are all the same color, you know, blood is red and money is green. Us battered women are all here for the same thing." This dynamic stance derives from creating meaning in context as women begin to see the commonalties of women's oppression. The spirituality of black and white women holds them together while, in the Women's House, they struggle to survive.

FIVE

"In a Spiritual Way, God Brings Justice"

BATTERED WOMEN AND THE PROBLEM OF EVIL

This is a man's world. One day men will come back to the Lord's
way. In a spiritual way, God brings justice. Now or later in life.

—Millie

INTRODUCTION

The suffering of battered women is sometimes staggering, sometimes subtle.
Millie served her husband meals, cleaned up after him, and tried not to make
him angry. He never hit her. Instead, he took her paycheck, spared her little
or no spending money, then left her at home alone for long stretches of time.
When he was at home, he routinely belittled her—her opinions, her appearance, her family, her friends. The abuse endured by Millie was not dramatic;
rather, it was a slow and steady stream of sometimes subtle, sometimes not
so subtle insults, indignities, and neglect. When she left him, Millie's husband destroyed their home.

Millie's new shelter friend, Abbey, sustained a different sort of suffering. Abbey was knocked off her feet with a blow to her stomach when she
was pregnant. When she miscarried a few days later, her boyfriend said he
was glad. He didn't believe it was his child in any case. No one who knew
about this or his many other assaults reported him, so he felt he was in no
jeopardy for his actions. Abbey left when he was not at home. He would
have forcibly kept her at home just as he forcibly demanded sex and money.

Both Millie and Abbey sustain deep and abiding faith in God. Like most shelter women, they look to God for strength. How do they reconcile their belief in an all-knowing, all-powerful, all-loving God with their painful circumstances? What do they believe about God's relationship to their suffering? In the language of theologians: To what theodicies or explanations do battered women subscribe when they consider God's relationship to their suffering?

In this chapter, I will explore the theodicies of shelter women. To determine a full range of explanations they offer, I will situate their words within a ten-category typology of both traditional and alternative theodicies.[1] Then I will identify the theodicies that most battered women articulate in the Women's House, a shelter in the upper ridge of the Bible Belt. To prefigure: Most shelter women initially function largely within a "Redemptive/Atonement" model or a "Suffering God" model. The Redemptive/Atonement model is the view that suffering is endured in expiation for the sake of others or out of obedience to God. Many battered women accept their suffering as part of God's plan for human salvation—at least in the early days of their shelter stay. Other battered women subscribe to the Suffering God model, an approach that recognizes that when human beings suffer, God suffers. The sufferer experiences compassionate care through both divine and human solidarity that strengthens her in situations of unjust suffering.

After presenting textual evidence, I will discuss some implications. For example, the Redemptive/Atonement and Suffering God theodicies gain further momentum because some features of the two models overlap with the gender socialization of girl children and women. Girls and women have been traditionally taught to endure suffering as part of their feminine duty: Sacrifices for family are a form of compassionate care. Thus, at face value, these models have little to offer for the recovery of women who have been only too quick to render silence, compassion, or obedience in the wake of family violence. Contrarily, however, these theodicies also have more or less potential to assist women in the healing process when women are in dialogue about the violence against them. Women influence one another. Further, some shelter women are able to offer alternative theodicies. As they heal, their visions expand. Like Rae, who now believes that change can happen through effort with God and other women, some battered women are able to reconfigure their explanations for unjust suffering by talking with other people in the shelter. Indeed, by the time they left the shelter, neither Millie nor Abbey articulated the purely traditional theodicies they had when they arrived. They had partially reshaped their outlooks to account for some of the social aspects of domestic violence.

WHY DO I SUFFER? THE THEODICIES OF BATTERED WOMEN

The battered women who pass through the Women's House may or may not be regular church-goers, but they are steeped in the conservative Christian subcultures of the urban migration from Appalachia and the eastern and central Bible Belt. Sanctified/Holiness and Baptist church doctrine forms a basis of their worldviews whether as ideology they resist or embrace. Even those women from other denominations, such as Catholicism or more mainstream Protestantism are more or less familiar with and function within some aspects of this socioreligious terrain. The culture is saturated with its conservative messages through face-to-face talk, radio programs, television evangelists, billboards, newspapers, and so forth.

Doctrinally speaking, white evangelical or fundamentalist Christians, as you may recall from chapter 4, at least nominally attest that suffering is related to the great cosmic battle between the forces of good and evil, between God and Satan. When the adherent obeys divine dictate (found particularly though not exclusively in the Bible), when she follows the path of righteousness, a way fraught with obstacles and pitfalls, her suffering is rationalized and minimized. She knows she will be rewarded in the afterlife for triumphing over evil. When she does not, when Satan prevails, her suffering is maximized and, as a sinner, she will pay for transgressions in the flames of hell. African American evangelical or fundamentalist belief generally agrees with this dualistic cosmology though it emphasizes the suffering of Jesus as the suffering of pure innocence. Jesus's suffering is often understood as an act of solidarity with believers, especially those who are marginalized.

Likewise, Holiness/Sanctified Christianity is based on dualistic cosmology: Doctrinally, however, the emphasis is on testifying and salvation through the works and gifts of the Holy Spirit. God the Father is perhaps viewed as a more benevolent creator than in fundamentalist/evangelical denominations because, when the Holiness/Sanctified adherent opens fully to the Spirit, she believes she has more control over her destiny.[2] She can successfully resist evil and its attendant suffering. Not surprisingly, at one church service I attended with a shelter woman who shortly thereafter returned to her abusive partner, the bishop counseled:

> If you are abused, relax, you are saved. [. . .] If your marriage down here didn't turn out the way you wanted it, don't worry. When you get to heaven, he'll [God] make it all up to you. [. . .] Don't lose your victory over a spouse that won't treat you the way you want. Don't think God is picking on you. People magnify their problems. Satan wants the person to think their problem is worse than the problem of anyone else. Say, "I don't depend on you. I got everything I need. I have my marriage [with Jesus]. I am smiling like Mrs. Jesus."

It should not be surprising that so many battered women return to their abusers. Church doctrine and Sunday sermons notwithstanding, however, the religious language of shelter residents covers a much wider theological spectrum. Their theodicies are not restricted to these views nor to the traditional ones, namely that suffering is: a test by God of their faith, a way of causing them to appreciate through contrast the good things in their lives, a hidden part of God's overall plan for the good of the world, or a punishment by God for the self-centeredness of human beings. Many battered women do not strictly believe that God allows their suffering because God will not intervene in human freedom. In short, most women do not consistently articulate one doctrinal position on suffering such as those spelled out in the doctrines, creeds, faith statements, or sermons of their own congregations. Instead, they ascribe to several or varying explanations.

This personal ambiguity about church doctrine has to do, certainly, with language heterogeneity or diversity: It involves the interplay between gender socialization, levels of religious education, the degree of adherence to official church doctrine, personal interpretation, lived experience, current religious practices, external expectations for discursive behavior, and other relevant contextual features. Yet, in attending to the words of battered women, I have found that their theodicies may be more or less elaborated through Kristine Rankka's modified ten-item typology. More specifically, fragments of shelter women's speech can be generally fitted into a ten-item typology of theodicies. These ten systems of belief are dualistic, Augustinian, punishment/retribution, redemptive/atonement, Irenian/evolutionary, remedial/instructive, faith (solution), process, suffering God, and liberation. In what follows, I will first briefly define these systems and provide illustrative quotations from the written and spoken words of shelter women.[3]

DUALISTIC

Many shelter women, of course, do live within a world based on a dualistic cosmology. In fact, it is a worldview many women simultaneously embrace and resist because, most importantly, it is a dominant view of patriarchal society, their religious subcultures, and their abusive partners. Yet they also sense the way dualism is used against them when womanhood is equated with weakness, sin, and evil. Again, for adherents of a dualistic model of belief, the universe is the arena for a great cosmic battle between the forces of good and evil. Suffering occurs because humans are caught in the struggle between these two polarities. Satan schemes for control over human souls and suffering is the result of succumbing to his overtures. Humans must struggle to resist evil. In fact, it is critical to do so because, if not, the forces of evil may eventually overcome the forces of good. However, God offers divine aid and intervention to humans who struggle to resist evil and, in the wings, he waits for them to make the right decisions and choices. Many women in the shelter articulate such theological dualism:

DANA: Domestic violence is the battleground over the good versus evil. The manipulating and anger are the evil terms. The faith and strength are the good tools. The devil can't handle [the] faith, hopes, and dreams [of women who resist domestic violence].

CORINNE: I learned that, being a battered woman, I had to depend on the Lord. Only through him have I gotten deliverance. The more I see where God has brought me from, I know he's always been there.

RAE: God told me in my ear to say to [my abuser]: "I rebuke you!" I said it!

Clearly, these women see their household and gender relationships as a microcosm of a dualistically aranged universe. Dana and Rae's partners have succumbed to evil and Corinne herself has been led out of the violence. Battered women can use faith to resist evil and to find "deliverance." The women rely heavily on divine intervention, particularly Corinne who finds relief *only* because of the workings of a benevolent God who lifts her out of abuse. This world is a hierarchical one in which God tells them what to do. Dana and Rae demonstrate some degree of agency, but it originates in and through God who battles against evil. Under God's direction, Rae rebukes her abuser. There are no ambiguities, complexities, or doubts in this universe of absolute good and evil. Significantly, however, the women invert traditional dualistic formulae: here, men and violence, not women, are identified with evil.

AUGUSTINIAN

Within an Augustinian cosmology, it is believed that humans are given free will by an all-powerful God; yet, humans often make destructive choices. Further, the lack of goodness is itself evil. God could prevent evil and suffering from happening but, in the interest of human free will, he does not. This system is marked by a mistrust of the human body as a primary source of temptation and destructive choices. Often, then, the adherent accepts privation as a way to avoid temptation and she accepts a hierarchy of religious authority for moral guidance. The words of some shelter women evidence strands of such a theodicy:

CAROLYN: My suffering stems from decisions that I have made that were incorrect. These decisions may not be important but the accumulation accounts for something. God will help you however with a wrong decision.

DELLA: I think that's why I'm having such a hard time now because I haven't been going to church or listening to the Word. I think

I know too much. They say nothing can be accomplished without God. Well, I haven't been putting him in my life so I'm having trouble.

KENA: [in answer to a question about whether she sought help from the police or public service to provide assistance she needed]: Prayer solves everything. I have a very strong mind and I'm staying positive and depending on the Lord. [. . .] I have so many regrets [for the choices I've made] it's unreal. I know through God that anything is possible and, so until I am able to go home, I will constantly seek help from the Lord. When I go home, I will continue seeking help and guidance and help my family find peace, faith, and righteousness through God.

In these remarks, Carolyn, Della, and Kena stress the importance of good decision making, implying at least a modicum of human free will. All three women express regret for poor choices. Della does not say she suffers because she was doing wrong, but because she was not doing *right*. The tension in the statements of all three women concerns the balance between good human decision making and dependence on God. Naturally, then, all three women look outside themselves for moral guidance. And, frighteningly, Kena ignores my question about seeking assistance from police or public services. She places all her hopes for release from suffering in prayer, supplication, and externally derived moral direction.

PUNISHMENT/RETRIBUTION

The Punishment/Retribution model is a variant of the Augustinian-influenced theodicy in that human choices lead to suffering. A powerful God keeps track of human sin, including individual or collective sin, and punishes it. Yet suffering does not always extend from bad choices even though human sin is still the cause. Through original sin, humans brought both human chaos and natural disaster down upon themselves. Natural disaster can be better explained than in a strictly Augustinian account. Inasmuch as human sin is the cause of human and natural chaos, however, it demands repentance. The next comments suggest Punishment/Retribution beliefs, most obviously in the emphasis on sin and its consequences.

PENNY [in a written prayer]: My God I have done wrong and I want to know my God that I used to know. . . . My God I am asking for forgiveness please! Lead me to your peaceful home. My God take away the Guilt that I have of myself and lead me to you My God.

Bring my family together and take away our pain and hurt and bring a family that prays together [and] stays together.

WANDA: I [wish I could] start my life over the way it started—with good firm loving biblical principles. But stay, and not stray from that teaching. Because I have learned God's way is not only the best way, but if you're looking for peace, it's the only way!

Penny and Wanda believe their suffering stems from sin. They believe that if they repent, they will enjoy peace. Penny pleads for forgiveness. Neither woman notes the systematic nature of sexism and violence: They are simply suffering the results of their own sinfulness. It is untenable, of course, for anyone to believe that domestic violence victims cause their battery through any action of their own—"sinful" or otherwise. Many battered women do and many more spouses apparently do too.

REDEMPTIVE/ATONEMENT

In a Redemptive/Atonement model, there is a willingness to accept suffering as part of God's plan for human salvation. Suffering is endured for a purpose: it is expiatory. So, like Jesus, the good Christian accepts it out of obedience to God. A good Christian bears her lot and she is strengthened by knowing that God will provide. God will reward. Below, Val, Samantha, and Lise's statements reflect strands of a Redemptive/Atonement worldview:

VAL: I think that everything will fall into place as long as you pray to God, pull yourself together, and concentrate on the positive things that happened in my life, have a good time with my family.

SAMANTHA: I know that my Redeemer lives. I need thee every hour of the day Most Holy One.

LISE: One week prior to my severe beating I told a friend if God does not take me out of this situation soon I'm not going to be able to keep going on. I prayed over and over every day, asking God to take the burden and the whole situation off my shoulders, that I gave it to him to bear. I felt like God was not listening to me because the abuse—instead of things changing—became worse. I really felt like giving up on prayers but, right when I couldn't take anymore, God took me out the situation. I was put on a plane, sent with people I didn't know. I left my home, children, job, et cetera. I finally had the strength from out of nowhere to leave the abuse. God answers our prayers in his own precious time not in our time. So now, I continue to give it all to him and wait for his answer or what will be sent to me next. I know my whole life has changed now I walk in faith. God is good.

Notice, first of all, the women suggest there is a purpose or plan to life.

everything will fall into place
I was put [by God] on a plane, sent with people I didn't know
I continue to . . . wait for his answer or what will be sent to me next

Second, suffering is to be endured until God rescues them in his own time:

right when I couldn't take anymore, God took me out the situation
concentrate on the positive things [that is, not the suffering]

Third, there is a suggestion of redemption or deliverance for enduring suffering:

my Redeemer lives
everything will fall into place
I know my whole life has changed now I walk in faith
God took me out the situation
I finally had the strength from out of nowhere to leave the abuse.
  God answers our prayers in his own precious time not in
  our time.

Surely, though Val, Samantha, and Lise may have additional conceptions of suffering and redemption, they simultaneously embrace some strands of a Redemptive/Atonement worldview.

IRENIAN/EVOLUTIONARY

In an Irenian or Evolutionary theodicy, suffering is seen to derive from the misuse of free will. It is the natural by-product of sinfulness. Yet, through suffering, God shapes souls by providing humans with a moral contrast between what happens as a consequence of sin and what happens as a consequence of goodness. Evil and suffering occur so that humans have the opportunity to develop morally in the face of affliction.

VANESSA: Our feelings, sometimes they overwhelm or depress us. Learn how to deal with them and not allow them to conquer us.

Learning how to overcome is the answer to knowing how to cope. To stifle them without proper processing we do ourselves much harm, physically, mentally, spiritually, and especially emotionally. So if God gave us feelings, it must be good even if the feelings make us feel bad at that particular time. Staying in touch with our Creator is the way to stay strong and accept and get in touch with our feelings he gave us. For me, this is God's way of making us in his image.

JOANNA: I love the Lord and he has always been a part of my life. I never blamed the Lord in what I went through, but it was very hard for me to talk to someone at church. I never questioned the Lord about what I went through because it felt like it was my fault and I didn't deserve to ask him for help when I knew I was wrong. I have always wanted to live a Christian life and serve the Lord, but all the men I encountered was not religious so it takes me away from what I believe in. I return to church and that's where I believe I got my strength to leave out of the relationship. I'm going to stay in church and do what I want to do. I know the Lord has never left me, but I did leave him. He was there for when I decide to come back to him.

SAMANTHA: If I learn to do his will not my will my life would be great.

In these segments of speech, Vanessa, Joanna, and Samantha believe they have misused their free will. Notice in particular these fragments:

> learn to do his will not my will
> Learning how to deal with them and not allowing them to conquer us.
> Learn how to overcome is the answer to knowing how to cope.

Note too that God teaches and they learn. God shapes their souls. They now know they must follow a path of moral goodness.

> this is God's way of making us in his image
> I got my strength to leave out of the relationship. . . . I'm going to stay
> in church my life would be great

Finally, notice that these women's responses to God's moral lessons entailed leaving their partners, at least temporarily. In the context of an abusive relationship, of course, this cosmology would be and is completely unsatisfactory. Many victims of domestic violence often try to ascertain God's lessons or will for them within their abusive situations—and they are gravely hurt, even killed because of it. This is true of other theodicies, including the next one.

REMEDIAL/INSTRUCTIVE

The Remedial or Instructive theodicy also entails a view of suffering as soul making. Suffering can be imposed by God or be self-imposed. In this version, however, there is a definite path leading from suffering to righteousness, compassion, and concern for others. Suffering leads not just to individual moral growth or development. It leads to what the sufferer believes is positive action taken on behalf of others. Suffering transforms to positive result:

LINDA: I think religion screwed me up big time. I hate that guilt I always have about everything. I think *it helps me to be a good person* but cripples me all the same time. I have the mentality that if I love John (truly love him), then *I will put up with everything that he is or does*, that I should accept these things. You know . . . *love* till death do us part.

ALLIE: Each day that I am away from home I am getting stronger and as I get stronger I become more comfortable with the changes that I'm making. My vision of myself in five years is to be a strong, confident woman in a career helping to make a difference in women's lives. My experiences are preparing me *for helping others.* God is preparing me for something good.

Clearly, Linda demonstrates confusion over the point of her suffering; yet, she believes it will have a positive outcome—at least for John. She will endure for his sake. For her, a good person may be crippled by suffering; nevertheless, it instructs her. It is positive for both partners: it remediates the relationship. Unfortunately, it may teach her the skills to endure even more suffering. Interestingly, she is a regular church-goer though she knows what she was taught about suffering and guilt is not healthy for her. Allie, on the other hand, has put a more positive spin on a Remedial or Instructive worldview. She made the break literally and conceptually from her abusive partner and, as she struggles to resituate herself, she believes her day-to-day suffering teaches her how to help other people.

FAITH SOLUTION

In this theological worldview, evil is a mystery. There is no adequate explanation for it. Like the Old Testament figure Job, the true believer surrenders to God. She may engage, like Job, in lamentation and protest; however, the ultimate response to God is trust and faith. Doris, Lisa, and Raeanne display strands of this worldview in the following comments:

DORIS: When my pain and troubles seem to get me down, I stand all amazed at the love Jesus offers me. Oh it is wonderful that Jesus cared for me enough to die for me. With God all things (problems–pain) ends. There is no end of God's great love for me and you. I write this in the name of Jesus Christ. Amen.

LISA: My name is Lisa and I am in pain. I just want to scream. I know it's time for me to carry my burden to God. Whatever the problem, I'll put it in God's hands.

RAEANNE: Suffering could happen without a reason. It can happen just like it happened to Job. No reason.

Raeanne clearly conveys the most explicit sense of evil as mystery. She does not question the reason for suffering or evil. Instead, she references Job who accepts his many miseries as mystery. Displaying equanimity, Doris also conveys a sense of the mystery of evil: She is amazed at the world even when it includes suffering. Lisa does not convey the same equanimity, but she does not probe evil. A true believer, she simply carries the burden to God.

PROCESS

For Christians holding a process view of evil, God cannot or will not control evil. Therefore, he cannot or will not punish evildoers now, later, or once and for all. He works by persuasion, not coercion. This is an emphasis of process theology. In this vision of reality, God depends on human action to effect goals he sets. Unlike in a more hierarchically organized cosmology, he is a cosufferer in unjust situations. He also takes risks to bring humans into community with himself and others in order to circumvent the processes of evil; likewise, humans need to take calculated risks. Some shelter women's speech indicate a process view:

DEANA: This time it's about my own mistakes. If I had been in the church, I wouldn't have such hardship. He would have guided me to make better decisions. But I'm not being punished. God gave me something to think about. You have to take that first step by yourself. If you take the first step, God takes the next ten. . . . God is supposed to guide you through the valley of darkness, but you're not supposed to do something foolish.

BEATTIE: Together we can accomplish all things! If we just believe in ourselves and trust in God! I am going back to school so that I can make things better for myself and my children.

MICHELLE: [God just won't take care of your suffering]. Well, I think you have to help yourself first.

Notice these particular segments of the women's statements by Deanna and Beattie.

> If you take the first step, God takes the next ten. . . .
> Together we can accomplish all things!

Deanna seems to suggest there is even some sort of contract between humans and the divine with stipulated responsibilities. "God," she says, "is supposed to guide you through the valley of darkness, but you're not supposed to do something foolish." In a similar vein, Michelle implies that God will not control suffering in the lives of battered women. They must be willing to take the risk of helping themselves first; then perhaps, she implies, God will assist. In each of the three cases, there is a sense of responsibility for one's own task in a cooperative endeavor.

SUFFERING GOD

Adherents of the Suffering God theodicy relinquish even further the notion of divine control over suffering and evil. When humans suffer, God suffers. God experiences the agonies of evil. There is a sense of God's suffering particularly over matters of injustice. Yet, the sufferer has hope because God makes available compassionate care. This, at least, God can do: provide for the victim of injustice. The sufferer experiences both divine solidarity and human solidarity to strengthen her in the experience of unjust suffering. Note the italics:

HEATHER: *God is my best friend and he's always there when I need him.* I talk to him and ask him for help. He has helped me through some tough times. He kept my son from dying after he was born and he's helping me right now. *He has put me in a Christian atmosphere with people who are Christians and in their own way they are helping* even if they don't know it. I love my religion and I hope someday I will get to heaven but until then I can just pray and read.

ROSEMARY: *Jesus stuck up for women* in the Bible. Such as Mary the Whore—when she was being stoned, he said, "Who [is] without sin cast the first stone."

KISHA: Africa God is going to bless [us]; don't give up. No more tears. No more mental abuse, fight, fussing, cussing. *[Of] all the men I loved, God loved me more.*

RHODA: *He comes through* the darkest days as well as the sunny days in any minute or hour or second or even in your sleep. All you have to do is know he is a Good God even when nothing is going your way because he is where he needs to be all the time. Just remember to pray and wait on the Lord. He is already there; he just can be really really busy. You are blessed just breathing.

JEWELL: I had to weep because I can't do anything by myself. I had to wait on the Lord because of what he had in store for me and I had to wait on him. I was crying and this man came up to me and I asked him if he was a Christian and he said, "Yes, praise God!" And I wept because I knew then that *the Lord brought him across my path to pray and lift my spirit.* I not only stopped crying but I was smiling. He had such a pleasant face and his voice was so at peace. *I know the Lord blessed me at that time in need.*

In a Suffering God model, suffering is a shared experience involving both God and humans. A victim of violence has this consolation: when she suffers, God suffers and responds. Ultimately, the solidarity strengthens battered women. The italicized segments make particularly clear this sense of solidarity with God. God can affect human activity. Not surprisingly, the divine appears nearly human—as if a coequal. Rhoda and Jewell imply that God attends to the suffering of battered women with compassionate care: guarding over, guiding others to render service to lessen suffering. It is the vehicle for divine blessings and human community.

LIBERATION

In a Liberation approach, suffering can be caused by the oppression of other human beings, not simply personal moral failure and shortcomings or Satan. In this view, some pain may be an inescapable part of life, but suffering is not. Suffering is caused by social factors. Sin is social and systemic; that is, social institutions can be oppressive. In this approach, God is revealed to the oppressed, particularly the poor, the marginalized, those who endure unjust suffering, such as battered women. The oppressed have a special relationship with God. Thus, the words of the sufferer are prophetic. Strengthened, she engages in complaint, protest, resistance. In fact faith leads to action particularly on behalf of the oppressed. God strengthens and assists. In this way justice will be delivered. For the sufferer, however, as in the Suffering God model, God is a "power-with" God, not a "power-over" God. Listen to the threads of a Liberation approach to the suffering in these women's utterances:

MILLIE: Man equals egocentric. They need to fulfill their masculine im-
                    age. [. . .] They get abusive if you try to make them feel less than
                    a man. This is a man's world. One day they [men] will come back
                    to the Lord's way. In a spiritual way, God brings justice. Now or
                    later in life.

DIANA: Everyone here is losing a little suffering. Little by little, we are
                    losing our suffering. Praise God who leads us out of exile.

MARLA: I left the church because I believe the patriarchal nature of it
                    leads to violence against women. In all my time at church, I
                    never heard any mention about abuse or domestic violence from
                    the pulpit. It's never mentioned. No one talks about it. It's the
                    biggest problem of our time. The church ignores it.

Millie and Marla point to the systemic nature of violence against women. For Millie, suffering stems from male socialization and male prerogative. For Marla, domestic violence is a social issue and she left the patriarchal church that contributes through a complicity of silence and neglect. Diana evokes the God of the Old Testament who leads and protects his people in the exodus, away from social oppression and slavery in Egypt. Like all shelter women, Diana knows (though she does not say it) that the reason shelter women are loosing their suffering "little by little" is because they are in community with one another, sharing stories, and reshaping their lives. This is human activity undertaken for a safe and just way of life. Millie believes that men will feel God's justice in this life—not necessarily in an afterlife. That is, the justice is delivered within a human context, through human activity or circumstances.

SUFFERING AND REDEMPTION:
THEODICY AND THE LIVED EXPERIENCE OF BATTERED WOMEN

The theodicies to which women like Diana, Kisha, or Beattie subscribe are not exclusive to battered women, of course; nor are the categories mutually exclusive. Persons who are not theologically trained, perhaps even those who are, may evidence contradictions in their cosmologies. As I mentioned ear- lier, this ambiguity or tension may involve the interplay between gender socialization, levels of religious education, the degree of adherence to official church doctrine, personal interpretation, lived experience, current religious practices, external expectations for discursive behavior, and other relevant contextual features. For example, their theodicies shift due to language heterogeneity or diversity in the shelter—a focus of upcoming chapters.

Although my findings are based on data gathered over an eight-year period, I do not believe that through these brief statements we can fully understand the dynamic theologies of the shelter women. If asked to present a systematic account, the women might very well work—more or less successfully—to realign their positions within the parameters of their traditional faith communities. At the same time, and in keeping with functional linguistic views of the intimate connection between word and concept, I believe these statements of shelter women, collected in largely naturalistic situations or open-ended conversations, do reflect some of their most authentic, unselfconscious thinking on the nature of God and suffering. These are the candid utterances of women who are not being asked to regularize or defend their statements. Their comments were gathered in many sorts of contexts and rarely in conversations in which faith, religion, suffering, or God were the focus.

This being said, I have discovered that many women in the Women's House initially function within a Redemptive/Atonement model or a Suffering God model of religious explanation for their suffering. The Redemptive/Atonement model, again, is the view that suffering is endured in expiation for the sake of others or out of obedience to God. The women often—at least in the initial days of their shelter stay—accept their suffering as part of God's plan for human salvation. The Suffering God approach is the approach that emphasizes that when humans suffer, God suffers. The sufferer experiences compassionate care through both the divine and human solidarity that strengthen her in the experience of unjust suffering.

Both of these models are typical cultural behavioral templates in the gender socialization of girls and women. Girls and women have been traditionally taught to endure suffering in silence as part of their feminine or maternal duty. A good mother suffers hardships for her children without complaint, for example, or she defers to the patriarchal lines of authority in the interest of family peace, harmony, and order.

In addition, these two models are also not at all unfamiliar to either white or black Holiness or Sanctified or fundamentalist/evangelical congregations (in which most of the shelter women have been raised and many still attend). In black experience, Jesus—the innocent sufferer—is a central divine image. According to theologian Jacquelyn Grant, black women have fervent feeling for Jesus as friend and cosufferer. And, although white and black women in Holiness Churches are principally motivated by the metaphors and images of the Spirit, the suffering Jesus is also a central image. By his suffering, he made full atonement for human sin. In fact, the Atonement is the only source of salvation. Those who suffer must repent and believe.

With somewhat different emphases, then, the suffering Jesus is an important image in the religious experience, the song and worship, of both white Sanctified/Holiness Churches and traditional black churches. Thus it is not completely surprising that the women have these two types of theological approaches to suffering. What *is* surprising are perhaps these points:

— First, given their traditional religious upbringing, gender socialization, and domestic situations, there are relatively fewer women in the Women's House who adhere strictly or primarily to potentially more woman-threatening theodicies such as Dualistic, Augustinian, or Punishment/Retribution theodicies.

— Second, as battered women review, rehearse, or reenact domestic scenes, their language suggests that their abusers lay claim to different theodicies. The abusers, it seems, often do subscribe to dualistic, Augustinian, Punishment/Retribution, or Irenian/Evolutionary explanations of suffering and evil. In women's reports of them, abusers are sententious and they use scripture to support their views. For example, abusers commonly cite scripture passages that reaffirm the patriarchal order and traditional lines of authority. They often cite Genesis 2 in which *Adam* is created before Eve, thus signifying his authority over her.

— Third, note the emancipatory potential of both the Suffering God and the Redemptive/Atonement models. These can instill passivity in the face of violence against women; they can also facilitate much more easily the growing social awareness and autonomy of battered women than other models. For example, if God is suffering with them, battered women may gather strength or confidence to make life changes. If they suffer as part of God's plan, they may believe that God's plan can change. They can be released from suffering.

— Finally, even theologically conservative battered women are surprisingly resilient in terms of notions of the origins of suffering and evil. Women who hold a dualistic view of goodness and evil can sometimes use polarity in creative ways. Recall Rae's words: *God told me in my ear to say to [my abuser]: "I rebuke you!" I said it!* And recall the words of Allie, a woman who subscribes to a Remedial/Instructive vision: *My experiences are preparing me for helping others. God is preparing me for something good.*

In dialogue with other women, there is opportunity for Rae, Allie, and others like them to develop new theological visions. In fact, the ambiguities, the contradictions, the internal inconsistencies in women's standpoints provide the opening for alternative theodicies. I will deal with this

point in upcoming chapters. Here, however, I would like to simply introduce the notion of the power of shared conversation to help women heal
and grow. An example is helpful. Rae, Marla, and Abbey are already familiar voices to us from the discussion earlier. Abbey and Rae were raised
in Apostolic churches (that is, Holiness/Sanctified). Marla and I were
raised as Catholics. On this evening, we talk about loyalty. Rae offers the
first opinion:

RAE: The big guy in the sky up there. He's more loyal than myself cuz
           I do bad. He stays by me no matter. He knows how to take us
           through life. He gives us the mindset to say, "Enough is enough!"
           He made me say that [to my abuser]. God had to give me a made-
           up mind. Love would have kept me there. He shows me the
           relationship is not good and he helps me out. He throws out the
           lifeline again. We want to be strong in a situation but God shows
           there's another possibility. He shows leaving is better. He shows
           you have to have real love in a relationship. You have to wait on
           God, but he's right on time. He touches us and relieves certain
           things. Battered women, we keep to ourselves. We don't have
           support but for God. We need a twenty-four-hour God.

MARLA: What does God mean by love in a relationship?

RAE: Love hurts. The other party [my abuser] had a generational curse.
           His [parents] were abusing to him and now he's abusing to me.
           I was trying to love him, but I didn't know it wasn't real love.
           God had to show me. God has to do it himself. He touched me.
           I got tired. I had to leave.

MARLA: My church said women should be obedient. You have to make
           sure you love your enemy. I tried to do what the church told me
           to do, but the hatred was killing me. It was my spiritual issue. I
           had to learn to stop hating and forgive. Get out.

ABBEY: The Bible says, "Likewise, men, love your wives." But men are so
           prideful. That's their sin—their pride.

RAE: Yes, they are prideful. That's their sin. They think they need to
           be in control of the family and they don't do their own part—
           "love your wives." God gave us a map but we have to be persis-
           tent. Like Job. There's suffering but Job stayed loyal to God.

CAROL: Do you mean that suffering can happen without a reason?

RAE: It could happen without a reason. Like it happened to Job. No
           reason.

MARLA: I left the church because of violence against women. I never
           heard any mention about abuse or domestic violence from the

RAE: pulpit. It's never mentioned. No one talks about it. It's the big-
              gest problem of our time. The church ignores it.

RAE: We had a pastor come to our church to talk about violence and
              abuse. She was a pastor of her own church. Some people do talk
              about it. My pastor he said you can leave! He told me I could
              leave. My abuser said every bad thing to me. God told me in my
              ear to say to him: "I rebuke you!" I said it!" [My abuser] turned
              around and didn't, couldn't, hit me. I felt so powerful with God's
              spirit. We're in this together. It's not a one-man show. God says,
              "You can!" I can!

ABBEY: The problem is we get isolated and we don't know about what to
              do. If he can get you isolated, the devil makes you feel alone.
              Then he can do anything. Think well of yourselves ladies. I
              didn't feel good about myself then, but God gave me the power
              to walk out. What my abuser's doing, he's not gonna get away
              with. God will make him pay. God will take care of it. My abuser
              will reap what he sowed.

MARLA: Well, I think you have to help yourself first.

RAE: God will not come down from the sky. God will not come down
              from the sky to make it all go away. You have to work with God.

In this extraordinary conversation, Abbey and Rae show signs of shifting
views. Rae puts creative twists on a dualistic worldview by associating evil
with violence against women instead of associating it simply with women.
She tries out more progressive stances related to the Faith Solution and
Suffering God theodicies. Early, she experiments with a nontraditional idea:
God shows leaving is better. Ultimately Abbey and Marla help Rae experiment
with new views, partly by teasing out opinions, partly by spurring her memory
of a woman pastor, and partly by suggesting novel ideas. Marla helps Rae to
finally articulate a more process-oriented view: You have to work with God.
This is movement well beyond her initial view that God has to do it himself.
For her part, Abbey shows signs of a Punishment/Retribution theodicy: God
will make him pay. Yet she also articulates a more social perspective: The
problem is we get isolated. With more conversation about domestic violence
in its sociocultural aspects, the women's views may evolve even further.
Plainly, there is potential for change in women's talk.

CONCLUSION

In my experience at the Women's House, survivors too often report being
held by their religious, social, and family communities, and particularly by

their abusers, to theological belief systems used to facilitate, justify, and sustain violence against them. Indeed, the women themselves adhere to theodicies, some of which simply are unhealthy for them. In our own culture, violence against women cannot easily be linked directly to theological notions any more than it can be easily linked directly to pornography or sexist advertisements. It is not possible to make such direct connections between ideologies and actions. Even fundamentalist women can quote select Biblical passages to support the view that husbands should respect and honor wives. But the path to violence against women is made much easier by notions of an omniscient God who, positioned at the pinnacle of power, indiscriminately punishes evildoers or weak or sinful women. Violence against women is made easier when women endure it for the sake of their children because their churches counsel them to withstand their spouses' shortcomings (actually, criminal actions) in the interest of traditional family life. The violence is made easier when women hold to notions of moral remediation or instruction through suffering or of afterlife retribution and justice. The feminist critique of patriarchal religion is desperately needed.

In the literature on domestic violence, little or no attention is given to religious beliefs outside of a general critique of patriarchy. Yet women sometimes resist harmful aspects of their subculture's religious ideology. In the next chapter I will widen my perspective to explore battered women's general notions about religion, faith, and family life. Many women make sense of the paradox of being violated as objects by men, churches, and scriptures at the same time as they remain subjects and namers of their own faith journeys as Christian women. I do not suggest that battered women have arrived at more mature, sophisticated theologies because of the violence against them. To do so would be to subscribe to an unacceptable theodicy. But the lived experience of battered women most fully legitimates their feet-on-the-ground theology. Their theological resilience is sometimes remarkable.

SIX

"In the Bible, It Can Be So Harsh!"

SHELTER WOMEN TALK ABOUT RELIGION

I don't want it to be too late before I start doing what I'm supposed
to do. In the Bible, it can be so harsh!

—Chloe

INTRODUCTION

Many battered women know that religion is a mechanism of social control.
At the Women's House, they talk about domestic violence and, as they do,
they show signs of recognizing that religion is used to sustain it. At the same
time, most women are believers. There is no shortfall of faith at the shelter
and the women accept suffering as part of their faith journey. Some battered
women adhere to theodicies that simply are unhealthy; other women have
or acquire more healthy views.[1] The women's lived experience hones their
perceptions and, in conversation, they may learn new ways to think about
how religion helps or hinders them.

In this chapter I wish to attend to shelter women's general language
about God, faith, and religion. In the last chapter I focused on theodicy and
argued that abused women increasingly connect social structures, including the
church, to their suffering. Here I look at other aspects of Christianity. Theodicy
is only one slender aspect of theology and theology is only one aspect of faith.
As Diana L. Hayes puts it: ". . . faith is more than just theology. It is also
worship and social expression. Faith is the lived out expression of a people's

hope and belief in someone or something greater than themselves."[2] To explore this "lived out expression," I turn to language practices. I will offer some themes, or repeated patterns, that run through battered women's language about God, scripture, the church, and its tradition. This is an interpretative process, of course, for myself as a participant-observer, for the women who reinvent their lives in acts of storytelling, and for the readers who share their stories.

In the first part of the chapter I will address a *hermeneutic of identity and relationship*. A hermeneutic is a method or style of interpretation. These questions surface: Who Is God? What should I do for God? How does God help me? Such questions are at the core of faith. Additionally, they address issues of mutuality and reciprocity that battered women are confronting in their abuse-torn marriages or partnerships. Thus the answers define a perceived process of exchange of being and doing with both human and divine dimensions.

In the second part of the chapter I focus on tensions in women's faith. Questions arise such as these: How is scripture related to my suffering? How is church or tradition related to my suffering? Briefly, I try to uncover a *hermeneutic of suffering*. The central issue is not God's connection to suffering (the focus of chapter 5), but the way church, scripture, and tradition map out a system of hierarchical relations between God, women, and men. Thus, I will touch briefly upon the issue of God-blame. Christian writers oft remark on battered women's anger toward God for their suffering. I offer an alternate reading: Women direct their anger toward church, scripture, and tradition—which they see as contributing to their suffering.

Finally, I will address the women's *hermeneutic of healing*. How do they navigate through impositions by churches, scripture, and abusers on women and on their relationship to God? Some themes are: women's special connection to God, their teaching role in church and society, and, finally, the consequences of ignoring their teaching and testimony. Some women survive or emerge more stable because of collectively evolved thoughts on these subjects.

A clarification: Shelter women do not typically address such topics head-on; rather, themes surface during conversations and writing sessions. On occasion, I make inquiries based on what I hear or I interview women for more specific information but, in general, their words come unbeckoned. Consequently, this chapter is broad. In subsequent chapters, I address battered women's healing processes and their local theology—that is, their theological responses to the problems of everyday life. It is useful, however, to consider the God-talk that forms the ground or base for those more specific processes. Battered women's thoughts on these issues cast both light and shadow on their ability to survive and sustain a violence-free life.

A HERMENEUTIC OF IDENTITY AND RELATIONSHIP

For shelter women in crisis, one relationship emerges as central—their relationship with God. Their words indicate they contemplate issues such as these: Who Is God? Will God help me? How? What must I do for God? They read the signs of their lived experience to formulate a hermeneutic of identity and relationship. That is, the women are interpreting and reinterpreting their ideas about God and their relationship to God through the lived experience of battery.

WHO IS GOD?

Images of God are significant.[3] There is a spectrum of assumptions about God's actual identity. Most women refer to God as gendered male. Often when I hear a woman use a gendered reference in their God-talk, I make inquiries. These are some of the responses:

— The Bible talks about him in a masculine way. We shouldn't correct the Bible.

— Most people, a lot of people, think God is a guy. But when you pray, you pray to God—not to the man, to God. I think in your mind, it is still a guy. Jesus is a guy.

— People think of God as a guy. I'm saying every picture is God as a man. You never see a woman as God. Guys think they are better than us [because of this].

— I think of God as a man. But not from a theological perspective. Then I don't think of him as a man or woman. [. . .] By repetition, I say "Our Father."

— God is a being. Not man or woman.

Clearly there is a range of response from biblically literalist to more theologically imaginative ideas about God and gender. A few women can imagine God as gendered female:

— A woman God is for women.

— Wouldn't it be wonderful if God was a woman?

— [Women] get all the pain. [A female God] would be sympathetic. If God was a woman, she would be sympathetic to women and give men all the bad stuff. God is a man. He made it easier on them.

Although the feminine attributes of the Godhead surface in scripture, the explicit gendering of God as female is not a practice in traditional religion[4] for it would reveal how religious ideology affects real world relations. It is not the norm in the shelter either, especially in women's initial conversations. The traditional view of God as gendered male and its attendant tensions and problems arise in the hermeneutics of abusers—a topic I will address shortly.

What Must We Do for God?

Shelter women have senses of responsibility toward God. For some women, unfulfilled responsibilities are directly linked to their suffering. For other women, their responsibilities are freely rendered as part of a relational exchange. To benefit from God's grace, they pray. They might go to church. They humble themselves and make sacrifices. They translate or teach God's word. They praise and worship. Some of these activities are affiliated with traditional gender socialization but, interestingly, shelter women often invest them with new meanings:

Women Should Pray

Shelter women believe in prayer. Some women pray for specific requests. With other women, there is an open-endedness to prayer—as if the rhythm or regularity of prayer counts more than the content. This unclosed aspect of talking to God connotes an authenticity or spontaneity lacking in their relations to men:

— You have to pray.
— Don't forget to pray.
— When your heart was broken, did you think to pray?
— Pray and wait on the Lord.
— Someone said prayer is not going to work when you want it to. Oh boy, I believe it now. But I am still praying because I believe everything is going to work out.
— Pray every night. Keep the faith that things will work out. . . .
— I go to my room in the quiet time and I sit and meditate for a while just to try to listen to God speak to me. I sing a few choruses of my favorite songs. Then I say the Lord's Prayer or a prayer that comes from the heart. I ask the Lord for forgiveness of anything I had done and pray for my family for health and strength. Guide me to do right, Lord.
— I pray everyday, morning and night.

— We [my children and I] were very prayerful. We knew God was going to take care of us.

— I was always in prayer. The prayer of the righteous prevaileth much. I kept the faith.

Women Should Go to Church

Most women make clear that church attendance is not necessary to have an authentic relationship with God. Stung by the church, its hypocrisy or sexism, many women will not go; other women believe it is crucial to go to church despite its problems. There is much pain and disagreement about it. In this exchange, it shows:

TINA: I don't believe churches work anymore. [. . .] They read the Bible and try to teach you their way. But they don't follow the rules themselves.

WREN: That's discouraging. They tell you one thing and do the opposite. You can't tell people to do one thing and then do the opposite.

MELISSA: You can't make up the rules.

WREN: The most abusive men are in church. They use God. My dad, he beat my mom over the head with the Bible. Literally! If my mom wanted to buy something, he would read from the scriptures about how she couldn't have it. My mom couldn't ask for anything. He literally hit her over the head with the bible. She couldn't ask for a stove, fridge, clothes. My mom was taking care of five kids. He gave her twenty or thirty dollars a week. What could she do? He went to church faithfully.

MELISSA: They are their own type of Christian. My uncle beat my aunt. [The church] told her it was her fault. They said, "Stay there and work it out." She filed for divorce. They told her she was aggravating him. She filed for divorce and so he shot her. And then he killed himself. When the congregation here heard, they turned their back.

WREN: Be subservient to your husband. That's what church is all about.

TINA: Some churches you go, you can feel God.

MELISSA: Not if it's led by men and men are power hungry. No one wants that stuff!

As Tina's words illustrate, the conflict about church surfaces not only between women, but within individual women. Many women believe they should go to church despite the pain and problems. In what follows (except perhaps for the woman saved at home), the speakers' theodicies appear to be such that failure to attend church is punished by suffering:

— I haven't been going to church or listening to the Word.
— I think if I went to church, I won't be having this trouble.
— If I had been in the church, I wouldn't be having such problems. You should do it now, go to church, read the Bible, make praises.
— I was lying in bed. I said: "Help me! You [God] are the only one who can help me! I am fighting the old man. Everything is mixed up." Then, something hit my head and went through my whole body. My whole body lit up. I felt so good! The next morning, I got my two kids ready and I went to church. And I go ever since.
— My abuser wants me to go back into church and I know I wouldn't have such a hard time getting my life together if I did.

Women Should Commit to God

Most women, particularly those who reject the sexism of the church and tradition, believe that a profound commitment to God is necessary. God should be central and, for some women, the centrality should be demonstrated. Remarkably, some women mitigate the traditional hierarchy of power and authority (that is, God over man over woman) by making God central. Such beliefs undercut the godlike authority of men granted by church and culture and taken full advantage of by abusive men. In a sense, the commitment to God is a form of resistance to social control by males.

— You have to be regular.
— You have to show you want him in your life.
— I wish that I could just make a commitment to serve God without choice of sin.
— First of all, before I committed myself to the Lord, to God, I had to be born again. Now I have committed and asked Him to come into my life and heart.
— If I had a chance to choose a man, it would be God first.
— I had too much faith in my abuser and not in God.

Women Should Humble Themselves

In keeping with the notion that they should demonstrate commitment, some shelter women believe they ought to show deference and humility toward God. Whether this attitude is acquired first through gender socialization is uncertain, but it is arguably augmented by it. Subtly but perceptively, however, the humility is part of an exchange for some women: God renders to women something in return. The relationship is akin to friendship—an arrangement of loving mutuality and reciprocity.

— I haven't been putting him in my life so I'm having trouble.

— If I learn to do his will, not my will, my life would be great.

— God does teach us to know self-control. The meek stuff.

— I never question the Lord about what I went through because it felt like it was my fault.

— You have to wait. God comes in his time, not your time.

— I talk to him and ask him for help.

— Asking God for advice was my major role of my daily activities. And then I put it all into his hands.

Women Should Sacrifice

Like humility, sacrifice may be a gender-socialized expectation. Women believe they must sacrifice to balance human-divine relations; yet, some women give this requirement a real twist. For them, sacrifice means to give up unrealistic dreams about love and marriage or even to give up their partners—not what churches have traditionally counseled. While some speakers are still idealistic, they are tempering their hopes with more realism about gender discrimination and partner abuse. Again, religious belief may be a form of resistance:

— [God] did something to show us he loved us, so we have to show him. Now I'm saying I'm giving this man [my abuser] up to show him I need him [God] to help me get through this. He'll reward me if I give this man up, [. . .] the man of my dreams. I learned from church and the Bible, he died for us, he gave his life for us. His life was precious and he gave it up. We have to give something up to show him. We have to give up something precious. Our man.

— I have always wanted to live a Christian life and serve the Lord, but all the man I encounter was not religious so it takes me away from what I believe in. I return to church and that's where I believe I got my strength to leave out of the relationship.

— I really think that for me and my son [a life] without a man would be a better life. I would give my son more of my time. We would definitely go to church.

— I dreamt to get married with a man whose loving and supportive whenever I need him and I will do also the same to him, but the things is not working good by now. We cannot expect everything [to be] perfect and I have to take whatever God gives to me.

— Since leaving my abusive marriage, I had to make heart-wrenching decisions. What was best for my daughter, but also what was best for me. Teaching my daughter along the way, how to make decisions based on [God's] inner guidance, what felt right, and what was expected. One of the most difficult times along this path was the step we made to relocate. It was such a scary, painful decision.

— All through my life, I knew everything couldn't be perfect. I would like to be physically and mentally stable. I want my son to grow up in a stable home whether it be a single- or two-parent home. Also, I would like this world not to have any violence because it would save me and a lot of people's problems. But this world won't be perfect so my real one wish would be for God to give me strength and health to raise my son the best way God allows me to.

Women Should Translate or Teach

All women are socialized by their churches. Marked in a particularly potent way are Holiness/Sanctified women who believe they have special connections to God to teach and testify. Even evangelical/fundamentalist women, who have scaled-down public duties, think they should help other battered women through bible study or scripture. The first three women below are Holiness/Sanctified; the next two are Baptist.

— God told [a woman in my family]. She translated the words.

— For my grandmother, it's like a natural thing for so many years. She's the one who talks to God.

— All the people in church have roles. There's some who cry. There are weepers and there are people who speak in tongues. [. . .] Women get the tongues.

— You have to tell [people] about God and what God's done for you.

— Why am I really here? I look at these women, they come to me, they break down, boo-hoo, on the verge of a nervous breakdown. I don't know how to handle this! I'm not professionally trained. I'm spiritually trained. [God has] been leading me to tell women not to worry. Trust God for the answer. As soon as I convince them to stop worrying so much and immediately something happens! I say, "Didn't I tell you? Is there anything too hard for him? Remember this day. He'll help you now and later on." Women have come to church with me, prayed with me. We sat up 'til six in the morning. I was answering questions [her roommate] had. The Lord would have me jump up for the biblical reference. I'd be almost asleep and then I'd jump up with another bible reference. She'd have another question. I wondered if I would ever get some sleep! 'Til six in the morning! Lord! Thanks for using me to serve, to help others, an instrument to help.

For the Baptist women, and most clearly for the last Baptist woman, God helps battered women escape marriages and other abusive partnerships. This is a revisioning of what scripture and their churches taught them about their duty to husband and family.

Women Should Praise and Worship

Other activities battered women observe in the exchange of offerings and services with God are praise and worship. A range of vocabulary describes this: testifying, tarrying, witnessing, glorifying, praising, worshiping. There are se-mantic, denominationally derived differences that accompany the lexis. Tarry-ing is Holiness/Sanctified language that entails speaking in tongues. Testifying more clearly originates in the black churches to signify publicly sharing the glories of God. Yet, among the words, there is also semantic overlay; that is, there is a sense of enlivening, quickening, or spiritedness to the words and to all the activity they denote. The commonality connotes public worship. It is a performed activity of giving thanks and testimony to the glories of God. The accompanying emotion is in contradistinction to battered women's alienation and depression. Indeed, the energy and connection is an aspect of healing:

— Now my grandmother is the kind of person who has her daily sessions throughout the day: She praises, she tarries, reads the scriptures. She gives God the glory. I mean if you hear my grandmother, she speaks in tongues. She's in her little joyous sessions.

— You [should be] right by God, praising and blessing and live right— by the golden rule.

— What experience makes me the wisest? I know for a fact that [it's] when I let God save me, filling me with that tongue talking, foot stumpin' Holy Ghost! This is in Acts 2:38, Acts 2:4. I tried this and this gift leads me. I know that the Mighty God is there.

— Society has to be getting back to praising God and living by the word of God. Who takes care of everything when the man leaves the house? The woman takes care of everything: the mother, the father, the sister, the brother. She has to take care of everything.

— I love and praise God for his love and forgiveness.

— God be the glory for the things he has done!

— [When I was born again] I got the knowledge. And I knew [God] was real. Hallelujah! And he is real. Before we were born from our mother's womb, we were blind. We couldn't see. But now we have our eyes that are no longer blind. And we can see. My mother was an evangelist. I am not a preacher. I am a prayer-warrior. That's what he told me I was. He said, "You are my prayer-warrior." I had an experience where I touched his heart. You know how people say God touched them, but I touched God. And he has blessed me spiritually. It is the most wonderful marvelous exciting experience that you can ever have with our heavenly father. My Lord.

These women are strengthened by their praises and worship that they perform publicly, enacting, embodying, or reexperiencing special spiritual moments, filled with gratitude and joy.

To sum up, shelter women create their own hermeneutic of identity and relationship to God. They believe that particular acts strengthen their relationships. They believe they should commit to God. They should humble themselves and make sacrifices. They should pray, go to church, and praise and worship. Some women, like mothers, church mothers, or grandmothers demonstrate good and appropriate behaviors to emulate.

What do such beliefs mean? How do they affect women's suffering, survival, and healing? Perhaps a narrowly defined theodicy would yield a belief system such as this: "I am suffering because I am not doing my part. I need to go to church," and so forth. A more positive rendering may be this: Battered women believe they should reorder or prioritize their relationship to God over their relationship with their abuser. As they consider their relationship with God, they may be considering what it means to have a better relationship with men and vice versa. As Nicole says, "We feel God is the man in our life, so we follow God, the strong man."

Such language may make a more socially aware person recoil; yet, some of the language is a form of resistance to traditional gender socialization despite conventional inflections. The language is reinvested with new meanings. Some women's words simply reflect a shifting consciousness about how religious ideology affects real world relations. Other women wonder how religious or spiritual practices benefit or impede their well-being. Recall the shift I discussed in the last chapter that some battered women make from the *redemptive/atonement* and *suffering God* theodicies to the *remedial/instructive* and *liberation* theodicies. Consider these words:

— It would help if we changed the religion.
— Let the women teach the way they want to teach. The religious scene would not be the same.
— Men wrecked the institution of marriage, of religion.

Anita and Lydia have this interesting and socially inflected exchange:

ANITA: Most churches are not okay. The men have the control.
LYDIA: They have the control, the power. How did we let them get that power?

Such language marks a significant shift in women's theology. While it might be argued that women's senses of responsibility toward God are dictated by their churches, it is also true that women inflect those responsibilities with their lived experience that tells them something is wrong with the traditional templates of prayer, sacrifice, and other female duties. For example, traditional or conservative church mores would not encourage a woman to "sacrifice" her husband in order to stay closer to God. Instead, traditional or conservative religious codes of female conduct pressure women to stay with their spouses—even abusive ones.

WHAT DOES GOD DO FOR WOMEN?

A good relationship is reciprocal. Although not many shelter women who are fundamentalist/evangelical or Holiness/Sanctified would agree that God and humans are actually interdependent, they do assume that God renders services to women who keep up their part of the relationship. In this way, the relationship does involve mutuality and reciprocity. Whether as grace or service, God's activities (among others) are to protect women, to teach and talk to them, to reward them, and to bring justice.

God Protects Women

Battered women have little confidence in law enforcement and judicial systems. Comments such as the following are routine:

— I was given a referral for the courthouse. But he would threaten me if he heard I called the police. So, the police didn't come into it. He has family on the force. They couldn't care.

— The courts don't care about domestic violence. This man is a raging drunk and two days before his first hearing he got stopped by the police again for a DUI. It's just escalating. I tried to talk to the prosecutor about it. They don't care. They won't care until he kills— kills me or my kids.

— What's a restraining order? They aren't gonna stop them. They'll be gone by the time the cops get there and your body will be all that's left behind. The restraining order pisses them off even more.

— I got "justice" only because he was on parole for something else and any contact with courts was bad for him. They put him back [in jail] because he made death threats on my neighbor's phone. He said she was kidnapping and brainwashing me. He thought she was helping me. Then he threatened her, so she wouldn't testify and she would not turn the tape over (of the telephone threats). She must have been scared by him. You never know.

With so little civil or societal protection, women turn to God:

— I have been in situations where I should be dead, but I believe in God because I should be dead and I am not dead.

— God shelters us women. He gives us somewhere to go. Here.

— God took me out of the situation.

— God would not want me to live in fear and anger and with the rage that [my partner] brought on me by beating and verbally abusing me.

— God is supposed to guide you through the valley of darkness, but you are not supposed to do something foolish.

— After that, the Lord got me out of there! [My abuser] became a wino. You can't do a blasphemous thing and get away with it. You reap what you sow. So, the Lord got me away from him. After all those years with the fighter, I fought back. I admit I fought back. Lord! I have the battle wounds to prove it. But you can't beat a man. He always gets the upper hand. My Lord has always saved me, rescued me, provided for me, sustained me, kept me. He never let me go, not for one second.

God Teaches or Talks to Women

God tells women what they need to know to survive, learn, grow, and change. Often, the interchange does not come via men, church, or scripture.

— God told her [her brother] was saved. [He was an abuser who re-
  pented.]
— God has to let them know it's no use trying to make it fit your beliefs
  like you want. You have to do all of it [that is, follow a Christian
  lifestyle].
— God gave me something to think about.
— God does teach us to know self-control. The meek stuff.
— God presents the situations to see what you will do.
— That's what [God] told me I was. He said, "You are my prayer-warrior."

These women have bypassed men, church, and scripture. Instead, their communication with God is direct and personal. In this way, women have a
chance to resist some of the more harmful aspects of scripture, church, and
its traditions. Further, God tries to teach and to protect them. Abusers must
repent to be saved. Notice that the women's language may still be taut with
tension or contradiction. For example, God teaches one woman the "meek
stuff" and God designates another woman as a warrior—the prayer-warrior.
These two images are polar opposites in terms of codes of conduct; yet, they
illustrate the potential and possibility accessible to the woman who is exploring her own relationship with God. Some women may still be influenced by
the sexism of church and culture, but they have at least opened channels for
direct, unmediated communication with the divine.

God Rewards Women

God is ready with rewards. The theological innovation for many battered
women is this: Reward comes with survival, not with conventional submission to male authority. These women have left behind the traditional two-
parent home for some safety and peace. The first speaker refers to her extended
family that her abuser forbade her to see:

— God, bring my family together. Take away our pain and hurt, and
  bring a family that stays together [because we pray together] back
  together.
— I lost everything like Job, but if I try to live right, God will give
  everything back to me tenfold.
— I didn't know about this place. I must have been right when I left
  because I got rewarded with this place.
— God Almighty will bless me and my babies to have a family in a
  healthy environment without a father.

— I used to wonder: God where are you? Then a blessing would happen.

— [It makes me hopeful that] I'm still alive and I'm not dead. That I have my kids with me. [. . .] I think it's God because we wouldn't be here with our kids if it weren't for Him.

— You are blessed just breathing.

God Renders Justice

In a world of so little concern for their safety and well-being, battered women often feel defeated. "There is no justice," one woman told me. She said, "These are bleak times." So many women believe only God can or will render justice. "For me, justice?" one woman asked incredulously when I made inquiries. She continued, "The law doesn't care about me." Only later in our conversation did she broach the topic again. "Wait till later," she said, intimating that God would render justice. For her, as for many battered women, justice can only come from God. These are typical utterances:

— He's gonna make it all right. The Father above. You have suffered enough. He's gonna make it right.

— In a spiritual way, God brings justice. Now or later in life.

— I could die. I could bleed to death. I'm not worried about it. If I do die, I will not see my kids! But they'll be okay. I'm like the martyrs in their fiery furnace. They knew that God would deliver them if he wanted to. If he wants to, he will. I trust him in all things. All things work together for good, according to his purpose. I know I am a child of God. No matter how much men, hell, obstacles, mayhem, no matter. I know God will work it out for my good in the end.

— The Lord said [to me]: "I will never leave you. I will never forsake you."

Surely, these women do expect God to undertake activities on their behalf. God protects women. God talks to women and teaches them. God will bring rewards and render justice. In these few and in a multitude of other language events, shelter women give witness to the many blessings God has bestowed on them. If God does not come through, they redouble their efforts to merit blessings sure to come.

A HERMENEUTIC OF SUFFERING

Although they believe God will render services if they keep up their part of their relationship, there are tensions in many battered women's religious belief systems. Perplexities surface around questions such as these: How is scripture related to my suffering? How is church or tradition related to my suffering? Interestingly and significantly, however, women tend to attribute their problems not to God, but to their tradition or scripture, their churches or abusers. This is a hermeneutic of suffering most Christian commentators on violence against women tend to ignore or to not duly recognize. In what follows, I would like to use the account in Genesis of Adam and Eve to illustrate my point.

SCRIPTURE: THE STORY OF ADAM AND EVE

Scripture has a role in the suffering of battered women. It causes suffering. Their partners commonly use scripture to justify their abusive attitudes and actions. The story of Adam and Eve (Genesis 1–3) is cited repeatedly by abusive men. The order of creation of Genesis 2 (in which God creates man first, then woman as his helpmeet) and the fall of Eve to the machinations of the serpent in Genesis 3 are cited over and over.

— The Bible starts out with Adam and Eve. The world thinks women are evil. Eve got Adam to eat the apple. Everyone says women are evil. So, the stories in the Bible are like that—against women.

— [Men] think they are better than us because of Adam and Eve! Man's downfall was Eve. That's what they think.

— Nuns wait on priests hand and foot! But that's what Eve was supposed to do. Sex him when he needed sex; feed him when he needed food! [Her tone of voice is derogatory]

— The stories that follow [the story of Adam and Eve] are messed up because it was blamed on Eve, but it was both of their faults.

— They misinterpreted those verses in the Bible. He ate the fruit too. They always put it on the woman. He wanted to. Adam. It's his own fault. So why are they blaming it on women?

— They assume it was from Adam and Eve. If you are Christian, it says in the Bible that Eve came from Adam. I've heard that from so many men: "You came from me, so I don't want you to forget it." If they are poor or rich, it's this attitude about women. They have authority. It feeds into that—religion.

— They try to put women down as if [women] don't mean anything by stating that women were born second to them and they were born first. So he is so much better than women.

— [My husband] was reading from a certain passage, a woman was a harlot. He constantly read it and made it seem like it was me.... He's not

> religious. He tried to use the Bible to justify his ways. The part about Eve,
> I heard that a lot. He used Eve as meaning I was less than him.

Clearly, the story of Adam and Eve is a central and highly symbolic story in the gender socialization in the culture. It surfaces in domestic strife and violence and it functions to socially order relationships according to lines of male power and female submission.

The lived experience of battery and abuse tips many women off to this hermeneutic; yet, not every woman criticizes or abandons it. As we have noted in the last chapter, some women try to improve their lot by realigning their beliefs and actions with a literalist or traditionally conservative interpretation of the Genesis story. This is especially true in their initial days at the shelter, before women have had a chance to ponder such theological questions with others. One woman, for example, told me: "It's in the Bible: There's a man who is the head of the church. Adam was the first one. They weren't created at the same time. Eve was created for Adam." For her, this meant that women were to be subordinate to men.

Not all shelter women, of course, are critical. When they are brought into contact with other women with other interpretations or beliefs, they will have a chance to listen and reconsider. Not all women are ready for the challenge.

SCRIPTURE, TRADITION, AND MALE POWER

Besides the story of Adam and Eve, other biblical passages figure in the dynamics of abuse in the women's relationships. In the following exchange, Denise, who was raised in a Baptist church, follows the literalist suit. But Earlene—who was raised in the Tennessee Holiness church and who has since abandoned the church, though not her faith—is certain that either Denise is using an inferior version of the Bible or she must not be following New Testament principles. Nothing else could explain the error to Earlene who has seen women preachers in her church.

DENISE: In the bible, it says women are to be silent. The Bible says . . .

EARLENE: It's a Catholic Bible.

DENISE: No, it's not.

EARLENE: Was it the Old Testament?

DENISE: No, it's not. If you don't believe it, then you don't believe the Bible.

EARLENE: Is it a King James Bible? It must be a Catholic Bible.

In their conversation, Denise is referring to St. Paul's injunction (in the first epistle to Timothy [2:8–15]) to women to learn and be silent in church.

Paul bases his teaching on the order of creation in Genesis 2:15–3:7 and not Genesis 1:25–27. In Genesis 2:15, Adam was first formed, then Eve. Adam was not seduced, but Eve was seduced; consequently, women should have no authority over men. Earlene contests Denise's reading. But neither Denise nor Earlene have embraced a critical hermeneutic. Denise holds literally to Paul's account and Earlene simply contests the entire biblical source.

Yet women refer over and over to their partner's or their church's practices of using scripture to gain power and control. In what follows, shelter women refer to the Bible or this practice in general:

— I think the rule of religion that states that women are supposed to be submissive to their husbands—[the idea that] any time that he wants, that your body belongs to him, not you anymore—interferes with my self-respect a lot.

— What do I think is wrong? Some men try to use what has happened in the Bible to justify what they do to you! [. . .] The only time I saw my husband read the Bible was after he done drank beers and then he beat me.

— Men try to throw thing things up that happened to people in the Bible and use it to defend the way they treat their women.

— [My abuser] would say he read the Bible all the time. The only time he read the Bible was when he done turned up twelve beers, go no-no-no to me [wagging her finger in the air], and wave the Bible.

— They do try to use the Bible to make it seem like they are like God. They have so much authority, like him.

— The biggest thing men remember all the time is the words, "Wives, honor and obey your husband." The words stick in their head. They can't think of anything else.

That many abusers use scripture and church tradition to support and sustain their abuse is not news to domestic violence scholars or workers. The point I would like to be noticed, however, is that most shelter women distance themselves from such rhetorical or interpretive strategies. This is especially evident after they have been in conversation with other battered women or with staff and volunteers who talk about the sociocultural causes of violence against women. After they hear such talk, battered women are less inclined to abide either by scripture or by scripture use that relegates them to secondary status, thus justifying violence against them.

Instead, in a hermeneutic of defense, they will often cite counterpassages or offer counterinterpretations. They do not believe God intended them to be regarded as secondary to men. They do not blame God. They are revealing their dissent to the use of scripture or church tradition to control their lives. Akesha augments gender roles as given in scripture:

> I don't think [men] are better than us. According to God, they have been placed in an authoritative role. The order is God, then men, women, then children. They are the tillers, and providers, according to God, and that's not to say Eve can't till the ground too or he cannot help Eve bear the children.

Sophie puts her own spin on women's roles in the Bible, ignoring or rejecting the inferior status usually designated to women in the Bible by its male authors and interpreters.

> What are women supposed to do? Again, everything is gonna come from God. Get the word of God! It can tell you everything you need to know on how to fight the enemy in your life. It has the greatest women in this book! The greatest women judges, ministers, are found in this book. The woman who found Jesus is in this book. Women are. . . . God uses women in awesome ways in this book. He uses women a lot in this book. Not in a bad way, but to touch others, help others. Women are very instrumental in God's plan and purpose.

Theodosia and Sasha invent their own biblical passages:

THEODOSIA: [Our abusers] are going to hell. The Bible says not to beat your wives.

SASHA: Faith says we are all created equal. The constitution, men wrote that up. But God says we are all created equal.

Vanessa and Myrtis contest church tradition:

VANESSA: That's why I don't belong to no church. I read the Bible. I feel in my heart what I have to do. I ain't going by his rules or her rules. No. I can't get into that.

MYRTIS: When I got married, I promised before God and everybody to love, honor, and cherish till death us do part.

Unlike Vanessa, Myrtis was initially faithful to the traditional church rules. Then her marriage became blighted with violence, and before she arrived at the shelter, her body beaten bloody. She left the marriage despite the recriminations of her conventionally devout Apostolic mother. Another woman,

Wilma, does not abide harmful tradition: "death do you part! Death will do you part if you don't leave."

Other women express disdain toward harmful aspects of their religion. Kelly, an African American Catholic raised Holiness, puts it quite bluntly:

> I look at the Bible as a good reference. Not the best book in the world. [. . .] I choose to be Catholic, but I'll always remember the role of the church in slavery. They helped. The Bible has been revised when there was corruption. So it's not perfect. I look at the Bible and say some of this is just chauvinist and, shit, I'm doing away with that.

Other women, in conversation, express fuller alienation:

VICKI: The church works for men.

RITA: I don't go to church anymore. It's not like when my gramma was pastor.

Kelly, Theodosia, Vanessa, and Rita, like many battered women, had partners who evoked the name of God during their beatings. Theirs is knowledge based on the lived experience of the connections between patriarchal religion and battery. Their rejection of harmful aspects of church, tradition, or scripture creates a reason for other shelter women and staff to celebrate.

ANGER AND GOD-BLAME

Christian commentators sometimes suggest that, in their anger and sorrow, battered women blame God for their troubles.[5] I disagree; certainly, there is a lot of anger in the shelter, yet, women do not engage in God-blame. These comments clarify its context and object:

— Today I was thinking about how angry I am. I am angry down to my very soul, I feel as if anger oozes from my pores, creating a cloud of gloom that envelops me. I walk through life engulfed in this haze that seems to cast a cloud on everything I see, everything I touch, everything I do.[6]

— How can I break this cycle of anger and self-pity? The people at whom I am angry don't care that they are responsible for so much hurt and loss. If only I could let go of this anger and move on. Must I carry this load that is not even my own forever? There must be someplace to leave it, something to do with it that is healthy and rational and doesn't involve destruction or denial.

— There's so much chaos here that even this place disturbs me. Not knowing where I'm headed disturbs me. I'm angry because I have no control over my life again!

— And I try hard not to be angry at myself for staying and not running away, for not being able to stop the abuse, for not trying to protect myself. I try not to be angry at myself for these things because they were not my fault. I have suffered long and hard at the hand of others, others who refuse to accept my anger. So I am still angry.

— I had a very frustrating day. Things I planned to do, I was unable to do because I couldn't find coverage at work [. . .] or childcare. A lot of anger and resentments come out in me when I have a day like today.

— I'm mad at myself for being such a people-pleaser and caregiver.

One time I asked two Baptists, Velma and Yvette, and a Holiness woman, Alma, about God-blame. Like other women, they were amused at the question. They are not angry at God.[7] They are angry about social conditions that disfavor women or disrupt their efforts to survive and heal.

CAROL: Do battered women blame God for their troubles?

EVERYONE: [laughter] No!

VELMA: We forget our faith and [the abusers] make you feel like you aren't worth anything. So, you don't feel like you're a child of God. You get the idea that you are nothing, or little, like you're an insect. Not worthy of His praises. You don't think of Him in your mind. It's not like we are blaming God.

YVETTE: Abusers are not God-abiding and they take you away from your church. It's competition to them or too much outside influence in your life. I was kept from going to church by a man. But I needed one man [God]. Believe me, they try to pull you away.

VELMA: They don't want you to have strength or courage. I don't blame God. I wanted God!

YVETTE: I blame me, not God. I blame me for the choices I make.

VELMA: You could learn a lesson from your abuse, and you can question why the lesson had to be so harsh. He puts everyone in your life for a reason—to learn something.

ALMA: We question, not blame, God. I say prayers and say, "God, why is this so hard on me? Is there another purpose? Let me be happy. I don't want gold or riches." We might ask what it's about—the suffering. But we don't blame God.

Velma, Yvette, and Alma were amused with my question. On another occasion, Wilhelma said:

> We don't blame God. Women don't blame God. We don't say, "Why did you do this to me?" We say, "Lord help me! Look at what I am dealing with!" He helps us. He don't cause this thing. These men are full of hell.

Lea offers this concise statement: "It's not that God's not fair, but men have interpreted God in their favor. We are taught what they have wanted us to learn. We haven't learned to take the power back." When women say they are angry, they are not angry with God. They lean heavily on God and celebrate his faith in them. Listen to Yvonne:

> I thank God for God. He is the source of all my strength. I can go to him at any time and he will never hurt me. When I cry, he cries with me. And he comforts me, renews my strength, and carries me when I'm weak. He's closer to me than anyone and he shows me love without pain. He never hurts or demeans me and accepts me no matter what.

Yvonne seems to compare her relationship with God to that with her abuser or other men. She has no God-blame. Battered women are angry with abusive men. They are agitated with indifferent family, coworkers, and neighbors. They are furious with unresponsive social, law enforcement, and legal systems. They are irritated at detached or preoccupied shelter workers and unhelpful churches. They contest practices or traditions used to keep women in secondary—thus vulnerable to violence—status. They are often angry with themselves for not leaving sooner. They are not angry with God. On the contrary, many women believe they enjoy a special relationship with God, often by virtue of their very oppression.

A HERMENEUTIC OF HEALING: STRATEGIES TO SURVIVE

In this last section I would like to address themes from battered women's *hermeneutic of healing*.[8] What themes surface as women devise or discover interpretive strategies to overcome the misogynist strategies of their abusers and church? Three themes that surface with regularity concern women's connection to God, their teaching role, and punishment or justice.

WOMEN HAVE SPECIAL CONNECTIONS TO GOD

Some women are remarkably certain that they enjoy a special relationship with God. This may be due to their denominational affiliation or to a particular line of gender socialization or analysis that attributes special ways of knowing to females as sensitive, effective language-users.[9] In either case, their gender affords special lines of communication with the Godhead.

— Not everyone can speak in tongues. For my grandmother, it was a natural thing for so many years. She's the one who talks to God.

— A man just shouts when the Holy Spirit comes, when he gets a quickening. He might not speak in tongues. A woman gets the tongues.

— A woman believes more in God. They have to. They have to take so much stuff! They have to have something to hold on to. Men have each other. Men stick together. They have one another.

— [Men are not better than women spiritually.] No, men think for the day. Women think for the future. God is the reward.

— I sit in the Lord's way. One day [men] will come back to the Lord's way.

— The serpent was the male species!

— Women don't know how powerful we are! We create life. We are most logical, most creative!

— The women are closer to God. Women is more in the Word of God and a woman does more of the right things.

— Women, we are more open, free to trust. I don't know what it is. God gave us a sweet spirit. Man is the one with the problem. It's just the spirit behind men and women. Men have more of bad spirit. They have this macho attitude.

WOMEN ARE CALLED TO TEACH OTHERS

In the Women's House, some women learn or learn to reinflect traditional responsibilities to teach others about God and salvation—from a woman's point of view. If men have "wrecked . . . religion," as one woman puts it, then women can reclaim it.

— Because I am a woman, I am special and different in my thoughts and reactions. It's easy to overlook the feminine way because we focus mostly on the masculine way. I am beginning to notice things in terms of women. I used to think masculine because I live in masculine conditions. Now I struggle to educate myself and other people about women's ways.

— At night when I be praying, I say, "Forgive me! I know I done wrong!" I want to tell someone. Then when you tell that person, they tell that person, and they tell that person, and they tell that person. Then everybody knows!

— The women take part in everything: preaching, singing, special prayers. They are just like a man. They do it all. They are missionaries, women preachers. I don't believe there's anything they can't do. Women do everything. They get up and start screaming, hollering for twenty minutes and then they'll run and jump over the seats onto the pulpit. They shout everything. Everything goes with them. Same as with a man.

— Let the women teach the way they want. The religious scene would not be the same.

GOD WILL PUNISH MEN FOR THEIR MISBEHAVIOR

If men do not listen to women's teaching, if they do not learn from their praise and worship, if they continue to use church and scripture to amplify their own power, they will be punished. The suffering of battered women may not be caused or condoned by God as punishment, but justice will be rendered for abusive men—if not now, then in the afterlife.

— My abuser believes in God. He thinks he will be punished. I know he will be punished.

— I know a lot of men would be going to hell.

— But when [men] die, they are going to get it!

— In the end, he'll get his judgment. If he is guilty, God will punish him.

— They are going to hell. The Bible says not to beat your wives.

— [God] can punish in this life too.

As their words testify, shelter women bespeak different religious values and concepts than those they attribute to their abusers, churches, and faith traditions. By virtue of their gender and their oppression, women believe they enjoy a special relationship with God. They believe women are called to teach others at home, in church, and in society. Their partners and others should listen to what God says—sometimes through women. If not, they will eventually suffer.

CONCLUSION

Out of suffering, battered women sometimes fashion their own theological themes—the makings of local theology to be discussed in chapter 9. At the onset, however, such themes arise when women speak more generally about religion. Shelter women talk about God, scripture, the church, and its traditions. Some of their talk is helpful and some harmful. Some talk accommodates traditional gender socialization and the theological status quo, some resists, and some reinterprets. Overall, however, the three types of religious interpretation or hermeneutics in the conversation of battered women seems helpful to healing. Undoubtedly, it is worthwhile for women to reconsider a hermeneutic of women's identity and relationship with God, a hermeneutic of women's suffering, and a hermeneutic of women's healing. Certainly, within these three basic categories, a range of meanings is made that filters into shelter conversation. Thus, a spectrum of such ideas spurs women to consider more critically their religious belief systems in the light of their shared lived experience of gender discrimination and violence.

Rather than ascribing a simple ontological basis to their suffering, many battered women ascribe a socioreligious basis. To them, our social and religious institutions and values seem distorted or corrupted. But in a world of authentic communication with God, in a world of mutuality and reciprocity in which women and God participate in a system of exchange of offerings and services recognized by their partners, families, churches, and society, life is made right. Relations are righted, both with God and with others. To many women, this is what it means to heal from the trauma of domestic violence.

SEVEN

"Waiting on God Can Be a Hard Thing"

SUFFERING AND THE PHASES OF HEALING

———————————————

I don't like to share my feeling.

—Hilary

I have no feelings at this time!

—Louella

I pray and I try to be patient. Waiting on God can be a hard thing.

—Reetta

INTRODUCTION

One evening a week, I go to the shelter. The mostly African American and white Appalachian women and I sit down together in a quiet place.[1] The women pick a topic, we write, and we talk about what we write. The intensity of human suffering inscribed with their words or, indeed, on their bodies is sometimes staggering. I witness the words of women who have been starved, beaten, burned, raped, knifed, imprisoned, pushed from moving vehicles, dragged by their hair, stalked, swindled, drugged, poisoned, and pimped. Now and then, a woman reveals her own anger and violence. Such women write and talk about how they themselves cursed, cut, punched, and poisoned their partners; typically, these women have suffered long histories of violence—often beginning with childhood physical or sexual abuse.

Whatever their personal stories, battered women's suffering is intense, often long-enduring, and always complicated. Still, a simple question often hangs in the stressful, hurt-filled shelter air: When will this suffering end? For social change educators, mental health care providers, pastoral care workers, and others who work with them, the question becomes: How can we facilitate the healing process for battered women?

This chapter is an attempt to address such questions by examining the healing processes of battered women. In chapter 5 we explored the theodicies of battered women, that is, the ways battered women theologically explain their suffering: its sources, reasons, and resolutions. In chapter 6 we analyzed the ways battered women try to move beyond their suffering through a reconfigured religious hermeneutic of self-identity, suffering, and survival. Many women are not immediately able or willing to engage in such strategies. Initially they suffer from fear, shame, and depression. They may not even want to talk. They cannot offer statements such as those given by women who have been in shelter for some time and who have benefited from conversation in a safe environment. The same women may clearly move beyond their immediate trauma. They try to integrate their traumatic situations into a healthier self-conception. How do they arrive at such reflection from states of silence and depression?

In this chapter I will attend to the healing processes of battered women. What is the nature of suffering in the early day-to-day life of a survivor? What characterizes the road to healing? How does language reveal or indicate healing? I will examine these basic questions in this fashion: First of all, I will set the subject of healing within scholarly, therapeutic, and pastoral contexts. Several disciplines have yielded forth interesting and utile scholarship on trauma and recovery. I will touch upon the work of several writers who have considered particularly the stages of healing. I will advance the discussion of chapter 2 (which introduced the connection between abuse and depression) by looking at the work of psychologist Judith Lewis Herman. Then I will touch upon the work of literary scholar and philosopher Elaine Scarry, sociologist Trudy Mills, pastoral care worker Marie Fortune, and theologian Dorothee Soelle.

This discussion is not intended to be comprehensive. I intend to be suggestive of the paradigms that shape domestic violence literature and caregiving theory and practice. Ultimately, I will turn my attention to the work of Dorothee Soelle, a German theologian. To clarify my intention: I wish to cast this discussion in theological terms because this is the language of choice of many shelter women. Clearly, the findings of mental health care providers on healing are immensely useful—indeed, critical for the practice of therapists and beneficial to the well-being of survivors. However, the theological imagination is the focus of my study and it ensues from the religious perspectives of battered women. Most battered women do not seek the help of mental health caregivers; instead, they talk to family, friends, or pastoral care providers. As we have seen, they often cast their dilemma in the discourse of religion and spirituality.

So the second task, and one of my main tasks in this chapter, will be to examine women's words through the lens of Soelle's phases of suffering and healing. There are three phases: isolation and silence, lamentation and anger, and solidarity and action. The beauty of this schema is its utter simplicity and clarity. There is a seeable road to recovery. Additionally, the schema is a relational one—thoroughly imbued with a sense of social contexts. I will critique and augment Soelle's schema with observations about healing in the shelter. The discussion will be grounded in the words of battered women as they move from phase to phase or back-and-forth within phases during their shelter stay. The next chapter, chapter 8, will analyze more delicately the way women are able to move from one healing phase to the next healing phase.

INTERDISCIPLINARY PERSPECTIVES ON HEALING

Across disciplines, scholars consider the process of healing. In what follows I will briefly sketch out theories of healing from trauma from several disciplines, including those of Judith Lewis Herman, Elaine Scarry, Trudy Mills, Marie Fortune, and Dorothee Soelle. These writers are representative of schools of thought within their disciplines, not exemplary of their entire fields. Aspects of their schemas are similar, but their basic perspectives or language sometimes differs significantly.

PSYCHOLOGY: JUDITH LEWIS HERMAN

In *Trauma and Recovery*, therapist and teacher Judith Lewis Herman is concerned with survivors of incest and childhood trauma. She sometimes refers to domestic violence, and though she writes primarily for therapists, her work has been widely influential in the battered women's movement.[2] Herman charts three stages of recovery for patients. Patients must establish a sense of safety, reconstruct the trauma story, and restore the connection between themselves and their community. The stages are recursive: A patient may revisit stages as she moves through the healing process.

The first stage, however, is critical to attain before any other work can be accomplished. Beset with terror, the trauma victim needs to find *a sense of safety* from harm. With the therapist as facilitator, she must regain a sense of control over her body and her environment. Essentially, she must have a safe place to live and she must have supportive relationships. Then the victim works with the therapist to restore a sense of power and control over her own life.

Second, the patient needs to engage in a process of *remembering and mourning*. She must give up the wordless nature of traumatic memory and replace it with testimony about her suffering. The therapist, as witness or ally, helps her to construct an interpretation that allows her to fully integrate the trauma into her life narrative. The victim mourns the loss of fantasies about relationships, including fantasies of revenge or premature forgiveness of the abuser.

Third, the trauma victim needs to *reconnect with the community*. In the second stage, there is no address of the social dimensions of the trauma. The primary task was introspection. In this third stage the survivor looks outward. She begins to fight for herself. For example, she may confront her family or challenge indifferent bystanders. She builds new relationships. In essence, she builds a new self, one that learns how to control fear and to move toward building relationships of mutuality and intimacy. A "significant minority" sees the political or religious dimensions of their suffering and make it a basis for social action.[3] For Herman, social action can be educational, legal or political involvement—a "survivor mission." It may be "pursuing justice" through attempts to hold perpetrators accountable for crimes. Like Marie Fortune, Herman guardedly offers the idea that forgiveness involves the victimizer's confession, repentance, and restitution. Recovery is never complete, but empowerment and connection replace isolation and helplessness. Self-esteem is rebuilt. The survivor begins to celebrate life.

Judith Lewis Herman's work reshaped the study of violence against women. She searched for and found coherent patterns and meaning in the frequently stigmatized experience of women's trauma. Though mental health professionals may quibble with aspects of her schema—for example, the difficulty of providing a sense of safety for the victim before providing a sense of solidarity or the dubious merits of designating forgiveness as a last step in recovery—Herman has influenced a generation of scholars and therapists. Further, and in no small feat, she offers hope to victims by providing a perspective on—thus a road through—recovery.

LITERARY STUDIES AND PHILOSOPHY: ELAINE SCARRY

Unmaking

In *The Body in Pain*, Elaine Scarry offers an account of the structure of torture and war. Her approach to evil phenomena, however, has found applicability across the disciplines. It offers an approach to physical violence against women, particularly prolonged severe brutality such as in some cases of domestic violence—a species of torture. The infliction of pain in torture is an inhuman act, Scarry argues, because it leads to the *unmaking* of human reality through grotesque, excruciating pain. Intense pain is world-destroying. The victim becomes all body as the psychological content of her mind—that which constitutes her self and her world—is obliterated (35). The perception of physical facts in her mind is destroyed. The trauma of torture, the annihilating power of pain, leaves the victim unable to create meaning. It demolishes language. The victim can only make inhuman groans and cries. It is the unmaking of her world.

The torturer, on the other hand, experiences a growing sense of self based on the infliction of pain. The victim's shrinking world is his enlarging world. His power grows. He is voice and expanding self; the victim is expanding body and annihilated self. He has no sense of responsibility outside of a sense of duty to inflict pain for some agency, for example, the regime he represents and its ideology. This frees him to objectify, deny, and destroy the victim. He makes her undoing his growth of agency, identity, and power. These events may be likened, in some limited but definite sense, to the silencing of a domestic violence victim by her abuser and the precipitating of her loss of self through repeated acts of degradation and brutality.

Making

Scarry's exploration of the unmaking of the world leads to an inquiry into the *making* of a victim's world when atrocity ends. The voice of the victim can be restored, particularly through the vehicle of the voice of a sympathetic other. If the pain is articulated, if it is brought into the world, it may be diminished and dissipated. A sympathetic voice can provide the hurt person with a self-extension. That is, the victim's pain can be expressed even when she cannot do it herself. One human being becomes the image of the hurt other. This is one way the loss of voice can be recovered. Scarry does not delineate specific stages of recovery; instead, she undertakes a phenomenological exploration of the process. Of interest, however, to this discussion are the two discernable aspects of making–that is, *making up* and *making real*.

Making Up

Recall that, in the unmaking stage, the infliction of pain forces the victim into a state of prelanguage. Pain unmakes language. It destroys the world by destroying reference to the world, by making the body the sole existent and its own enemy. The victim feels her body, not the weapon upon it. At the other end of the spectrum—its extreme—is imagination. When the victim is released from physical pain, she can engage in mental imagining. She can remember and reference the world. She can engage in *making up*. When her body ceases to be an object of concern, then she can extend her consciousness. She is able to imagine objects, relations, the world.

Making Real

In *making real*, the survivor endows the object of imagination with a material or verbal form. She opens into a wider frame: invention. She articulates her pain, for example, and has the ability once again to find, make, and endow with significance objects in the world through images, words, and ideas. She can self-express and self-extend. She can modify her relations. In this phase, the victim can offer counterfactual revisions of the traumatic event she suffered. There is a redescription of the trauma in her own terms. She is able to reconstruct her world.

Although Scarry is concerned about the inhumanity of political torture and the analogue between torture and nuclear war, her work is relevant to other discussions of pain, suffering, and trauma. Domestic violence victims go through stages of silencing, alienation, rediscovering their voices, and recreating their identities and worlds. Interestingly, Scarry's schema has been critiqued for its basic "Christian existentialist morality."[4] This would not seem to be a disadvantage for the many battered women or their advocates who look to Christian paradigms to understand pain and suffering. Additionally, by underscoring the critical need for reinterpreting and giving voice to traumatic experience, Scarry's schema sheds significant light on the recovery process for women who hold out hope for some sense of justice in the public forum.

A SOCIOLOGICAL VIEW: FIVE STEPS FROM VIOLENCE TO RECOVERY

For sociologist Trudy Mills, domestic violence victimization is a gradual process. It includes five steps. The woman enters a violent relationship, manages the violence, experiences a loss of self, reevaluates the violent relationship, and restructures the self.[5] Mills's schema was devised twenty years ago, but this sort of schema has proven useful in counseling or self-help sessions. It offers the opportunity for women to explore with integrity the reasons they stayed in an abusive relationship for any length of time before they finally fled—a situation for which they are often berated by those people who do not understand the economic, religious, and other cultural pressures battered women face. Most women try for a time to keep the family together. Later, they feel ashamed or, especially if they have children, guilt-ridden. Friends and strangers alike aggravate the situation by not acknowledging or comprehending the obstacles.

Second, the schema addresses the day-to-day management of domestic violence. This is a survival issue since shelter women often return to abusive relationships, perhaps multiple times, before the final break. Indeed, Women's House staff and volunteers are instructed to let residents make up their own minds about whether they wish to return to the relationships. If violence starts, women can minimize injury. They are taught by staff to always be prepared (with bags, keys, documents, and so forth) to flee the house and seek temporary shelter or to call police immediately when violence begins. Such strategies could be lifesaving.

Of particular interest to this discussion, however, are Mills's thoughts on the last three steps: the loss of self, the reevaluation of the violent relationship, and the restructuring the self. In the stage of *self* or *identity loss*, Mills argues, the victim gives up identities without taking on new ones; meanwhile, the woman's remaining roles or identities are undermined by the abuser. For example, the woman may give up her identity as a friend, student, sibling, and so forth to placate her partner. There is a loss of the *observing self*—the one that authentically knows and feels without an abuser's coercion, resulting in the victim's confusion and isolation. Many women, numb and confused, may not be able to manage the escalating violence.

In the stage of the *re-evaluating of the violent relationship*, the woman experiences contradictions from the disjunction between her own and her partner's definition of the situation. With outside validation, and some specific triggering event, the woman begins to conceive the situation as unacceptable. The triggering event allows the victim finally to perceive the violence as unallowable or unsustainable. She breaks through habitual ways of dealing with it.

In the stage of *restructuring the self*, the woman begins to understand herself as either a victim or a survivor. This conceptual move allows her to take action on her own behalf. She recalls memories of her own strength and she establishes a support network to validate a new sense of self. This is particularly true if she self-identifies as a survivor rather than a victim.

Accurately, Mills notes the stages are "ideal types." She writes that, "while the stages are chronological, not all women go through all the stages. Furthermore, a woman may reach a stage and then return to an earlier stage" (105). My own research on the language practices of battered women confirms this recursiveness. However, although Mills acknowledges the social self— roles, identities, and so forth—the social context is not well integrated into the structure of healing. The schema ultimately emphasizes the individual: A woman enters a violent relationship. She must reevaluate the relationship. She must restructure the self. Such steps are not inaccurate; yet, one may be tempted to think the woman is the responsible party. She enters and must extract herself from a limited intimate situation—with perhaps little help from her friends. One may be tempted to forget the pervasive social aspects

152 THE LANGUAGE OF BATTERED WOMEN

and structural elements, the social construction of gender, and the ideologically saturated context within which sexism and oppression are normalized and violence is socially energized and culturally accepted.

Thus, a related and more specific shortcoming of Mills's schema—at least for the analysis and benefit of Women's House residents, is its entirely secular nature. It does not account for the ideologies shot through male-female relations, including religiously based ones. So it cannot easily handle complications and contradictions like the damage caused by patriarchal religion as well as the strength women gain from their faith in order to secure "survivor" status.

The Church and Pastoral Care Giving: Marie Fortune

Christianity is a primary source of patriarchal ideology and, institutionally, it has not adequately addressed the consequent problems it creates for women. Feminists fought for years to force the church to even recognize domestic violence as a significant social issue. It still refuses to recognize the depth of its own complicity. Pastoral counseling training in seminaries often disarms feminist analysis of battery by adopting a clinical discourse that ultimately blames the victim. For example, the term *codependency* was long used to cast domestic violence as a dynamic in which both partners contribute to intimate violence. The woman could not bring herself to leave and eventually might suffer from post-traumatic stress disorder—a more current therapeutic diagnosis—in which fear and confusion compromise survival measures.[6] Yet it is ultimately ineffectual, perhaps even harmful or dangerous, to rely on purely therapeutic approaches because they tend to focus on how the woman needs to change.[7] As historian Linda Gordon suggests, psychological approaches implicate individuals rather than social structures.[8] Predictably, forgiveness is the last step of healing[9]—a potentially dangerous prospect for women who have forgiven their abusers time and again in the face of escalating danger.

Marie Fortune, a United Church minister, is a well-known figure in the field of pastoral care of battered women. She has done pioneering work in bringing particularly the perspectives of middle-class battered women to the attention of the church. Her work is imbued with Christian values. Healing begins with an acknowledgment that harm has been done: the victim confronts, the abuser confesses. Second, the abuser must demonstrate repentance and changed behavior. Third, the abuser must make restitution to those whom he has injured. This may include, for example, paying for damages or for the victim's therapy. Forgiveness, the last step, is a means of restoration to wholeness for the battered woman. Confession, repentance, restitution, forgiveness: this is traditional Christian language for overcoming sin and evil.

Notice the agency in these steps is realized largely by the abuser. If the abuser is not present for these steps in the process, the therapist stands in so the woman can tell her story and receive validation. Fortune advocates pastoral encounters, including treatment, therapy, conversion, and mediation (in appropriate cases). Only the first and last steps involve the agency of the victim. The last step, forgiveness, revolves exclusively around her agency. She is asked to confront and forgive, both highly risky actions for a victim of intimate violence though Fortune does emphasize preliminaries, such as the cessation of violence and the accomplishment of justice, "even in a limited way."[10] Of the four steps, the two middle steps are transformative for the abuser—if he engages at all. If he does not, a proxy might appear in the guise of the therapist. Healing is cast as a relational issue between an abuser and his victim.

As a pastoral worker, Fortune, however, does recognize the role of faith in a woman's recovery. She calls on victims to use their strength and the help of others to move away from violence. She calls on victims to recognize their responsibility to care for themselves with God's help instead of passively waiting for God to protect them. Finally, she calls on victims to have hope and a passion for justice. They are invited to reject injustice and act.[11]

DOROTHEE SOELLE, FEMINIST THEOLOGY

WHAT DOES SUFFERING MEAN?

One contention of my study is that, contrary to the starting point offered by some theologians and pastoral care workers, battered women typically do not question why they suffer. They know why they suffer and they wonder why their suffering is not adequately addressed by the people and the institutions able to offer support and relief. If religious, they wonder why scripture is used against them by individuals and by church institutions.

Elisabeth Schussler Fiorenza, Elizabeth Johnson, Marie Fortune, Emilie Townes, and Lisa Sowle Cahill—to name just a few—have written about the role of the church in women's suffering. For example, Elisabeth Schussler Fiorenza believes that male violence is caused by men's need for patriarchal control and their jealousy. Because the church is a stronghold of patriarchal control, Fiorenza believes women must work for church reform.[12] Some theologians shift attention away from the causes of suffering—theodicy—toward the meaning of it. Herman, Scarry, and Mills offer secular attempts to explain the meaning of suffering by examining victims' experience as they try to survive and overcome it.

In pursuit of its spiritual meaning, feminist theologian Elizabeth Johnson elucidates two types of suffering: the consequence of freely chosen action and the consequence of inflicted personal degradation. The suffering of the person who knows she will experience retaliation for working for social justice is different from the involuntarily experienced suffering of the person who knows she will experience random or unjustifiable violence by an abusive spouse.[13] Marie Fortune concurs though she still believes battered women blame God in some way.[14]

In the work of Fiorenza, Johnson, Townes, and Cahill, there is great sensitivity to the social, systemic nature of violence against women and the way social injustice becomes inscribed or embodied in women's bruised flesh. They know that domestic violence is a matter of male aggression in the interests of maintaining power and control: both personal and societal or structural. Their theological reflections confirm the practical and intuitive wisdom of battered women who know that patriarchal control of their bodies, their pocketbooks, and their churches causes a great deal of their suffering.

Feminist theologian Dorothee Soelle offers a discussion in *Suffering* with extraordinary applicability.[15] She looks for meaning in the language of victims of involuntary suffering, mostly Holocaust victims. Soelle sees three phases of response: a silent phase, a lament phase, and an active phase. Her framework for the stages of suffering is not unlike the frameworks particularly of Judith Lewis Herman, Trudy Mills, and Elaine Scarry.[16] But Soelle's framework is developed with sensitivity toward victims' spiritual dilemma. She attends to their religious imagination. For this reason, her perspective is very amenable to our purposes.

How Do Battered Women Talk through Suffering?

Three Phases of Suffering

Language reflects, if imperfectly, community and culturally influenced interpretations of external circumstances, internal states, changing perceptions. Not surprisingly, then, battered women's language changes as they move through the healing process. In some respects, the language change *is* the healing process. Because language communicates slight nuances of meaning, it is sometimes ambiguous, contradictory, and polysemic. The world of shelter women is itself transitional, intense, shifting, and uncertain. Residents come and go; new discourses are introduced, encouraged, or discouraged. The women's language is reflective of this shifting, changing state. In addition to every other sort of upheaval—the loss of her partner and perhaps her children, home, and job, a battered woman experiences a sort of linguistic upheaval as well. She is trying to sort through and name a raw crisis experience.

I would like to address these shifting language practices of battered women and their possible meanings. In particular, I would like to consider Soelle's phases of suffering in relation to these language changes. I find it beneficial to use, emend, and add to Soelle's schema. In what follows, I will present her category or phase, my emendations, and the language of battered women that exemplifies each phase. There are further correspondences to the schemas of Herman, Scarry, Mills, and Fortune that I intend to point out as I illustrate the actual language of shelter residents. There is a purpose to this project. Our social reality is largely constituted by language; hence, language practices both mirror and mitigate the state of suffering. To begin to understand these practices is to begin to address the lived experience of battered women.

Phase One: Silence and Isolation

In the most intense phase of suffering, argues Soelle, the sufferer cannot articulate her pain in language. Language is destroyed. Pain and suffering crush it. The victim is silent. She is isolated from others—unable to relate. The pressure of suffering turns the sufferer into herself. Her feelings may be numbed. Concurrently, she may experience periods of explosive feelings. In the throes of intense psychological (and/or even physical) pain, she may engage in moaning or animal-like wailing. The sufferer of domestic violence is psychologically dominated by her situation and, hence, she may retain such reactive behavior for some time after she leaves her partner. She cannot organize her own objectives. Ultimately, she feels powerlessness. She believes her personal autonomy of thinking, speaking, and acting is lost.

Soelle's first phase prefigures the work of Elaine Scarry. As you recall, Scarry argues that intense suffering cannot be expressed in language. Terrible pain wrecks language wholly, turning it into silence, or rerendering its expression as preverbal cries.

I agree. I have seen battered women lying motionlessly, almost catatonic-like, on common room couches or in their beds, unable or unwilling to talk about what has happened to them. They physically or psychologically re-move themselves from others, hiding in their rooms or walking through public spaces without responding or responding fully to overtures to talk. In group sessions—if indeed they are willing or able to be present at all—they do not speak. They might leave abruptly or prematurely. If they stay, they watch and listen and sometimes they weep silently. Other times, they can be heard to cry themselves to sleep at night.

Most women who come to the shelter, however, are moving beyond Phase One suffering. They gathered enough courage to get out of the isola-tion typical of abuse situations—frequently motivated by fear for themselves, their children, or even their partners. Later they may recount that they were afraid they might be killed, they might kill their partner themselves in an act of anger or self-defense, or their children might be physically or psychologi-cally injured. They flee the relationship and seek to establish safety for them-selves and their children.

Indeed a woman, especially a woman with children, is, in some sense, not allowed to succumb completely to the void and darkness of Phase One internal states. A mother knows she must keep herself as intact as she can in order to care for her children. Later, battered women repeatedly refer to the needs of their children when they reflect back on their own survival and recovery processes. At the Women's House, residents will often tell me how they prayed and prayed for God's help to keep from falling apart completely and to protect them and their children. Not infrequently, they interpret shelter services as the divine answer to their immediate crisis, a proof of divine providence.

This is getting ahead of the story, however. When she first enters the shelter, a Phase One domestic violence survivor often is not especially inclined to communicate with others. But she is invited (indeed, strongly encouraged) by staff and other residents to enter into the social stream of shelter life. For the woman who is still reeling from injury and loss, this is not easy. She may show evidence of hopelessness, meaninglessness, and depression. Her language may be somewhat incoherent, fragmented, or inchoate: at least, this is how it might appear to staff or more stable residents. But, of course, this is a woman who has been trying to rationalize or repress her battery experience and she has not had time to restructure her memories for shelter consumption. In fact, as Trudy Mills notes, there is loss of selfhood: Not only can the victim not easily imagine herself as a human agent apart from her partner, but she cannot easily construct or recall a self, a past, or a future outside the narrow confines of the abusive relationship. There may also be an inability or an unwillingness to perceive her abuse as a problem of ontological, social, or structural origins. That is, she cannot easily entertain the idea that her partner is the person with the problem or that his problem might extend from social, cultural, and institutional systems. Indeed, the Phase One survivor cannot easily analyze her situation at all. She is in the grips of terrible pain and it diminishes analytical thinking or rational discourse. The pain simply is. It is nearly all there is.

The storytelling sessions I hold at the shelter yield plenty of traces of Phase One experience. The following exchange between Lynn, Mary Jo, and Pam took place during a storytelling session. Together the women are rehearsing the dynamics of the suffering of Phase One. Notice that these are recollections or reflections of the battered women's Phase One internal states (that is, of mind or feeling) while they were being abused.

LYNN: We talked about that last week. That part of you that says, "This is cool. This isn't cool." We numb that—when you first start getting abused.

MARY JO: Man, it feel[s] like a dream. When am I gonna wake up? It feels like I'm sleeping and when am I gonna wake up from this bad dream?

PAM: This is really depressing me right now. I'm, I'm just being honest with you. You know, we live the nightmare, and it's—it's depressing.

Lynn, Mary Jo, and Pam are recalling and interpreting their experience. Their capacity to share in conversation indicates that they have moved beyond this particular phase. They are actually in Phase Two and they are remembering their Phase One experience: their loss of agency, their numbed emotions, their inability or unwillingness (for reasons of survival) to reason. Both Pam and Mary Jo liken Phase One to sleep, a dream or trancelike state. Pam names it "the nightmare." This is a depressive state akin to what Soelle describes as the "drowsy stupor" experienced in extreme suffering, such as in concentration camp life.[17]

In a private interview, Phebe also recalls a performance of Phase One dynamics. She says, "One time my husband put a pillow on my face and didn't take it off until I played dead. My husband isolated me. He knew I had no family in the area. I completely relied on him." At first glance, it would appear Phebe had largely lost her agency or autonomy as Soelle and others would suggest of early trauma victims. In my interpretation, however, Phebe (like the woman with children who knows she needs to survive and takes steps to do so) does use agency, her own intelligence and cunning, to survive her partner's life-threatening attack. She had to play dead to live. She knew she needed to escape and, even without family to help, she did manage to escape.

Thus, for many if not most battered women, the suffering of Phase One must include respites, revivals, or periods of increasing and subsiding agency. It may include decisions about the performance of agency, its relinquishment or resurgence, according to the exigencies of the moment. I believe few battered women ever relinquish their agency in its totality. To do so would be to invite certain death. Instead, battered women must hide their own autonomy or agency, deny, or subsume it—until they are finally unwilling or unable to continue to do so in the interest of their own survival. Then they leave or sometimes they die. Death from domestic battery—which claims thousands of victims worldwide each year—is the ultimate loss of human agency.

Even without enduring death-dealing blows, even in the throes of a survival performance, women forfeit parts of autonomous selves to survive violence. The experience of serious, prolonged pain takes its toll on those women who flee to the shelter. Fortunately, by virtue of communal life in the shelter, they are challenged to articulate their suffering. This is movement toward asserting their full autonomy.

Phase Two: Lamentation

In Soelle's view, the Phase Two sufferer has become more aware. She actually experiences her own autonomy. She can perceive her suffering as arising from a specific situation and she can analyze the situation. Being more aware, she is able to speak, to communicate, to express her suffering. In her expression, rationality and emotion are communicated together. She laments; that is, she expresses sorrow, sadness, mourning. She also uses psalmic language—a language both of lament and of praise and worship of God—because theological expression becomes possible after the silence or muteness of Phase One. In prayer her objectives are utopian. She may wish God would rescue her from her sorrows; yet, in day-to-day life, she seeks acceptance of her situation and the conquest of it through existing social structures. She has begun to integrate her experiences into her own sense of selfhood. Ultimately, in Soelle's view, the sufferer needs language in order to change. The Phase Two sufferer has come to voice.

Battered women do exhibit features of Soelle's Phase Two. At the shelter, they try to bring to language the tribulations, the injustices, the outrages they often previously endured in silence or expressed only with fear for their safety. If they were battered women who "fought back" either verbally or physically, their language and other actions were accompanied always with anger or dread; that is, with compromised senses of agency.

There are qualifications. When battered women move out of the isolation of a violent relationship and the attendant confusion and alienation of Phase One suffering, they do not move linearly to autonomy. Instead, throughout the healing process, most women will move recursively or cyclically through periods of greater and lesser autonomy and lucidity. Previously they hid from public gaze. Now they move rapidly through periods in which their ability or desire for public self-assertion, autonomy, and selfhood fluctuates.

Further, they gain autonomy by attending to relationality; that is, they must relate to others to see that they themselves have a unique selfhood worth others' attention. In short, the language must be language addressed to other people. It must be witnessed. Further, it must be heard sympathetically, responded to, and shaped by its successful reception. It must be shaped by a give-and-take characterized by varying degrees of autonomy, diversity, creativity, vision, or aspiration. Soelle argues that the communication must take place within the context of a group of people who share their lives, including their suffering, with one another. This is an astute observation; at the same time, however, the language needs to involve transaction. Soelle believes that the sufferer must herself put her suffering into words. Unlike in Scarry's schema, no one can speak for the battered woman. This is commonsensically true, but the interaction must be genuine interaction, dynamic, dialogic. In fact, I will explore this idea in detail in the next chapter. It does indeed matter "where they find the language or what form it takes."[18] Soelle does not believe it matters.

As Soelle concedes, however, the basic form of the language of the Phase Two sufferer is psalmic language or lament. Her own definition of the language of lament is thus: it emphasizes one's own righteousness or innocence; it laments, petitions, or expresses hope. Further, it is painful. It can initially intensify suffering. But it is not toned down or humble. Rather it is direct and straightforward. In theological terms, the language of lamentation includes features not only of complaint, but of praise, worship, and even divine retribution. In the Old Testament Book of Job, Job struggles with ideas of retribution in the face of his own perceived innocence.[19] These features do indeed appear in the language of shelter women. Depending on context, there may be a change of tone or emphasis on one or more the features. The following are examples of shelter women speaking in the language of lament:

CHRIS: The Bible says the meek will inherit the earth and ladies we know this is not true!

LORA: Some men try to use what happened in the Bible to justify what they do to you!

MARIANNE: God shelters us women!

KARA: I said to myself, "I'm God's child. I don't need to have abuse. I need a ride out of here with me and my children."

To move beyond Soelle's insights about the language of Phase Two: In these laments, shelter women distinguish clearly between the work of God and the workings of the patriarchy. These laments name their reality, an inequitable world wherein men profit from, for example, the misuse of scripture. Further, the women's language of lamentation is a staple of their stories.

In acts of storytelling, women reclaim their own anger, sometimes expressed as a desire for retaliatory violence for the devastation they now easily see as caused by their partners. In this phase, the survivor perceives the partner's behavior in sociopsychological terms, as dysfunctional socialization, or in religious terms as an ontological issue or as personal sin. One day a woman said, "If God were a woman, it would be wonderful! I know a lot of men would be going to hell!" In the following utterances, the women admit feelings of vengeance and anger.

LYNN: You have every right to hate this person for what he did. I was afraid of killing somebody.

MARY JO: Did you ever think about burning the bed? I thought about that many times.

ANNIE: You think about everything you could do to 'em.

WANDA: It might be very disturbing, but it's very normal.

ANNIE: I'd think he's gonna get old and I'd cut his goddamn throat.

In their exchange, Mary Jo, Annie, Lynn, and Wanda admit to their overwhelming feelings of anger. The anger brings them together and draws them out of their sleep. It awakens them and, as they relive their experiences together in the act of storytelling, they are able to experience the attendant feelings as righteous anger. Annie is no longer guilt-ridden about her rage; instead, she sees it as the last (and functional) straw. Like many other women, she would not stay because she began to be afraid that she would kill her partner.

Rose evokes the anger she feels toward the abusive partner who beat her and molested her daughter for years. In the following passage, she recalls the anger—at one time a murderous rage because she wanted to kill her husband for sexually abusing their daughter—to call other women out of their denial, their slumber, their avoidance of the issue of violence against women.

> I coulda been on death row. I could have and it wasn't that far away because my daughter was bleeding out of her rectum. [. . .] The only thing I could say was, "Lord have mercy. You've been killing my child!" Then I had to look at her when she asked me, "Mama,"—she's twenty-one years old now—"You were my mother. Why didn't you know?" Wake up ladies. Wake up. He bad.

Rose is able to evoke anger; then she uses its evocation as a call to action. She is moving into the third phase of suffering.

Phase Three: Solidarity and Action

The woman in Soelle's third phase of suffering has radically changed. Unlike the Phase One sufferer, she is not rendered ineffective by the sheer brutality of the suffering and, unlike the Phase Two sufferer, she is not rendered less effective by her strong reactions against it. Instead, according to Soelle, the pressure of her suffering now results in solidarity. She can organize: that is, her objectives can be organized. She uses rational language. Finally, she experiences an autonomy of action that produces change. She engages in active behavior as she helps to shape or reshape her situation. She accepts the reality of her situation, but she seeks to conquer it through changed social or personal structures. Prayer has had a role in this healing process for prayer is a subversive process that "allows people to handle their suffering differently from the way society recommends to them."[20]

In my work, I note some variations in the basic contours suggested by Soelle's schema. First, Phase Two language draws battered women into Phase Three language. One is not suddenly in solidarity or rational. Instead the sufferer is drawn forward slowly into solidarity by small negotiations in conversation. The pressure of the solitary suffering of the woman with a black eye and a lacerated face does not produce solidarity. The release of suffering comes from satisfaction about being heard and understood, of giving and taking: an evolution of empathy. The confirmation of self even in the state of transition brings a sense of solidarity.

Further, for Phase Three shelter women, rational language must give way to an imaginative, creative language with social, communal, and political dimensions. Indeed, rational language must be understood to entail affective and imaginative elements. This creativity regards their senses of self, other, and God. As such, it speaks to both their autonomy and their relationality. The sufferer must have hope and vision even in the midst of pain and suffering. The creativity is not necessarily or primarily characterized by reason; it is characterized by its open-endedness, its possibility and spontaneity. This transformation begins with talk, with storytelling, as battered women's initial distrust of strangers and outsiders turns into trust in sister kin, allies, and friends. The need for autonomy transforms into a need for critical interdependence, that is, for reciprocity and mutuality between themselves and other women. A loose sense of relationality extends and deepens to a sense of commonalty and compassion with others. Many third phase women begin to see how their individual well-being is related to the social good, the social well-being, of all womankind. In short, the frightful first phase loss of selfhood transforms into a willingness to give of oneself, to make a gift of self to others as long as it does not compromise one's own integrity. In theological terms, it signals a widening of referentiality; women see their suffering as related to the suffering of particularly other women and girl children.

With specific regard to their abusive partners, some Phase Three battered women can sometimes feel forgiveness without a need to be in relationships with them. Here forgiveness means that they have a desire for the well-being of their abusers—a desire that does not include reconstituting the relationship. The women can begin to feel forgiveness because they can now perceive their partners' behavior in terms of its nature as a social depravity or a structural, systemic issue. The Phase Two desire for conquest (a will for "power-over" a situation) has become a desire for affinity with (a will for "power-with") others—particularly others who suffer. Their language is less psalmic, more prophetic. Third phase survivors of domestic violence have been able to transform fear and anger into hope and joy. In its expression it is often cast in religious or prophetic tones. Mary says, "One day [men] will come back to the Lord's way! In a spiritual way, God brings justice—now or later in life!"

Many shelter women will not wait. They want to help usher in their idea of the kingdom—that is, social transformation—now. They experience their changing self as a grounded identity, directed toward political action—however minor it may appear—for societal change. After having benefited from its resources, many shelter women express a desire to work for the battered women's movement. Others attend "Take Back the Night" walks or other local events. A few women confront their pastoral care workers about the poor advice that, fortunately, the women did not heed. Nearly all shelter women express an understanding of the need to work for social, structural change. Patricia expresses the feeling concisely: "We should have a Million Lady Walk!" The following are excerpts from storytelling sessions. Note the evidence of Phase Three language, in particular, a fuller sense of self, a sense of social connection with others, and a willingness to take action for social change:

EMMA: I was hearing and seeing the idea I had from God in what [my shelter friend] said to me. After that, I had such a great confidence. I refuse to become someone I am not. I am a trusting person. I like who I am. I like being friendly. I must be gentle, but wise. [. . .] I got to share [my story] with my sister and I got to rejoice. I told her how I was strengthened by it and how I had grown and seen myself grow. . . . And from where I was—not truly caring!

SHARON: I would wish for world peace. I would wish for my kids to be educated and grow up to be very sweet and caring and good young men. I would wish to be a person who can reach out and touch other people's minds. Oh Father . . . bless my wishes!

VANESSA: [In five years, I want to be] working in the social work field, helping others achieve their goals, helping families stay together through struggling times, and assisting them in any way possible with the red tape in our system. To see smiles on faces, instead of desperation and no hope. [Helping] broken spirited persons will give me joy and [make me] eager to get up to go to work.

These women have reached a frame of mind quite different from their earlier (Phase One and Two) selves. They are speaking a different kind of language—one with reference to others, with vision, and with hope. Emma encodes the distance she has traveled by way of her last emphatic statement: "And from where I was—not truly caring!" Vanessa sees her former self in the desperate faces of the families she envisions she will help. Sharon imagines a violence-free world, locates herself in it instead of alienated and outside of it, and positions herself within caring and influential proximity to others. These are changed women in a changed world.[21]

CONCLUSION

The scholars we discussed in this chapter—Judith Herman, Elaine Scarry, Trudy Mills, Marie Fortune, and Dorothee Soelle—have more or less impacted the battered women's movement and the literature on domestic violence. Aspects of their descriptions of the healing process of trauma survivors are similar. The schemas are from different disciplines so their focus, language, and basic perspectives differ, sometimes significantly. All are useful. Indeed, as trauma studies continue to mature, we will see further cross-disciplinary discussions of the healing process.

Applied to domestic violence survivors who conceive their dilemma in religious or spiritual terms, Soelle's schema is particularly useful. She knows the far-reaching effects of concepts of God in religious practices such as prayer, liturgy, and petition. She recognizes the role of religious language—of prayer, lament, psalm, and prophecy—in the language of sufferers. Soelle also recognizes healing as a function of language practice. She focuses on women as central agents in their own healing process. She recognizes the radical shifts necessary to end suffering. These shifts may involve crossing boundaries of class and of religion.[22] That is, she sees (though she does not develop) the importance of dialogic activity that moves beyond cultural expectations of "normal" religious activity, "normal" social activity.

Other schemas, such as the ones of Judith Lewis Herman, Elaine Scarry, Trudy Mills, and Marie Fortune, contribute greatly to our understanding of different aspects of the healing process. Judith Lewis Herman, a prominent contributor to the women's movement, contributes to a fuller understanding of the psychological processes at work. Herman knows fully well the importance of safety and of connection. She particularly values the role of memory and mourning—staples of shelter storytelling. Trudy Mills involves us in the fact of the gradualness of the process of victimization. Elaine Scarry's emphasis on the phenomenology of suffering and pain compels us to recognize the nearly incalculable distance which battered women must travel, the challenges they must face, in order to "make up" and "make real" a new world. Marie Fortune shows us the importance of religion in women's lives in this process. Dorothee Soelle, of course, straightforwardly acknowledges the radical revision necessary in church and society for a religious worldview to be a force for justice.

A word of forbearance, however: In my experience, some shelter women do enter wholly into the late stages of such healing schemas as those we have examined. Many more women are not able to do so within the relatively short period of time in which they are allowed to stay in the shelter (approximately six weeks). Some women simply do enter into Phase Three language and action. Still women may enter it provisionally and, as they become aware of other hitherto unreckoned dimensions of their abuse, fall back into the earlier phases only to sometimes reemerge into Phase Three conceptualization again some time later.

This is why an opportunity for storytelling—indeed, any continuing opportunity for community—is so critically important. Language is a key factor in the healing of battered women. Some women may be able to experience aspects of third phase thinking, and sometimes enter more fully into it, if only other women beckon them. By hearing one another's stories, battered women invite one another to heal. For this reason, I will to look directly and in-depth to show how it is possible for women—sharing anguish, fear, and much more—to imagine new identities, new relations, new futures. In the Women's House, it happens. Jebba succinctly names it while her new friend, Raylene, concurs: "We laugh together, we cry together, we support each other, we strengthen each other every day."

EIGHT

"The Prayer of the Righteous Prevaileth Much"

LANGUAGE CHANGE AND HEALING

I feel relieved when someone listens to me—like my life voyage has
a hidden message for them. I've learned a lot of things the hard way
and maybe they won't make the same mistake as me.

—Henrietta

INTRODUCTION

A white woman of Appalachian ethnicity, Alice Clare, tells me the horrendous story of ten years of marriage with an abusive partner. How did she
survive all those years of hurt and humiliation? How did she survive the
slaps, shoves, and beatings? "I was always in prayer," says Alice Clare. "The
prayer of the righteous prevaileth much. I kept the faith." I admire her
strength and resourcefulness and I am dismayed by the role of religion in
keeping women in states of suffering and oppression. When Alice Clare
came to the Women's House, she showed the signs of ten years of abuse. She
was silent and withdrawn. Initially she did not interact with other women
and, mostly, she stayed in her room. Then Edwina came to the shelter to flee
the father of her children. By the time Alice Clare left for her sister's house
in eastern Kentucky, she had made friends with Edwina and other residents.
She sought legal advice about her domestic situation. She came to our story-
sharing group and spoke. She even went to church on Sundays with Edwina
and a few other women. Edwina drew Alice Clare out in a way the staff and

volunteers did not do. It was an unlikely friendship: Alice Clare, a skinny middle-aged white Appalachian stay-at-home wife without children, and Edwina, a robust young African American high school drop-out with two children who worked as a grocery clerk. In the end, they helped one another heal. Edwina's words reveal the delicacy, the compassion, with which she approached Alice Clare and other residents: "In the shelter, you have others and their feelings. What kind of feelings are we dealing with today from someone else? Their feelings as well as our own determines your and my attitude, and how and what will be said to that person."

With these remarkable words, Edwina discloses some of the dynamics of healing. She has a clear sense of communal influence and energy and the deeply collective nature of language practices. I wish to continue, in this chapter, to analyze this language of healing. Thus far, my argument has been that the mostly urban African American and white Appalachian women in the shelter attempt to survive abuse and to begin to heal by engaging in a similar series of rhetorical or linguistic strategies and communicative practices. That is, survivors move from states or tendencies of personal alienation to tendencies more amenable to community integration. This process sometimes leads to solidarity and action-oriented accompaniment with other women.

In this chapter I will attend more immediately to the interpersonal aspects of language. My argument is this: During their conversations or storytelling[1] about domestic violence, the use of hybrid language by battered women helps them to heal. *Hybrid language* is conjoined or jointly constructed language. It is a mix or melding of two or more registers (that is, types of language) that results from negotiating, compromising, and creating shared meanings with other women in the shelter.[2] Hybridization can lead to changes or shifts in what women think and say. It can lead to meaning shifts that facilitate women's recovery from the devastation of domestic violence. A meaning shift is a conceptual change (in as much as we can witness it through language). This early stage of hybridization is what Edwina reveals to us about talk with other women: "Their feelings as well as our own determines your and my attitude, and how and what will be said to that person." She intuits the dynamism of language, the compromise and shared meaning. Conversations shape our attitudes. We influence one another's worldviews.

To illustrate hybridization and shifting meaning, I will look at a conversation between three women—Chloe, Vanessa, and myself. I will focus on the mixing of secular and religious language. I choose this particular mix to illustrate my argument because, in some respect, it is typical. First of all, most residents attend or have been raised in Holiness/Sanctified or fundamentalist/evangelical churches, that is, conservative traditions that distinctly affect how women perceive suffering.[3] They tap into this language when they speak about domestic violence. Traditional religious concepts about gender often fuel the family tensions that lead to violence. Thus the women's language is suffused with the semantic shadings, metaphors, and concepts of traditional religious socialization (in addition to other linguistic markers—class, race/ethnicity, education, age, and so forth).[4] Second, the women use secular language learned from staff, volunteers, or one another to analyze their situations. The staff and volunteers use specific registers to discuss domestic violence—such as the registers of law enforcement, self-help, or feminism. I will subcategorize these registers shortly. Both religious and certain secular languages circulate freely in the shelter. They mix and mutually influence one another.

In addition, I choose this particular mix of language because I will ultimately argue that it is instrumental in the recovery of some battered women. Shelter women often resist or subvert traditional meanings about gender taught by their churches in order to heal. Thus, the healing of battered women from the Women's House often involves theological meaning shifts. They sometimes move from an acceptance of religious concepts that facilitate abuse to a rejection or reinvention of those concepts. Sometimes battered women create their own theology—an idea I will explore in chapter 9. The secular/religious language mix is significant in the process.

In this chapter, I will begin by explaining hybridization. I will examine it in a storytelling episode between two shelter women and myself. Storytelling provides the opportunity for the language of healing. I will briefly consider the matter of theodicy because women's ideas about suffering are honed by their lived and shared experience. Finally, I will conclude with some remarks about the universality or applicability of my findings to other survivors.

One significance of the analysis of the previous and this present chapter is the attention to the dynamic movement of the language of healing. The language of healing makes apparent—in a poignant and socially relevant way—the way in which all human language functions to greater and lesser degrees as the dynamic site of ideological action. That is, the process I will describe is not restricted to the language of healing. It is simply the nature of language. However, in our effort to understand the nature of the healing process of battered women, it is useful to look carefully at the specific elements involved for survivors of domestic violence.

HYBRIDIZATION

What makes it possible for Alice Clare to move away from states of silence or near silence? What makes it possible for Emma, Sharon, Vanessa (that is, the women in chapter 7), and other women like them, to move away from states of near silence to the articulation of such degrees of self-consciousness and social awareness? Clearly, the process is phenomenally complex. In some sense, we can never fully know; yet, we can consider some suggestive linguistic patterns in battered women's language. The evidence suggests that storytelling is critical because it allows for the mixing and melding of various types of language—hybridization—that may assist healing. To deal with the language complexity, I make several working assumptions. One assumption was identified in the last chapter: that is, the movement through the process of healing by survivors is socially motivated activity that is nonlinear and multidimensional. In this chapter I will show that the movement is energized by hybridization.

In traditional linguistic terms, a hybrid *language* is a mix of two or more registers or types of language. It is a process of word formation. A hybrid *word* has elements that come from more than one language.[5] In linguistic philosophy and literary studies, hybridity concerns all language formation, including new combinations within one language. Indeed, in literary studies, the term is sometimes expanded to include combinations at any level of the meaning system. I use the term to signal differences, contradictions, or heteroglossia *within* one person's language and *between* more than one speakers' language. That is, I mean to signal combinations or stratification (layering of types of language) from the mixing of voices in dialogue. *Heteroglossia*, a term from literary studies, is the mix of different languages. My use of the terms hybridity and heteroglossia is in consonance with the language and literary philosopher M. M. Bakhtin when he makes the case for the heteroglossia of all language—the internal stratification of language into various constituent social languages that make it heteroglot, multivoiced, multistyled, multilanguaged.[6] The languages intermix—dialogically—and result in new concepts or new languages. Bakhtin argues that ". . . dialogic orientation of discourse is a phenomenon that is, of course, a property of any living discourse."[7] Further, he writes:

> Thus at any given movement of its historical existence, language is heteroglot from top to bottom: it represents the co-existence of socio-ideological contradictions between the present and the past, between differing epochs of the past, between different socio-ideological groups in the present, between tendencies, schools, circles and so forth, all given a bodily form. The "languages" of heteroglossia intersect each other in a variety of ways, forming new socially typifying "languages."[8]

This process is the crux of language change. Yet, in my view, some language seems fraught with overt instances of hybridity. The language of healing is noticeably replete with instances of hybridity because, as survivors of domestic violence move from one stage of the healing process to the next, they carry along instances of prior or parallel worldviews, diverse life conceptions, or articulations. For example, they carry along the registers of their church communities or religious background. And, as they take part in new kinds of social activity in the shelter with new conversational partners, survivors assimilate new languages. For example, survivors may begin to use the feminist and/or self-help language of the shelter workers. The degree to which battered women are able to assimilate and mix language registers has important implications for their recovery. The crises of domestic violence, the loss of a partner, home, sometimes children and jobs, may lever open the meaning-making practices of survivors as they struggle to make sense of their destabilized situations. "The inner dialectic quality of the sign comes out fully in the open only in times of social crises or revolutionary changes," argues V. N. Volosinov.[9]

Many types of languages or linguistic concepts may function side-by-side in the language of survivors. Hence contradictions, semantic anomalies, and conceptual tensions abound. The contradictions are open to reflection or to question by interlocutors. Consequently, the borders between concepts, the linguistic interfaces, implicitly hold the possibility of transformation and change. Hybridity and its inherent contradictions can also result from negotiating, compromising, and creating shared meanings with other women in the shelter. Slight semantic shifts may occur as the survivors transfer words and meaning from one context to the next, thus thrusting language into new forms and functions and the speakers into new linguistic territory. The destabilization of their life situation and pressure from new acquaintances (that is, house residents, staff, and volunteers) may contribute to a metaphorical *spiraling movement* of meaning shifts or language changes—from silence to lament and anger to increased social connection or solidarity. I use the term *spiraling* to suggest that the process is not unidirectional, linear, or permanent; rather, the process is dialogic and thus not predictably or uniformly realized. Yet the dialogic activity between previous, current, or possible frames of mind about their lives and experience can result in language change for survivors. It can result in the opening of imaginative space for the realization of autonomy and self-in-healthy-relation: that is, healing.

RELIGIOUS AND SECULAR LANGUAGE HYBRIDIZATION: AN EXTENDED EXAMPLE OF LANGUAGE CHANGE AND HEALING

To illustrate the concept of hybridization and its function in the healing process of survivors, I will focus, in one storytelling session, on one particular type of mix in the language of the battered women: secular and religious. I choose this particular intersection because the interplay of religious with secular languages is more frequent in the language of battered women than most scholars and cultural workers have acknowledged. Indeed, scholars have tended to focus on the negative effects of religion on the situation of women.

By *religious* language, I simply mean language relating to the divine or transcendent or to Christian beliefs and practices. I will try to make qualitative differentiation between *religious* language and *spiritual* language. Spiritual language expresses a sense of self, authority, or agency above and beyond the dogma, traditionalism, or rituals of religion and its institutions. Broadly speaking, *secular* language is nonreligious language; however, I will limit my focus to distinguishable varieties such as the languages of self-help, folk wisdom, human rights, and courts/criminal justice. These registers are from the women's life experience or assimilated from other residents or the staff and volunteers who advise, advocate, or teach sessions on domestic violence, drug and alcohol abuse, codependency, and so forth. I will reserve the term *social language* for language that features a sense of the community rather than solely the individual.

The distinctions between secular and social and between religious and spiritual are admittedly rough distinctions but, ultimately, helpful ones. In the terminology of chapter 7, secular and religious language are linguistic evidence of Phase Two concepts; social and spiritual languages are evidence of Phase Three concepts.

The following conversation is excerpted from a storytelling session. A word about the participants: Vanessa is an African American woman raised Baptist and native to the city. Chloe is a caucasian woman of Appalachian descent, raised Holiness. I am a white caucasian from a northern state, raised Catholic. Chloe and Vanessa are roughly the same age—in their thirties. I am ten years older. With respect to heteroglossia, notice how secular and religious language mix or interweave in the exchanges between Vanessa, Chloe, and myself:

1 VANESSA: I always had my faith. I say my prayers at night. I put more faith in God and
2 not in him [abuser]. Do you know how I know? Because I was torn enough to get out
3 before it got too bad. I was torn about [my abuser] and God helped me to get out.
4 CHLOE: It's different for Vanessa than for me. Vanessa came up in a loving family. I
5 had a bad life. . . . I had to try to believe in God. I had to try. . . .
6 VANESSA: I felt it in my heart. You have to feel it in your heart. You can't do it with your
7 head.
8 CAROL: What do you feel in your heart when you feel God?
9 VANESSA: I feel happiness in my heart. When it comes to God it seems like, when I'm
10 walking down this dark road, I can see this light at the end. I know there's a light ahead!
11 CHLOE: I don't want it to be too late before I start doing what I'm supposed to do! In
12 the Bible, it can be so harsh!

13 CAROL: Do you find out about God from the Bible?

14 CHLOE: The Bible is very complex and real scary and other people look at it as being the
15 truth but the Bible contradicts itself.

[A discussion about how most people think God is male, leading some men to think
they are better than women. Both women disagree with the image of God as male.]

16 VANESSA: [Men] do think they are better. Do you know the saying, "Behind every good
17 man, there's a woman"? It's never the other way around.

18 CHLOE: They think they are better because of Adam and Eve. . . . Women believe more
19 in God. They have to. They have to take so much stuff. They have to have something
20 to hold onto. Men have each other. Men stick together. They have one another.

21 VANESSA: A woman doesn't have anybody. Suppose you are just out there by yourself.
22 God is the only person you can believe in.

23 CHLOE: Me too. I don't have no girlfriends when I get into trouble. . . . If God were a
24 woman, it would be wonderful! I know a lot of men would be going to hell!

25 VANESSA: Me too. I know I would be standing. I try to be a good person.

26 CAROL: Does that mean God [as a man] lets men get away with stuff?

27 VANESSA: God lets men get away with stuff! Women pay more on earth, more than men.
28 Guys don't think about it. They are not going to get their consequences till after they
29 die. Women get it now. But when [men] die, they are going to get it.

30 CHLOE: A woman God is for women!

31 VANESSA: In my case, I called the police. I was the one being abused. He snatched my
32 sons. I called the police and they said he can do it because he is their natural dad. That's
33 not fair! Turn the tables. I would go to jail for kidnapping them. The laws are so messed
34 up. If a woman kills a man, she gets fifteen to twenty-five years in jail. If a man kills
35 his wife, he gets six years. I don't understand that! It's not fair. They don't get what
36 they deserve. We get punished a lot harder than a man.

[A short discussion about penalties for different legal charges, followed by a discussion
of the O. J. Simpson trial. The gist of this second discussion is twofold. First, it
concerns the bias in the way whites report black crime. Second, it concerns the way
men are apparently able to harm women with impunity. The central concerns are the
media and the legal system. Vanessa, an African American, and Chloe, an Anglo, are
both dissatisfied with the outcome of the trial because they think Simpson is guilty.]

37 CHLOE: Anyway, there's biases because of who has control. The country is run by rich
38 white men. The church too.

[A discussion about the patriarchal nature of one of the other shelter woman's church.]

39 VANESSA: That's why I don't belong to no church. I read the Bible. Now and then I read the
40 Bible. I feel in my heart what I have to do. I ain't going by his rules or her rules. No, I
41 can't get into that.

42 CHLOE: I am having a problem with the Bible all the time. Most people do, but they
43 just believe anyway. They don't admit the story is wrong. [. . .] The Bible starts out with
44 Adam and Eve. The world thinks women are evil. Eve got Adam to eat the apple.
45 Everyone says women are evil. So the stories in the Bible are like that—against
46 women. It is not right.
47 VANESSA: [My abuser] thinks God is on his side.
48 CAROL: It's like a blank card to do anything.
49 VANESSA: There's your freedom to do anything you want to do.

In this series of exchanges, the language hybrids can be identified on the
rhetorical or narrative level. That is, words are not blended; rather, some
sentences take on aspects of the content of the previous sentences—regardless of which speaker offered the last thoughts. In this way, Chloe and Vanessa
engage in dialogic language activity with both religious and secular content.
On the level of the clause, the secular languages can be subcategorized as
those of folk wisdom (lines 16–17), criminal justice (lines 31–33), legal/
judicial (lines 33–36 and O. J. Simpson trial discussion), politics (lines 37–
38), popular psychology (lines 16, 27–28, and throughout), domestic violence (line 31), human rights (lines 31–46). Subclausally, there are secular
themes and metaphors regarding the journey or escape (lines 2–3), the moral
trial (lines 4–5), and justice/punishments (lines 34–36). The following
section lists these discourses:

SECULAR REGISTERS

folk wisdom
[Men] do think they are better. Do you know the saying, "Behind every good
man, there's a woman"? It's never the other way around.

criminal justice
In my case, I called the police. I was the one being abused. He snatched my
sons. I called the police and they said he can do it because he is their natural
dad. That's not fair! Turn the tables. I would go to jail for kidnapping them.

legal/judicial
The laws are so messed up. If a woman kills a man, she gets fifteen to twenty-
five years in jail. If a man kills his wife, he gets six years. I don't understand
that! It's not fair! They don't get what they deserve. We get punished a lot
harder than a man.
O. J. Simpson trial discussion

political
Anyway, there's biases because of who has control. The country is run by rich white men.

popular psychology
Women pay more on earth, more than men. Guys don't think about it. [Men] do think they are better.

domestic violence
I was the one being abused.

human rights
In my case, I called the police. [. . .] We get punished a lot harder than a man.
O. J. Simpson trial discussion
Anyway, there's biases because of who has control.
I ain't going by his rules or her rules.
Everyone says women are evil. It is not right.

journey/escape
Because I was torn enough to get out before it got too bad. I was torn about [my abuser] and God helped me to get out.
When it comes to God it seems like, when I am walking down this dark road, I can see this light at the end. I know there's a light ahead.

moral trial
I had a bad life. . . . I had to try to believe in God. I had to try. . . .
I feel in my heart what I have to do.

justice/punishment
If a man kills his wife, he gets six years. I don't understand that! It's not fair. They don't get what they deserve. We get punished a lot harder than a man.

The secular language in the conversation is from past and recent experience—as Bakhtin puts it in *The Dialogic Imagination*—"the co-existence of socio-ideological contradictions between the present and the past, [. . .], between different socio-ideological groups in the present . . ." (291). Although it is not possible to absolutely trace its (assuredly multiple) origins, the secular language undoubtedly also derives from the shelter, including the self-help, feminist, and perhaps the criminal justice, legal language, and the metaphors of justice/punishment. The secular language is heteroglossic.

Chloe and Vanessa contribute to the mix from their own standpoints. As Chloe points out, *It's different for Vanessa than for me. Vanessa came up in a loving family. I had a bad life. [. . .] I had to try to believe in God* (lines 4–5). Indeed, Vanessa is the one who (initially at least) articulates the most conventional or uncritical religious perspective: *I say my prayers at night* (line 1). Initially, her language appears to be largely Phase Two language. Recall its features: a growing awareness, autonomy, and relationality. There is a developing ability to speak and communicate about the suffering. For Phase Two speakers, there is noticeable sensitivity from and an analysis of suffering, but rationality and emotion are communicated together. Expressions of anger and lamentation abound and there is sometimes a will to violence or vengeance. Survivors perceive their partner's behavior as ontological, that is, as personal sin or dysfunction. Their words belie utopian objectives. Generally, survivors accept and seek conquest in existing social structures—as noneffective as those structures may be.

Chloe uses the most Phase Three language though she definitely does not use it always or consistently. Recall some of the characteristics of Phase Three language: It is rational and sometimes imaginative, creative, or prophetic. It is politically and socially oriented. Suffering evokes within the survivors a sense of relationality and solidarity with others. Phase Three survivors perceive their abusive partners' behavior as social sin or as related to structural issues. There is evidence of active, directed behavior intended to shape situations or produce change. They begin to accept the idea of and work for changed social structures. Consequently, there are traces of the transformation of the survivors' original fear and anger into senses of hope and joy.

Influencing one another, the women approach Phase Three language. Notice, however, there are Phase One traces in the language of both Vanessa and Chloe. They recall a prior world—before they arrived at the shelter—in which they were isolated and alienated (lines 21–23): *A woman doesn't have anybody. . . .* As she relives her Phase One experience, Chloe chooses the present tense: *I don't have no girlfriends. . . .* In the actual present, she counts Vanessa and other shelter women as her friends. In contrast, Vanessa's language is speculative: *Suppose you are just out there by yourself. . . .* The chosen frame—an imaginative world—indicates she now considers herself beyond [what I am defining as] Phase One; additionally, she is inviting her interlocutors—through storytelling—to imagine this circumstance, to enter emphatically into it, as she rehearses a past life that no longer exists.

I wish to argue that the tension of the mix of phases and the secular-religious hybridity creates a spiraling or recursive effect that results in both women engaging, if momentarily, in Phase Three worldviews. To illustrate, I will first briefly consider the language of each of the women, then I will discuss the ways their contributions propel the conversation forward.

VANESSA'S LANGUAGE IN TERMS OF THE PHASES AND MEANING SHIFTS

When she is not reliving her suffering, Vanessa initially uses Phase Two language about religious and secular issues. Lines 1–3 reveal a somewhat uncritical religious perspective:

> *I always had my faith. I say my prayers at night. I put more faith in God and not in him* [abuser]. *Do you know how I know? Because I was torn enough to get out before it got too bad. I was torn about him and God helped me to get out.*

Vanessa leans on religious explanation for her survival. She doesn't consider psychological or physical expediency. She has a growing, not full, awareness of her own autonomy.

Likewise, lines 16–17 reveal a limited though growing Phase Two awareness of her social situation: [Men] *do think they are better. Do you know the saying, "Behind every good man, there's a woman"? It's never the other way around.* She reveals clear anger toward her abuser and, in lines 16–17, her view appears to be shaped solely from her experience with him (for surely, not all men think they are better than women and "behind" some women are supportive men). That is, she initially does not have a grasp of the social aspects of her personal situation. There is no full social analysis. Still she is coherent and cohesive: Emotions and rationality are cocommunicated. Yet anger sometimes overwhelms her ability to see other possibilities.

There are additional Phase Two modalities in her language. There are traces of righteousness in Vanessa's anger. Her abuser has violated moral, criminal, and legal codes; yet, the legal and criminal justice systems and God protect men, at least on earth. Still her language is psalmic. It is lamentation, composed of both complaint and praise. In Vanessa's language, in addition to the plaintive modality, there is a tone of praise and worship. When asked how she "feels God," she says, *I feel happiness in my heart. When it comes to God it seems like, when I'm walking down this dark road, I can see this light at the end. I know there's a light ahead!* (lines 9 and 10). God is praised even though, she complains, the road is dark.

Ultimately, Vanessa counts on God's justice and, overall, her objectives are utopian. Why not? She cannot count on the criminal justice or the legal systems to help her. However, pragmatically, she accepts her situation and, despite the recalcitrance of the criminal justice or legal systems, she seeks to change her own situation through existing social structures (for example, *In my case, I called the police* [line 31]). More precisely: she does not imagine alternative, more effective social structures, but she does imagine retribution—if only in a religious sense—and a better life for herself. *But when they die* [men], *they are going to get it* (line 29).

By the time Vanessa utters the last exchange of the conversation, how-ever, she has substantially altered both her religious and secular language. In lines 27–29, Vanessa is applying a modest sociocultural critique of religion. She says: *God lets men get away with stuff! Women pay more on earth, more than men. Guys don't think about it. They are not going to get their consequences till after they die. Women get it now. But when* [men] *die, they are going to get it.* By lines 31–36, she is forming a critique of social institutions. She says:

> In my case, I called the police. I was the one being abused. He snatched my sons. I called the police and they said he can do it because he is their natural dad. That's not fair! Turn the tables. I would go to jail for kidnapping them. The laws are so messed up. If a woman kills a man, she gets fifteen to twenty-five years in jail. If a man kills his wife, he gets six years. I don't understand that! It's not fair. They don't get what they deserve. We get punished a lot harder than a man.

Further, by lines 39–41, Vanessa is performing a full Phase Three sense of her own authority in spiritual matters: *That's why I don't belong to no church. I read the bible. Now and then I read the bible. I feel in my heart what I have to do. I ain't going by his rules or her rules. No, I can't get into that.*

Finally, by line 49, Vanessa performs a full critique of religion: *There's your freedom to do anything you want to do* [that is, if you believe God is on your side like men do]. In short, she is demonstrating some clear Phase Three sensibilities. Her secular language has assumed a fuller social analytic; her religious language has been elaborated as more critical and more maturely spiritual. She recognizes that, when her abuser uses the Bible to justify his actions, he is giving himself an undue, unlimited freedom (lines 47, 49). Yet Vanessa asserts her own authority in spiritual matters rather than relying on her abuser's authority or a church's rules or dogma: *I feel in my heart what I have to do! I ain't going by his rules or her rules* (line 40).

CHLOE'S LANGUAGE IN TERMS OF THE PHASES AND MEANING SHIFTS

Chloe displays somewhat more Phase Three language overall in the session, particularly regarding secular matters. She evidences less anger toward men. She more evenly balances rationality and emotionality in the conversation: It would seem Chloe has slightly more willingness to think with equanimity about gender and relations. She does believe women are more "spiritual" than men and she thinks women are closer to God, but this is because, as she said in another context, men have a different temporal frame of refer-ence: *[M]en think for the day. Women think for the future. God is the reward.* Though she has had "a very bad life," she appears more willing to forgive.

Chloe is not paralyzed by anger or simply reactive. She looks beyond her personal experience.

Ultimately, Chloe's perspective on both secular and religious matters is more fully socially analytical. She repeatedly offers a social analysis of religious matters. In line 18, she is offering a critique of dogmatic or fundamental religious views that surface in biblical interpretation: [Men] *think they are better because of Adam and Eve....* She understands that men have an advantage because they enjoy solidarity: *Men have each other. Men stick together. They have one another* (line 20). The implication is that women suffer because they do not enjoy solidarity with one another. Chloe understands the consequence of the lack of solidarity on women's lives: *Only God can be depended upon.* In lines 23–24, she is again rendering a social/cultural critique by implying that justice is a gendered concept: *If God were a woman, it would be wonderful! I know a lot of men would be going to hell!* Apparently justice on earth is gendered male. Chloe clearly understands that critical institutions (including, assumedly, the legal, criminal, political, and religious systems) are dominated by wealthy white males: *Anyway, there's biases because of who has control. The country is run by rich white men. The church too* (lines 37–38).

Although Chloe's view is more than simply religious or religiously doctrinaire, she is initially spiritually somewhat unsure or, more precisely, she evidences contradictions in her thinking. Notice lines 11–12—*I don't want it to be too late before I start doing what I'm supposed to do! In the Bible, it can be so harsh!*—in contrast with lines 14–15: *The Bible is very complex and real scary and other people look at it as being the truth but the Bible contradicts itself.* She does not share Vanessa's initial dogmatic religious point of view, but she initially accepts her basic perspective and so her own sensibilities fluctuate. By line 30, however, Chloe's language is, in fact, imaginative, creative, prophetic. *A woman God is for women!* she declares, calling prophetically for a universe rectified or ordered by female justice. These are signs of a Phase Three consciousness moving toward critical interdependence with other women. By lines 45–46 Chloe is performing a more fully mature spirituality, that is, she has assumed her own authority in spiritual matters: *It is not right to use scripture to limit or control women socially.* She also says: *Everyone says women are evil. So the stories in the Bible are like that—against women. It is not right.* Her statements seem to broach issues related to the meaning of life and her place in it. She has broken the earlier tendency of seeking the approval of others, including the scripture writers or the doctrines of the church. Her religious experience appears to have social or communal aspects. Indicating traces of political consciousness, she says, *If God were a woman, it would be wonderful!* (lines 23–24). Apparently women would collectively benefit if men were collectively controlled or punished, if posthumously.

Neither Chloe's nor Vanessa's senses of the need for social connection or solidarity with women are rendered, however, in explicitly political terms (that is, in the sense of understanding the need to organize or engage in concrete communal actions). They do understand the problem of the lack of solidarity: Recall Chloe's statements *Men have each other / Men stick to-gether / They have one another* and Vanessa's statement *A woman doesn't have anybody* (lines 20–21). But the women appear to seek to conquer this through cosmic structures rather than through social structures. For example, Chloe implies that if God were female, justice would be better served. Vanessa trusts only in divine efficiency: *God is the only person you can believe in* (line 22). The two women do not offer political ideas for social change though, clearly, Vanessa and Chloe understand the need for change. Indeed, as they told me more than once in our interactions, they viewed sharing their words in this study as a contribution to the battered women's movement.

Still, within this set of exchanges, the conversation moves on a general trajectory from worldly to religious matters and from legal to sociopolitical matters. The trajectory is not unilinear. Rather, it proceeds with recursive "movements of mind" as Chloe and Vanessa return again and again to basic issues of fairness, justice, and right living interspersed with moments of their own sexism, anger, and religious dogma. The ideas advance and recede. They are rearticulated and recast. The critical point, however, is this: In the end, Chloe and Vanessa have participated in a kind of dialectic activity that results in the coproduction of a more liberatory worldview (temporary though it may be).[10] Perhaps neither domestic survivor could have arrived there without the other: The conversation pushes on and on.

A word about my own contributions to the conversation: I add three questions:

Line 8: *What do you feel in your heart when you feel God?*

Line 13: *Do you find out about God from the Bible?*

Line 26: *Does that mean God lets men get away with stuff?*

The first two questions are probes for information. Of the three inquiries, line 26 is most suggestive. Still the question plays on Chloe's speculation that if God were a woman, justice would be differently rendered. My intention was to draw out more information about the women's concepts of God and gender. Chloe perhaps is most responsive to the inquiry. She continues her religious speculation. More pragmatically, Vanessa elides the religious into the secular by describing the sexism of the police (and, thus, their inability—apparently like a male God's inability or unwillingness—to render justice on earth).

I offer one statement in the conversation: [When men believe that God is on their side], *it's like a blank card to do anything* (line 48). The statement comes at the end of the conversation and it is a rejoinder or coda to Vanessa's claim that men believe God is on their side. It also shares a strategy played out earlier when Vanessa elides a religious concept into its secular parallel (line 31 and following). To liberally paraphrase this semantic pairing: As a male God is male-biased, so the male police are male-biased too. Within a sentence, I offer a confirmation of Vanessa's religious language (that is, *God on their side*) by linking it with a secular analogy or simile (that is, *like a blank card*). Similar to the conversation as a whole, these two statements offered by Vanessa and me are specific instances of secular and religious hybridity—a mixing of concepts and terms from two different registers. In the end, however, Chloe and Vanessa are responsible for the primary conceptual work of the conversation.

DIALOGISM AND SOCIAL CHANGE

I have noted repeatedly that the phases of healing are nonlinear or curvilinear. There can be no certainty that conceptual knowledge (as reflected through language) is always moving progressively in one direction. In fact, it most assuredly does not. In their thoughts and ideas, people backtrack. They may return to earlier positions. They may hold on to two irreconcilable positions simultaneously. As speakers take ownership of concepts, those concepts and other concepts shift and change. My conversation with Vanessa and Chloe demonstrates these characteristics of nonlinearity. There are contradictions in the worldviews of both domestic violence survivors. For example, Vanessa does not question the discrepancy in the way God appears to divvy out justice to men as opposed to women. Other parts of the conversation (not recorded above) reveal both women's fundamental sexism against women though they decry the sexism of men. *You can't trust a woman*, Vanessa says; Chloe adds: *Women are conniving*. Still, both women's language shows signs of more expansive views about God and gender. Their language shows signs of the healing process.

In fact, Chloe and Vanessa's relationship seems to negate their own sexism. They do not treat one another as untrustworthy or conniving. They listen respectfully to one another and to me. They learn from one another. Indeed we were all learning from one another. We attend to relationality by listening carefully, agreeing or accepting, modifying or yielding, challenging and meeting one another's challenges as we jointly construct a mutually acceptable worldview composed of some clearly differing worldviews or languages. The willingness to create shared meanings creates the spiral or recursive activity and the energy or impetus to stir and move each woman's level of perception or awareness. Important moments happen at specific junctures or locations. Chloe adds significantly to the movement beginning in lines 18, 23–24, and 30.

Lines 18–20   [Men] *think they are better because of Adam and Eve. [. . .] Men have one another.*

Lines 23–24:   *If God were a woman, it would be wonderful! I know a lot of men would be going to hell!*

Line 30:   *A woman God is for women.*

Generally speaking, in these moments, Chloe is applying social analysis or cultural critiques to religious matters. She is creating hybrid statements. Significantly, and importantly, Vanessa engages and responds respectively beginning in line 21 and lines 31–36:

Line 21:   *A woman doesn't have anybody. Suppose you are out there by yourself.*

Lines 31–36:   *In my case, I called the police. I was the one being abused. He snatched my sons. I called the police and they said he can do it because he is their natural dad. That's not fair! Turn the tables. I would go to jail for kidnapping them. The laws are so messed up. If a woman kills a man, she gets fifteen to twenty-five years in jail. If a man kills his wife, he gets six years. I don't understand that! It's not fair. They don't get what they deserve. We get punished a lot harder than a man.*

The exchanges are being meshed together: Each time a religious register arises, a secular register is conjoined to it and vice versa. A spiraling motion is created as the ideas turn around on each other and push each other forward. Notice that between lines 29–30, between lines 36–37, and certainly by the last utterance, Chloe and Vanessa are in positions of agreement and accordance: A kind of coproduction has been made by acts of negotiation, respect, or reciprocity.

Line 29:   Vanessa: *But when [men] die, they are going to get it.*

Line 30:   Chloe: *A woman God is for women.*

Line 36:   Vanessa: *We get punished a lot harder than a man.*

Line 37:   Chloe: *Anyway, there's biases because of who has control.*

Last line: Vanessa: *There's your freedom to do anything you want to do.*

With Chloe's help, Vanessa moves from a relatively uncritical to a more critical religious and secular view. At first she takes consolation in divine (if posthumous) retribution. By the end, she critiques the social system that—with the religious system—allows men to do as they please. By her last statement, she is not waiting for God's retribution. She is critical of the entire social and religious order. She has righteous anger—in short, a fuller social and spiritual awareness.

With Vanessa's help, Chloe moves from an ambiguous to a more fully authoritative spiritual stance. At first she has contradictions in her thoughts about God. She is unnerved by biblical dictates and thinks she needs to mend her ways. Then she recalls the Bible's internal contradictions. Vanessa does not object and even concedes that she only sometimes reads the bible. In the end, Chloe is convinced the Bible is in error. It is "against women." She is more certain of God's justice—if only God were a woman. But Vanessa helps her to see she can follow her heart rather than scripture or biased arbitrators of justice.

The women move in such directions because of the energy of one another's contributions. The dialogism helps them to recast their initial articulations into language more self-consciously aware and mutually accommodating. In short, together they create a new worldview. They help one another see problems with scripture, its use, God's distribution of justice, the law, and the legal system's distribution of justice through the police and courts. Interestingly, Chloe and Vanessa are able to imagine this new world because they subvert traditional religious formulations that, they imply, unduly impact gender relations. In effect, two spiritually minded women use religious resistance or subversion to reorder their worlds. They become more autonomous through relationality. They do not abandon God; they recreate God. Through hybrid language forms and meaning shifts, they render God as female and her justice as sure.

THE MATTER OF THEODICY

It is not possible to discern with certainty the original or foundational theodicies of Vanessa or Chloe from this conversation. Respectively, they were raised Baptist and Holiness. Both women drifted in and out of church communities as they became adults, moved to new locales, and gained or lost interest in organized religion. Within the conversation, both women weave several types of religious explanations for evil. Certainly, there is evidence of a punishment/retribution theodicy or mentality. In this theodicy, human choices lead to suffering. Suffering does not always extend from bad human choices, but human sin is still the cause. Sin demands repentance. When Vanessa and Chloe imagine the final hellish destiny of males, they are tapping into a punishment/retribution religious worldview. There is some evidence of a remedial/instructive theodicy. In this theodicy, suffering is believed to be soul-making. It leads to righteousness, compassion, and concern for others. It can be imposed by God or it can be self-imposed. Chloe seems to adhere to this view when she says: *Women believe more in God. They have to. They have to take so much stuff. They have to have something to hold onto.*

By the end of the conversation, both women are articulating, in brief fashion, a liberation theodicy. In this theodicy, suffering is caused by the oppression of others. Sin is social; that is, social institutions can be evilly oppressive. In this theodicy, God is revealed to the oppressed, the poor. God is a "power-with" God, not a "power-over" God. Recall chapter 5: This theology often works in conjunction with the "Suffering God" approach. So the sufferer engages in complaint, protest, resistance. Her words are prophetic. Faith leads to action.

There are clear characteristics of this liberation theodicy in the women's words. By line 30, Chloe makes a crystalline liberatory statement: *A woman God is for women!* This is less utopian than pragmatic. It is based on the lived experience of the inequality between males and females. By line 40, Vanessa asserts her right to make her own ethical decisions. It is a statement of faith leading to self-determined action. Both statements are grounded in the lived-experience of violence and oppression by men and their institutions. The protest or complaint is clear. The resistance takes the shape of rejecting the patriarchal aspects of religion and its central text, the Bible, and leads to a new spirituality or a new theology—a woman God for women. These are imaginative, prophetic words.

CONCLUSION: THE APPLICABILITY OF FINDINGS

In terms of developing both the autonomy and relationality of survivors of domestic violence, conversation seems to advance the healing process. Through hybridization, that is, through the shifting and mixing of language— opportunities for new concepts are created. Epiphanies may happen. *A woman God is for women!* Transformation may occur. New languages may emerge. The dialogism or the energy of hybridization may move women to more social or communal (rather than primarily personal or individual) frameworks of awareness.

This transformation from a personal to a more fully social awareness is the essential feature of Phase Three language. One of the many possibilities of Phase Three sensibility is that secular language is transformed into social language. As I mentioned earlier, in Phase Three, the emphasis on personal situations gives way to a new emphasis on social concepts, structures, causes, and solutions. For example, by the end of the conversation presented above, Chloe includes all women in her dream of justice. Both women are aware of the role of church and society in their plight. This is not to say that the personal is henceforth neglected or that full healing has been achieved. It only suggests that secular languages have a fuller realization with emphases on the communal or social. The speaker is more self-conscious and socially conscious. A woman might continue to speak of her *desire* or *need* for a violence-free life, but she will also begin to speak about her *right* to it and the responsibility of society to ensure it.

Empowerment and social change can derive from this new awareness: Individual women suffer domestic violence because our society and its institutions condone all sorts of violence against all women. As neighbors, teachers, caretakers, and friends—that is, as people who accompany battered women on the road to safety and recovery—we might be more fully aware of the healing power of language. One final clarification, however: I do not suggest that all women in the shelter engage the linguistic trajectory I have described.[11] I do not suggest that all battered women move through such phases of healing. I do not predict universals in the language of healing. Anthropologists, linguists, and sociologists study the profundity and profusion of crosscultural variation in social behavior and language practices. Indeed, this study is an attempt to describe the effect of religion on a particular segment of the population of domestic violence survivors in one shelter in the upper South. Patterns or ranges of human behavior do cross cultures, however, inviting us to think in terms of universal or strategic similarities based on social structure similarities.

Hence, I propose that many women (even outside the Women's House) do evidence some movement along the trajectory I describe in this study. I suggest that similar linguistic patterns may surface crossculturally based on universals in women's positions vis-à-vis men's positions. To the extent that women occupy similar spaces in religious doctrine and the sociocultural imagination, with similar constraints on behavior, they may speak or act in similar ways at the strategic level I describe in this study.[12] Granting individual variation based on degrees and kinds of adherence to religious and gender socialization, we could expect similarities across situations or contexts in which sacred text or scripture is used by those with the power to relegate women to a secondary status and to police women's social behavior by any means necessary, including the brutality of domestic violence. It is widely recognized that domestic violence—even as it spawns resilience and resistance—results in women's loss of personal self-esteem, social isolation, and political alienation. This situation, of course, exists in innumerable places crossculturally. In this study, we get a glimpse of language in a specific community that may speak to other women, other situations, and other ranges of a human language of healing.

In this particular shelter, most women are African American and white Appalachian women from Holiness/Sanctified or fundamentalist/evangelical denominations. They do share some cultural and religious practices and beliefs including the centrality of scripture and a conservative reckoning of gender roles. The advantage of being at the shelter is that, by virtue of the effect of the many and diverse stories, the secular and religious may assume fuller and felt realizations on their way to being social and spiritual quests, liberation, or transformations. This is because there is more opportunity to revisit and analyze Phase One, Two, and Three conditions or language tendencies in community. More simply: There is opportunity for creating intersections when there are women of diverse situations willing and able to speak and listen. There is opportunity for healing when there is opportunity to collectively consider suffering, its aftermath, and its openings for fresh starts. At its best, the shelter provides this opportunity. Women in crisis may have, for the first time, unbroken opportunity to do so—given the extent to which their partners tried to isolate them from friends and family, from social interaction.

In the end, however, the sharing of stories is more than simply a rehearsal of past events or an exercise in emotional release; storytelling is sharing and shaping possible worlds. When we tell our stories to one another we are, metaphorically, etching a map of where we have been and where we might be in the future. When storytelling has a religious component, it can lead to new theology.

NINE

"If God Were a Woman, It Would Be Wonderful!"

LOCAL THEOLOGY AND SOCIAL CHANGE

Imagination is a gift from God.

—Priscilla

The more I see where God has brought me from, I know he's always
been there. He's been a father to me, a mother to me.

—Corinne

INTRODUCTION

In the last chapter I suggested that the language of battered women often
initially reflects aspects of redemptive/atonement and suffering God theodicies.
The first model proposes that suffering should be endured for the sake of God
or others. Thus, in their early conversations, battered women often accept
suffering as part of God's salvific plan. If the women's approach reflects the
second model, they recognize they suffer unjustly and that, when they suffer,
God suffers. But shelter women talk with other survivors about suffering and
the communal talk is healing. Adel succinctly put it: "For support, we've
done it amongst ourselves. The women help each other." They meet others
with new ideas about society, violence, religion. Consequently, their language often shifts toward more socially oriented remedial/instructive and

liberation theodicies. In short, women sometimes cocreate new theological language.

In this chapter I look at this dynamic from a broader perspective. I suggest that women develop "local theologies," their own particular views concerning God, religion, and revelation. Local theologies—particularly ones that challenge the status quo by considering women's problems and oppression from social, economic, and political perspectives, are initiated through dialogic activity. Sometimes a shift happens.[1] To investigate, I first discuss local theology. I probe its features in the women's language: cultural context, unsatisfactory theology, and new theological explorations. Second, I discuss nascent models of local theology in the talk of battered women: praxis and the ethnologic models. Third, I discuss complications. For example, in some women's language, there is evidence of dual theological systems or no linguistic evidence of change. Fourth, I make further observations about dialogic changes in terms of some traditional theological categories: evil, sin, grace, salvation or redemption, and relations with God and others. Plainly stated: battered women rethink the problem of evil.

LOCAL THEOLOGY: WHAT IS IT?

Traditionally the term "local theology" has been applied in missionary contexts when missioners or practitioners recognize that aspects of the theology inherited from traditional mainline churches does not fit their cultural circumstances. New theology develops. Recently (since the1970s) theologians apply the term more widely. The process is labeled with different terms, including local theology, contextual theology, local contextual theology,[2] inculturation or enculturation, homemade theology, and theology of the people. William Dyrness calls the process "vernacular theology,"[3] the theology people commonly do as part of their everyday lives. It is "a symbolic complex of ideas, objects, events, and *language* that both express and define what we mean by Christianity" [italics mine]. Vernacular theology is "constructed, often intuitively, by Christians seeking to respond faithfully to the challenges their lives present to them."[4]

I use the term "local theology" to define this process in the language of battered women. Theology is part of the knowledge, sometimes tacit, with which battered women confront violence and cope with their lives. The key to a community's framework—its implicit theology—is found in its predominant ideas and practice. Thus, I look for evidence of local theology in the women's language—strands of religious language that derive from the blending of the diverse languages of the shelter. In this context, local theology is an innovative composite that derives from the women's personal and collective experience and it seeks to address their particular situation of gender oppression and domestic battery. To be sure, the evidence is not always direct or concise. Local theology stands in "continuous interrelationship with all social factors and consequently is subject to the influence of conflicting interests."[5] Accordingly, it is not always clear and articulated knowledge; instead, it is often fragmentary. Yet, it involves "a web, or framework, of symbols in terms of which people make choices about what is important to them."[6]

While the linguistic evidence is not always neat and simple, there are broad features. The situational context, including lived experience, is critical. It involves at least three considerations: socioeconomic and political factors, the cultural situation, and the ideological and religious situation.[7] As I have argued in chapter 8, these are precisely the factors that stimulate battered women toward new ways of thinking about their situation and their suffering.

WHO DOES LOCAL THEOLOGY?

Traditionally only theologian scholars were considered knowledgeable enough or authorized to do theology. Within its newer and broader usage, however, the term *local theology* applies not only to their work. Ordinary people who reflect on the connection between their faith and their lives are feet-on-the-ground theologians.[8] Language analysis makes it plain: They theologize though they would not use the term to define their God-talk. Instead, they would say, for example, that they are witnessing, testifying, or simply talking.

In the Women's House, local theology is not generally a solitary activity; rather, it takes place in conversation. As women interlace the stories of their lives, their own abuse, women's oppression in society, and their faith in God, they are sometimes able to jointly construct a new and local theology. There are two general circumstances for this activity. First of all, shelter women create local theology when they recognize as inadequate the theodicies and other theological arguments foisted on them by abusive partners who try to justify their dominance or by pastors and church communities that try—as so often they do—to effect reconciliation in the interest of family "stability" or supposed scriptural mandate. As I have shown in previous chapters, the linguistic evidence suggests that battered women often are estranged from aspects of traditional theology or even their churches. They recognize their churches as patriarchal institutions and they see how scriptures and liturgies are used as the tools of their batterers. "They twist the scripture to get what they want! Twist it!" says Lisa. Battered women theologize when they critique such practices and other aspects of the church, its tradition, and scripture—or uses thereof—that facilitate violence against women.

Most battered women at the Women's House, however, are deeply faithful. Their critiques are faithful critiques. They try to make sense of the Christian message within the context of local circumstances, that is, within a context of the tremendous cruelty and harm perpetrated by men and their institutions. However, battered women do local theology, I suggest, not only when they critique. Their language reveals the role that particular circumstances play in shaping creative responses to scripture. So, secondly and often concurrently, they do local theology when they try to imagine freshly what their relationships with God and others would look like without rules, orders, mandates, dogma, assignments of character, essence, or gender-based proclivities and other authoritative explanations imposed upon them from an abuser, the church, or scripture.

In short, women do local theology when they communally consider their situations within the light of a rekindled, critical, and creative religious imagination.

THREE RECURRING CONCERNS OF LOCAL THEOLOGY

In their conversations and writing, shelter women do not engage in popular religion; rather, they engage a consciousness that adapts their theological concepts to their personal and collective experience within a social, political, and economic context.

According to theologian Robert Schreiter,[9] there are three recurring concerns for which to look in identifying local theology: Questions are raised about the broader culture, unsatisfactory theological explanations (theodicies, for example) are dismissed, and new ways of being Christian are explored. The concerns surface in the talk of battered women.

First, local theology begins with an examination of the cultural context. Local theology begins with analysis. Energy once devoted largely to metaphysical issues or to worship begins to engage social, political, and economic issues. Not unusually, battered women learn to see the injustice in their own domestic situations; then they begin to reckon with the systemic nature of it. To explain: Initially, battered women often think their partners' behaviors are both unique and uniquely deserved. Through talk, they begin to see that their partners act in well-known behavioral patterns—in ways familiar to other battered women. Then, as the women reach out for help beyond the family system, they learn about and agonize over the apparent ineffectiveness of civil society to address their problems. They see the ineffectiveness of the law enforcement, judicial, and penal systems. "There is no justice," Lisa says to Holly and me one day as she tries to figure out how her abusive partner had gotten released from jail just days after severely assaulting her. Later in the conversation she fantasizes that, if God were a woman, there would be childcare and more resources for domestic violence survivors. She also criticizes men for interpreting or constructing images and interpretations of God that bolster their own privilege. Still, when asked what gives her hope when secular and religious institutions have failed her, she immediately answers: "I think it's God."

To push this further: Local theology derives from an analysis of the dynamic interaction among the church or tradition, scripture or gospel, and the culture. The dynamic is dialectic: one that moves back and forth between these three components. This, I argue, is exactly what Chloe and Vanessa engage in as they talk about their situations within the context of shelter culture and influence one another's religious/spiritual perceptions. Recall this excerpt of their conversation:

VANESSA: In my case, I called the police. I was the one being abused. He snatched my sons. I called the police and they said he can do it because he is their natural dad. That's not fair! Turn the tables. I would go to jail for kidnapping them. The laws are so messed up. If a woman kills a man, she gets fifteen to twenty-five years in jail. If a man kills his wife, he gets six years. I don't understand that! It's not fair. They don't get what they deserve. We get punished a lot harder than a man.

CHLOE: Anyway, there's biases because of who has control. The country is run by rich white men. The church too.

Over and over, shelter women like Chloe and Vanessa critique their situation and the situation of women in society. As they do so, they slip easily back and forth into religious discourse or discourse about religion. In another conversation, Millie and India talk about sexism. Notice how the cultural critique slips effortlessly and seamlessly into God-talk.

MILLIE: Man equals egocentric. They need to fulfill their masculine image. If they can't, they can't think straight. They get abusive if you try to make him feel less than a man. This is a man's world. Everything is for him. He doesn't have babies. Nowadays it's changing a little. We're here because we know abuse is wrong. But society makes the masculine images. Little girls you buy dolls, little boys you buy guns. No matter what you do yourself, the majority does it that way.

INDIA: I like commercials when the men feed the baby, when the men change the diapers, when the men make the dinner. . . .

           [Scenarios of child raising are recalled in which the women are imaging or recounting episodes of teaching children not to be violent.] India then offers this statement, seemingly to recall the Christian principles upon which her child-rearing practices are founded:

INDIA: I believe in God. I sit in the Lord's way.

MILLIE: One day they [men] will come back to the Lord's way. In a spiritual way, God brings justice. Now or later in life.

In this conversational coda, the women are theorizing a God who acts on behalf of women. As in so much of the talk of battered women, there seems to be no boundary between the sacred and the secular. Millie recalls the moment she decided to leave her partner: "I said to myself, I'm God's child. I don't need to have abuse. I need a ride out of here with me and my children." India nods her head, pensive but pragmatic about the future: "I'm thinking about my new apartment. I'm thinking of my heaven on earth!"

For Millie, and many other women, being a child of God entails access to basic human and material necessities. The words of Millie, India, Vanessa, and Chloe illustrate the cultural critique that underlies battered women's talk about God. This is an essential aspect of local theology.

Second, unsatisfactory theological explanations (theodicies, for example) are dismissed. In chapter 6, we explored some of the shelter women's general notions of God, religion, and faith—both their own notions and those of their abusers. Many women examine and find inadequate those beliefs. Recall the dismissal of traditional interpretations of the story of Adam and Eve by the many battered women who have been verbally or physically assaulted by abusers who quote Genesis. Recall, for example, the words of the woman who says: "[Men] think they are better than us because of Adam and Eve! Man's downfall was Eve. That's what they think." Clearly she does not agree.

Many women find scripture or church tradition inadequate in the light of their own experience. Often this is true even if the women come from denominations that ascribe to scriptural inerrancy—such as Lisa, Tina, and Rita, who are talking about the Bible and their church communities in this conversation:

LISA: Be subservient to your husband! That's what church is all about!

TINA: Where does that leave us?

LISA: How can you remain faithful?

TINA: I dropped out of church when I was twelve years old: I was a sinner!

CAROL: Does it mean women aren't spiritual? Does it mean women can't have religion?

TINA: Giving birth is a religious experience.

RITA: It's the most beautiful thing! It brings tears to your eyes!

In these few conversational exchanges, there has been an implicit repudiation of scripture and tradition. The more assertive Tina and Lisa dismiss the institutional church—at least its definition of faithfulness, its rules regarding proper female conduct, which they seem to see as irrelevant or unjust. The Genesis 3:16 passage in which God condemns Eve to suffer in childbirth is inverted.[10] This is not a repudiation of faith: All three women are spiritually minded and engage in acts of witnessing. They simply are not faithful to aspects of tradition and scripture they find biased and used against women. The more religiously conservative Rita does not contribute to the critique of the church and scripture. She does, however, take ownership of the jointly construed renunciation of the traditional interpretation of scripture of childbirth as punishment and suffering; instead, childbirth appears to be an experience of religious ecstasy. Here are other isolated examples of the dismissal of inadequate theological perspectives:

KESHA: I think the rule of religion that states women are supposed to be submissive to their husbands in any way that he wants, that your body belongs to him not you anymore, interferes with my self-respect a lot.

ROSEMARY: Some men use what's happened in the Bible to justify what they do to you.

DONNA: Men try to throw things up that happened to other people in the Bible and try to make you believe that [the Bible is] talking about you.

MARI: I left the church because [I believe the patriarchal nature of it leads to] violence against women. In all my time at church, I never heard any mention about abuse or domestic violence from the pulpit. It's never mentioned. No one talks about it. It's the biggest problem of our time. The church ignores it.

JANNA: The preacher tried to tell me what to do. I left home because of that [but] I'm going to stay in the church and do what I want to do.

Apparently, many shelter women are scrutinizing church, tradition, and scripture and their usage to sustain sexism and to justify abuse. Given that so many of the women are from evangelical/fundamentalist or Holiness/Sanctified churches, that is, churches that have held conservative notions about the inerrancy of scripture, their words are remarkable. They are finding suspect scripture or traditional scriptural hermeneutics. Their theological imaginations are being kindled by the inadequacy of tradition in the light of their experience of domestic violence. When they share such standpoints, they can initiate new ways of thinking.

Third, new ways of being Christian are explored. The third concern of local theology involves theological imagination. In the light of experience and under the influence of communally shared words, the theological imaginations of battered women are stirred. Surely Tina, Lisa, Rita, Janna, and other shelter women are exploring new ways of being Christian. They find redemption in the struggles of their own lives and they creatively recast their religious perspectives to accommodate their experience. When they think of the future, they think imaginatively or prophetically. This is one sign of local theology. For Tina, Lisa, and Rita, childbirth is not punishment for original sin—as in traditional or classical Christian theology. It is an aesthetic experience. Recall too Chloe's words in her conversation with Vanessa and me. She says: "A woman God is for women." Here are other isolated examples:

SADDIE: We are crossing to the Promised Land. We're in the Promised Land [shelter].

ROSEMARIE: When I got married to my husband, I promised before God and everybody to love, honor, and cherish till death us do part. But how can you stay with someone and have them literally destroy your self-esteem, your body, mind and soul? [. . .] I left. Jesus stuck up for women in the Bible.

RHODA: He thinks his religious is best of all religions. If a man argues with you about religion, to me he is not for me, because God does not bring any type of pain when he is spoken of—just joy. Think twice about [him] because he may very well become abusive.

Before they came to the shelter, Saddie, Rosemarie, and Rhoda were instructed by scripture, church traditions, ministers, and abusers. Not infrequently, they were told to stay in the abusive relationship and work to change it. In a new community, they are now thinking creatively about what it means to be a Christian—a safe one. Rosemarie and Rhoda know that abusers and some churches use scripture and tradition to limit the full humanity of women. They oppose. Though Rosemarie has not read feminist theology, she shares some of its interpretive strategies: She conceives the ministry of Jesus as concerned with gender-oppression—not an interpretation her church would abide.

But the women know they must find new interpretations. They must change or suffer, perhaps die. Their faith helps them to survive and to change. The foundations for local theology occur with remarkable frequency in their conversations: They question the culture, they dismiss unsatisfactory theological explanations, and they explore new ways of being Christian.

MODELS OF LOCAL THEOLOGY

What kind of local theology do battered women do? Aside from the three broad recurring concerns just presented, is all local theology the same sort of reconceptualization? Stephen Bevans was one of the first theologians to consider types of local theology. He outlines six models.[11] These are the translation model, the anthropological model, the praxis model, the countercultural model, the synthetic model, and the transcendental model.

A model is a framework, or mental construct, for thinking about reality. Yet because it is not reality, there is some slippage and this will be addressed shortly. However, of the six models of local theology, the praxis model is perhaps one of the most relevant—and the most enticing—to consider for language change in the Women's House.

In this model new theological concepts are grounded in tradition, scripture, and the context of people's lives. The praxis model emphasizes political action, reflection on action in the light of scripture, and renewed action in the light of reflection. The practitioner takes into account, for example, oppressive material conditions that hinder full human development and she seeks to change the conditions through human activity. Bevans identifies some feminist theological movements with the praxis model, particularly third world feminism. In the light of a feminist understanding of the causes and conditions of violence against women, the praxis model would be an ideal new development for shelter women who very frequently come out of traditional fundamentalist/evangelical or Holiness/Sanctified backgrounds.

However, battered women do not often participate in political activity because they are struggling with day-to-day issues of survival and do not immediately—if ever—become involved in activities such as lobbying, boycotting, and so forth for social change. This does not mean the women do not become politically active at some other point in their lives (though long-term change is not within the purview of this study) or that their language activity is not political. (I will discuss this again.) Still, the praxis model applies to some shelter women, especially women who later become involved in the shelter movement or who, for example, attend the "Take Back the Night" events. In addition, if words are considered action (a viewpoint to which linguists, since speech act theory, subscribe), the language activity of shelter women may be considered to fit the praxis model. In this context, reflection and action take place mostly on the language or interpersonal levels of meaning. Certainly, language use is political activity.

Yet, given the complexities of language and behavioral change, I find it useful to consider as well another schema for thinking about local theology. Richard Longenecker identifies seven models: the transferal model, the translation model, the anthropological model, the ethnological model, the transcendental model, the semiotic model, and the synergistic-developmental model. Of these models, the transferal and the ethnological models are most fitting to the language practices of women in the shelter.[12]

The transferal model most aptly fits the language of women who are functioning within the most conservative concepts of their abusers, scripture, religious communities, or traditions—for example, women in Phase One of the healing process have not yet been challenged to think more critically about domestic violence by other shelter women, volunteers, and staff. In this model, God is sovereign and all-powerful and scripture is heavily emphasized. Revelation is found in scripture. Consequently, there is no or little attention to sociological, political, or economic factors. Instead, there may be a lot of attention paid to whatever scripture or tradition—as it is imposed from context to context—displaces. Thus, for example, when abusive partners tell women that they are being beaten because they are not appropriately submissive, as Genesis 3:16 would seem to justify, there is a transferal from the scriptural-mythological context to the contemporary context. Shelter women may initially accept these more conservative theodicies or explanations of their suffering. They may believe their suffering is deserved or at least functional and that only grace is needed to cope and survive. I will discuss this model again but, briefly, I consider it an early or initial model under which many fundamentalist/evangelical and Holiness/Sanctified shelter women at least partially function. It also shows up in situations where "dual systems" of theology are functioning and I will illustrate this common occurrence in an upcoming section.

In the ethnological model, revelation is seen as God's ongoing activity in history. It is not confined to scripture or tradition though these are not ignored. The task of theology is to discern where God is acting and to try—through scripture, tradition, and reflective action, to act as God's partner. The analysis begins with human conditions, then turns to scripture, to work out political and social problems. Longenecker regards liberation theologies, including women's liberation, within this category. I consider it the model which many shelter women explore during their shelter experience partly because of the influence of more socially and politically minded women.

Overall, however, I find that the prophetic is not emphasized enough in the work of Longenecker or correctly in the work of Bevans as it is in, for example, Schreiter's attention to new kinds of Christian identity. Both Longenecker and Bevans consider liberation theologies, including feminist theologies, as fitting within their schemas as, respectively, ethnological or praxis. Neither theologian lingers on the prophetic. Bevans specifically flags the prophetic as a feature of the countercultural model. The countercultural model has a critical function that allows it to be prophetic both in terms of the culture and the church itself. It finds itself "over against the culture" and its task is to unmask antigospel elements. Yet, Bevans sets the countercultural model against the "neopagan," (123) even diabolical nature of the contemporary North American context. For him, North America has become "a culture of death (119)." Indeed, Bevans refers nostalgically to traditional American values in his description of the task of the countercultural model without recognizing that traditional American values kept women at home, under patriarchal control, and more oppressed than they are even today. Thus proponents of a countercultural model may very well be working at odds with proponents of a praxis or an ethnological model. They may be working at odds with battered women's advocates who struggle for full human rights for women—a countercultural struggle in a country still dominated by patriarchal politics and culture.

Still, along with the transferal model, the ethnological and the praxis models fit aspects of the language of healing in the shelter. At its best, the theological language of healing moves from the transferal model to the ethnological model to the praxis model—a continuum of sorts of overlapping to superseding language practices.

Scholars of contextual theology do not, inasmuch as I am aware, consider movement along these lines. My argument concerning the language of healing, however, entails a movement from conservative to more progressive models of theology. In short, as the lived experience of suffering is taken into account, the belief system of the sufferer becomes more fluid, more malleable. Belief systems are not static—as the categories of the contextual theologians might suggest. Instead, belief systems—under pressure from the lived experience of crisis and influenced by the lived experience of others—change.

This is the meaning of healing. A battered woman who is healing (and who actively functions within a Christian perspective) moves from an acceptance of transferal or conservative theologies to a reinvigorated language that recognizes the role of the social, economic, and political, to a reinvested, prophetic, or clearly creative language to reimagine God, evil, suffering, and other key concepts in Christianity.

In this chapter I will discuss this movement. I will deal with the transferal model in an upcoming discussion of dual systems. In the next sections I will deal with the ethnological and praxis models. Some women's language records with clarity the economic, social, and political; other women's language leans toward the prophetic.

THE ETHNOLOGICAL MODEL: ATTENTION TO THE SOCIAL, ECONOMIC, AND POLITICAL

In the shelter some women (learn to) emphasize the social, the economic, or the political in relation to God-talk. They associate or refer to God as they consider the secular-cultural context of domestic violence. These women are beginning to operate within an ethnological model of local theology.

Their words highlight different features of the model—the social, the economic, or the political. Below I will comment and provide illustrations of each emphasis—though, assuredly, it is sometimes artificial to separate them.

The Social

In chapter 6 I discussed the remedial/instructive theodicy. In this theodicy, suffering is considered soul-making. It leads to righteousness, compassion, and concern for others. It can be imposed by God or sometimes it can be self-imposed. Allie provided an illustration:

> Each day that I am away from home I am getting stronger and, as I get stronger, I become more comfortable with the changes that I'm making. My vision of myself in five years is to be a strong confident woman in a career helping to make a difference in women's lives. My experiences are preparing me for helping others. God is preparing me for something good.

Allie's words show traces of a move from a more individually-oriented theodicy into a more socially oriented theodicy. She seems to view her suffering ("my experiences") as more than a mystery, more than soul-shaping, more than expiatory. Instead, she has a more integrated perspective of both her suffering and her relationship with God. In short, Allie's words indicate more than theodicy; they suggest a new and local theology. Transformed by her shelter experience, she is concerned about more than her own suffering or the reasons for suffering. She learns from it. She engages new decision-making processes: She is making changes in her life. She has a vision of the future and it involves the risky venture of recreating her social and political identity. God and her lived experience impel this future. The vision includes care for women who are not as strong, confident, and socially integrated as she.[13] Allie learned about such women by living among them and recognizing herself as one of them. With a new social awareness (for which God is at least partly responsible), she is ready to press forward.

Millie's words also highlight social aspects of the ethnological model of local theology. She reenvisions gender or, perhaps more aptly, she tries to resocialize her conventionally socialized female conversation partners. That is, she conceives of herself and other battered women as courageous instead of fearful, active instead of passive, and legally informed instead of virtually isolated and alienated. Women should communicate with God through prayer and get on with the healing process. She says, "You shouldn't let fear overtake you! If you let it overpower you, you won't accomplish anything. Say a prayer, get legal advice, and take a risk."

Both women have come a long way from the relative silence and isolation of their first days at the shelter. They are recreating themselves, their concepts of appropriate behavior, and their relationship with God and others. Attending to social context, they link it with God-talk.

The Economic

When battered women function within an ethnological model of local theology, they attend to economic issues. Bettie is one of many women whose words relate an economic context with God-talk. She writes:

> Together we can accomplish all things if we just believe in ourselves and trust in God. I'm going back to school so that I can make things better for myself and my children. There's no man in my life because of my domestic situation. Maybe a man's not needed for now. But a car is!!! Joke. (:

Bettie has learned to see the economic aspects of her oppression. She renews her trust in God, but she knows she needs to be realistic. Without transportation, her life is unnecessarily complicated—even with her faith. Her words reflect a pragmatic concern and she resists considering—as she probably did consider when she lived with her abusive partner—that a man would take responsibility for her. Typical of the ethnological model in the shelter context: God—and not a man or husband—is seen as the suitable partner; yet, this is written with lightness or humor. Bettie fundamentally knows she needs to believe in and work for herself. Had they known each other, Bettie may have agreed with Chris's words: "The Bible says the meek will inherit the earth and [slaps hands], ladies, we know this is not true." Cinthia also associates God-talk with the economic context:

> I'm struggling for survival. I'm climbing the ladder, I have all these obstacles in my way, and I'm still struggling to get up and go around that ladder so I can live above the poverty level. Starting today, I, Cinthia, vow not to take the down [that is, that which makes me feel depressed] to heart but to take God to heart. I vow to get myself at a[n] economical status that I can cope with. I, Cinthia, decide to deal myself the Ace, K[ing], Q[ueen], J[ack] and to become all I can be in this lifetime. If women can conceive it, then women can achieve it.

Cinthia writes a manifesto of sorts. Like most shelter women, she has lost whatever financial resources her abusive partner provided. Yet she attacks her economic suffering or vulnerability head-on. She enlists God as her financial partner but, in so doing, she does not evade any responsibility. She is the one struggling, she is the one dealing, and she is the one envisioning the new future. Still her words suggest a sense of the collective strength or power of women: "If women can conceive it, then women can achieve it." The remarkable aspect of her language is the joining of God-talk, feminist-talk, and economic resolution: an ethnological approach.

Cinthia no doubt learned this new language from women like Nina. In the following short conversational excerpt, Loretta, Nina, and I are talking about violence against women and male misuse of power. Nina rejects Loretta's fundamentalist approach:

CAROL: Is it the devil making them do it?

LORETTA: It is.

NINA: It's about money, not the devil.

Yet the pragmatic Nina is as faithful as Loretta or Cinthia. She says, "I try to pray everyday." Clearly, these women are concerned with their economic situations. They don't accept economic deprivation as merited, remedial, or mysterious. Instead, they believe God is also concerned. This is one sign of an ethnologically oriented local theology. Economics matter and they matter to God. Simultaneously the women's words bear the traces of the healing language of the shelter: a sense of the interconnectedness with others, particularly for girls and women.

The Political

An ethnologically based local theology is implicitly, frequently explicitly, political. In fact, a criticism of this kind of local theology is that it tends to lean away from the gospel and toward the sociopolitical. When women change the way they talk about domestic violence and religion (for example, when they shift views about theodicy, as we discussed in chapter 5, or when they move through the phases of healing, as we discussed in chapter 7), they are subscribing to a different kind of linguistic politics. Still some shelter women begin to imagine the advantages of actual political activity. The following are isolated (that is, not from one conversation) examples of nascent political activism:

CAROLE: Now I think it's not worth it to indulge too much in misery. I think I want more action, less tears, more action, less pity.

IDA: If I had my way, I'd have a picket sign that says: "You can't do women that way!" You know, I feel this time [I left him] I really went far. I didn't care how he feels. I got justice and I got to start my life over. That's a lovely thing to look at! I'm going to get my degree! I'm going to go to school. I can really be myself.

PAT: We should have a Million Lady Walk.

TAMMY: Fight back legally. Not physically: You won't ever win. Come here and learn to fight back.

In one conversation, this exchange took place, indicating an attention to politics, an attention simultaneously laced with pragmatism, anger, and humor:

MICHELLE: Men run the government, the law, the state for the man.

HAZEL: For the man, of the man, by the man.

MICHELLE: I think we should have the '68 riots. For women. Sex riots. It should be a sex riot. We could close up [the city], the whole of us. Just stop working. No women go to work. The country will close up.

These women recognize the need for political action and social change. They know the status quo (that allows violence against women) needs to be challenged through activity. Although the exchange does illustrate it, Carole, Michelle, Hazel, and Ida are deeply faithful women. In a subsequent interview, Hazel provides these clear words: "I want to be remembered! I want something to say: Hazel was here! [. . .] I just hope the Lord gives me enough time to do something before I go." Later, she says: "I'm not really sure what. I have to figure out what. I want to know if, with what I've been through, is there something I can leave to someone else to save them from hurt? [. . .] Me and Patty were talking about it today."

Hazel cannot yet fully imagine a personal or political contribution. But she wants to alter the status quo. Indeed shelter women who talk about men and violence and, in the same breath, God and religion, often arrive at an ethnologically based local theology. They have arrived at the threshold of later stages of the healing process. Their problems are oftentimes overwhelming; yet, they see God's ongoing activity in their lives. They turn to the gospel to work out their problems, but the gospel is more than scripture or tradition. Revelation surfaces within the context of their own problems. The point of departure is the context itself—a context of suffering and injustice for women. In working for social, economic, and political change, they find God. They discover or uncover God as their partner for change.

Interestingly, the reinvigorated views of the women, especially those of Bettie and Allie, are not completely foreign to traditional Appalachian (or traditional African American) religiosity. As Mary Ann Hinsdale, Helen M. Lewis, and S. Maxine Waller argue, ". . . before it was overlaiden with the theme of salvation through personal conversion (which was really the message of the colonizing church and the Nashville recording industry), the early religious music of the Appalachian mountains was laden with themes of salvation through struggle." Hinsdale et al. argue that, in local theology, God is seen as a "creative partner."[14] This surely is how Bettie, Allie, and other shelter women see God.

THE PRAXIS MODEL: ATTENTION TO THE IMAGINATIVE AND PROPHETIC

Battered women sometimes imagine new ways to think about God and religion in their lives, ways not common to the traditional faith views of the congregations in which they were raised or worship. When the imaginative is brought to the foreground, I consider such language practices as evidence of a praxis model of local theology. In Bevans's praxis model, he notes the importance of the dialectic movement of reflection and action. That is, he accentuates political activity. Typically, battered women cannot engage in actual political activity: They are struggling with day-to-day survival issues. In my view, and in keeping with the view of language as action, when battered women theologize in imaginative or prophetic ways, they are doing the hard work of action and reflection in the light of their situations. Another feature of this language is a sense of the basic goodness of women rather than their innate or original sinfulness. It is not easy for battered women to reject these traditional views for these more creative—if sometimes unsystematic—views. When they do so, their words are well-received in the shelter, if not vigorously applauded. These are isolated (that is, not from one and the same conversation) examples:

CHLOE: If God were a woman, it would be wonderful!

ALMA: God shelters us women. He gives us somewhere to go. Here. I didn't know about this place. I got rewarded with this place.

WANDA: Do I think God is a man? I think he is whatever you want him to be. He's been a mother to me.

CARRIE: If God were a woman, a lot of men would be going to hell.

JAYLENE: The [church] mother is like a spiritual mother and you can tell her anything. Mother is probably the wisest person in the church and there's always a church mother. [The pastor is not] more reliable than the mother.

DELA: They know she's been talking to God. She's the one who talks to God. A man just shouts when the Holy Spirit comes. A woman speaks in tongues.

Prophetically, the women invert tradition. Here battered women are select, God's choice. Imaginatively, the women suggest that women, not men, are made in God's image; women, not just men, hold teaching status; women, not men, commune with God. Ultimately, men will have to answer for their shabby treatment of women as inferior or subordinate.

Other women, speaking imaginatively, clarify God's partnership. In the following short conversational excerpt, Rae and Manni are reinvesting the meaning of a relationship with God. They are not just recipients of punishment, remediation, or mystery. For Manni, especially, the relationship must entail women's basic self-sufficiency. She moves Rae to acknowledge that even a partnership still entails women's basic independence and responsibility:

RAE: [My abuser said every bad thing to me.] God told me in my ear to say to him: "I rebuke you!" I said it. I said, "I rebuke you!" [My abuser] turned around and didn't, couldn't, hit me. I felt so powerful with God's spirit. We're in this together. It's not a one-man show. God says, "You can!" I can!

MANNI: Well, I think you have to help yourself first.

RAE: God will not come down from the sky. God will not come down from the sky to make it all go away. You have to work with God.

Manni, Dela, Jaylene, and other women are working imaginatively, creatively, sometimes prophetically. They push at the edges of ordinary or traditional views. To greater and lesser degrees, they lay aside the sexism of their churches and abusers and they welcome more imaginative and creative relations with God and others. They aren't afraid to add some intensity or vigor to their understanding of justice. One woman, Deena, said, "Baptists are hard on women. They make it hard to be equal. You know, Jesus was a guy. But, honestly, you know, he went as far as to protect Mary Magdalene. She was a prostitute. He stuck up for women. The crowd wanted to hurt her. He said, "You dare if you are without sin!"

THE DEVELOPMENT OF LOCAL THEOLOGY: AN EXTENDED EXAMPLE

In the last chapter, I characterized Vanessa and Chloe as moving away from Irenian/evolutionary (that is, misuse of free will; teaching by moral contrast) theodicy and toward liberation theodicy. In terms of local theology, I would characterize their words as ethnologically based, but tending toward or approaching a praxis model. Recall these words:

CHLOE: The country is run by rich white men. The church too.

VANESSA: That's why I don't belong to no church. I read the Bible. Now and then I read the Bible. I feel in my heart what I have to do. I ain't going by his rules or her rules. No, I can't get into that.

CHLOE: I be having a problem with the Bible all the time. Most people do, but they just believe anyway. They don't admit the story is wrong. [. . .] The Bible starts out with Adam and Eve. The world thinks women are evil. Eve got Adam to eat the apple. Everyone says women are evil. So the stories in the Bible are like that—against women. It is not right.

Through dialogism, Chloe and Vanessa arrive at fuller and more fitting theology. In another example, the talk yields up elements of transferal, ethnological, and praxis-oriented theologies:

PRISCILLA: For me, it starts with having a strong foundation with spiritual principles and beliefs, not necessarily religion, not necessarily traditional, or orthodox, or family values. It's about raising our children differently. It's about loving-kindness as part of a daily routine. Education is important in terms of educating about different groups of people, individuals, and groups. Even more, it's loving yourself.

CAROL: What is spirituality to you?

PRISCILLA: Spirituality is consciousness or contact with a higher power, believing and knowing and accepting there's a force out there. It's greater than yourself and it works through you and gives you the power to change yourself. Thus changing policy, some form of policy. It gives you the power to change policy. If you have a spiritual foundation, you can do things. So a higher power is the answer.

CHARLENE: I know that by being here I feel extremely strong. Stronger than I've been ever. In terms of speaking up for myself. Education is the big thing. I lived for years in abuse without knowing I was in it. I've gone through hospitals, twelve step programs, all kinds of programs. They all helped me but knowing the truth, being here, and living with other women who have experienced abuse has enlightened me and made me strong. I don't deserve this [abuse]. This is the first time I've felt this way. That's from being here, and talking to other women, finding out I have other options. I didn't know I had other options. The biggest thing that will stop [violence against women] is education. Educate the men, educate the women, and pray a lot. Faith helps me get strong.

PRISCILLA: Society tells you everything: how to dress, how to think, how to do everything. How can you change society?

AMANDA: If society could feel or know what the abuse is like. Men should experience what abuse is like. Women take a lot of mental abuse. It almost destroys them. Maybe they wouldn't be abused, if men experienced abuse. To me this is my home. I feel safe, wanted, and loved here. I hate to leave. I intend to come back as a volunteer or as a social worker. It makes me feel like I am a person. Abused persons feel alone. You think: No one will understand me. Here, it makes me feel human again.

PRISCILLA: I'm not gonna let anyone do anything with me or to me. It comes back to our value system. Because we live in a democracy, I think people understand what that is. We have to empower ourselves and the groups we live with. We need politics. The judicial, the legislative. It's politics. We need to vote in people who vote in our values. For instance, with domestic violence. It should be a felony. You need to get the people elected to change the policy.

CAROL: Do you think women ever will really be equal to men?

PRISCILLA: No, they'll never be equal.

LISA: I won't say women won't ever be equal. I will be.

PRISCILLA: Society is set up in a triangle and very few are up in the triangle. You know that triangle you learn about in sociology? Carol, you know that triangle I mean? They teach about it in school.

CAROL: Yeah, I know it.

PRISCILLA: You can't change it.

EMILY: Talking is cheap. You have to do something about it. You have to try to least. Then you can say: I tried. You have to keep trying. Women do not stick together. They don't want anyone to know about their shame, their abuse. They are ashamed. You got to stick together. Women got to act together. Go to the streets.

MICHELLE: Like then. Like before.

CAROL: Like in the civil rights days?

MICHELLE: Yeah, like fighting for civil rights.

AMANDA: Faith says we are all created equal. The constitution, men wrote that up. But who is controlling the system? Man is running the system. Man and women are created equal. The

Bible says: Man and woman are created equal. God created them the same.

LISA: We need a woman president.

EMILY: Why can't women get together and protest? Why don't we get together out there and change the laws? Women are scared. We need to march in the streets.

AMANDA: Women have to voice their views until the policies are changed. The judge doesn't deter men from domestic violence. I would make it a felonious assault. Women are afraid to speak up. They think men will hurt them. He gets a DV [domestic violence citation]. Does a few weeks in jail. She thinks he will change. He won't because he sees it don't cost him. The law needs change. The woman needs to speak up.

EMILY: Women chicken out. Women are scared of the system. They belittle them. You think you might as well stay where you are.

AMANDA: I knew this man he beat his woman. He done beat her brains out once. No woman can beat on a man. No woman can beat on a man like that. I know what I would do if it happened to me.

LISA: I called the police. It was like a joke.

CHARLENE: The police don't care.

EMILY: They always ask: Aren't you going to leave? I want to say: Are you going to take care of me?

AMANDA: They say you have to go downtown. They don't care if you are bleeding and you have to go to the hospital. At the last minute, I chickened out. The first time, nothing. If the person has a history, then the police will sign the warrant.

PRISCILLA: You have to be almost dead. Police, she'll be dead when you come back. In a body bag.

LISA: The police only asked questions. [My abuser] knew they wouldn't be trouble.

AMANDA: Did you speak out?

LISA: I did speak out. They did nothing. As a result, other things happened and my life is fucked up totally. They told him to leave the house. Go cool off. Go calm down.

MICHELLE: There has to be a protest. You have to do something like march it out.

AMANDA: Like women trying to get the vote. All the women protested in marches.

MICHELLE: Men think they are the dominant sex and women has no say so. They need to get that out of their heads.

AMANDA: They misinterpreted those verses in the Bible. He ate the fruit too. They always put it on the woman. Adam, it's his own fault. Why are they blaming women?

AMANDA: Society has to get back to praising God and living by the word of God. Who takes care of everything when the man leaves the house? The woman.

MICHELLE: There was this woman defending herself. She hit him with a bottle. They arrested her. He beat her. They locked her up instead of him.

LISA: They need a self-defense law. Women are too afraid to go to the police.

This lengthy conversation shows clear and distinct signs of unfolding local theology. All the features of an ethnologically based local theology occur, including serious and prolonged attention to social, economic, and political issues. The views are filtered through the women's personal experience of battery, but they are honed in the communal task of making sense of women's oppression. A strong sense of faith runs through the talk, mostly upheld by Charlene, Priscilla, and Amanda. Traditional religious views—that is, signs of a transferal model originating in scripture, tradition, or the abuser—are rejected. For example, Amanda rejects the Genesis passages about Adam and Eve and those men who use it to oppress women. Priscilla also offers an explicit rejection of traditional views. Replacing such transferred concepts with praxis-oriented concepts, she links God (that is, "higher power," in the language of twelve step programs) directly to politics: ". . . it works through you and gives you the power to change yourself. Thus changing policy. . . ."

There is other evidence of praxis-based theology, including the attention given to the civil rights struggle, human rights, feminist street action, women in politics, voting, and education. Traditional sexist biblical hermeneutics are rejected and feminist (or at least woman-oriented) hermeneutics are admitted to the conversation. Though the women also intertwine less progressive ideas in their reflection and call to action, they are perceptibly entering a praxis-oriented theology. That is, despite the dual belief systems, they are moving toward a more local and liberatory theology.

EVIDENCE OF DUAL SYSTEMS: CHANGE AND DIALOGIC ACTIVITY

THE TRANSFERAL MODEL

Battered women (my basic research argument holds) devise alternative theodicies or theologies by way of the interplay of diverse languages and lived experience. Given that most women enter the shelter in late Phase

One or early Phase Two stages of the healing process, I am admittedly making an argument for considerable change. In linguistic/semiotic theory, however, change is not considered the total elimination of one system of signs. It's the incorporation of new signs, messages, or codes in an already existing system of signs. In the shelter context, there may be operant dual systems of belief in which older theological systems continue alongside newer systems. Clearly, this is what frequently happens in the shelter. When Tina wonders that a female God might have "the PMS thing" in one breath and in the next says that a female God would make her life better, she's clearly operating out of two belief systems—if not more. But there is a shift, and from a feminist healing perspective, a shift with potential.

The language of many other women yields forth evidence of dual belief systems. Dela, an African American Pentecostal woman, talks about church rules and regulations. She says:

> You are supposed to be away from worldly things, not wear pants. My grandmother would wear no makeup. But I think if you don't feel guilty, it's okay. I hate the color of my lips. I want to change the color with lipstick. But if my heart is right, by God, I'll be all right. My uncle, he says, "Don't eat pork." But when God says if you are saved or not, he doesn't think if you eat pork or don't eat it. He [my uncle] thinks his diet is going to come in question! I doubt it! But I won't wear big earrings. My face wouldn't be made up like Tammy Faye. God has to let them know it's no use trying to make it fit your beliefs like you want. You have to do all of it. My aunt used to be a Muslim, but she's Apostolic now. She knows it has to be real. There's a feeling in the church. She's filled with the Holy Spirit, speaks in tongues, praises. . . .

Dela struggles with the Apostolic tradition. She holds contrary views. On the one hand, she believes rules can be bent or broken. For example, God will not ultimately care if dietary laws are broken. She knows the church calls for modesty in appearance, but she cannot afford dresses. So she goes to church in pants, not an appropriate choice for Apostolic women. Her compromise is to wear a hat. On the other hand, Dela maintains that one should not tailor beliefs. "You have to do all of it." She says, "The Bible is right about women" though it may appear sexist. Yet she also believes that women "get the tongues" when the Holy Spirit comes and that a man "just shouts." In short, her lived experience cuts through tradition and scripture at some points, but not others. Consequently, she lives with contradiction or dual systems.

In one remarkable conversation, Mari and Deidra disagreed heartily in their perspectives on suffering. Deidra is Baptist and she believes Satan is responsible for suffering and evil. Mari is a Catholic with a well-developed social perspective. She argued that "systems and not Satan" are responsible for some of the tragedies she's experienced: child incest, domestic violence, and sexism in the church. By the end of the conversation (which I can only summarize here and not quote because I did not have a recording device that evening), Deidra admitted systems such as the police, the courts, and culture are partly responsible for her troubles too. But Satan, the epitome of evil, stood outside her concession as a decontextualized, depraved, ultimate source.

In a different conversation, Wanda seemed slightly more willing to question. Raised Holiness, she is now Baptist. Her father, a Holiness minister, was abusive. Wanda functions within dual systems of belief. With a deeply fundamentalist predilection, she says,

> What causes domestic violence? All evil comes from Satan. We wrestle not against flesh and blood. I am not waging war against my father, my abuser. We are dealing with the force driving that person, the power making the person do what he does.

Later, with a strong sense of the injustices done to women, she says,

> I have a special responsibility to women and girls. I look at these women, they come to me, they break down, boo-hoo, on the verge of a nervous breakdown. I'm not professionally trained. I'm spiritually trained. In their lives, they are worrying and worrying. As soon as I convince them to stop worrying so much and immediately something happens! I say, "Didn't I tell you? Remember this day. He'll help you now and later on." Lord, thanks for using me to serve, to help others, an instrument to help.

But she also says, "According to God, [men] have been placed in an authoritative role. The order is God, then men, women, then children. We can't turn our sons into women." Wanda yearns for social change, but she is caught in tradition. She has a dual belief system. One system may weaken enough to collapse into the other.

At the shelter, dual systems are continually challenged: an advantage of interaction. Sometimes the interventions are immediate; thus, the contradictions are apt to be resolved quickly. In the following conversation, Tara, Diamond, and I discuss coping strategies. The talk turns quickly to religion. Tara, a member of a white Holiness church, offers a more progressive perspective than Diamond, who grew up as a Seventh-Day Adventist and is now Baptist.

DIAMOND: I don't trust men, but I don't really trust women either. Still I put my trust in men. God is a man.

TARA: Who said that? God is no [gender.]

DIAMOND: The Bible says, "The father, the son, and the holy ghost." If Eve hadn't done what she did, everything would be fine.

TARA: That's what men believe!

DIAMOND: They have been used like we have and we can't trust each other.

CAROL: If women can't be trusted, where do you get the confidence to go on? You think the pastor is more trustworthy or wise than the church mother?

DIAMOND: The pastor isn't wiser than the church mother.

Challenged by her interlocutors, Diamond hedges into a dual belief system. Ultimately, Diamond reformulates her words as she reacts to scrutiny. Peer influence does its job and, arguably, initiates some ideological change. If Diamond is simply caving in, she has at least been invited to scrutinize her position—the first step toward reformulating it.

No Healing and No Change

One night a young Baptist woman, Ellie, joined our writing session. She addressed our topic—how God has helped me as a battered woman—in this way:

> I believe in God and prayer, but I wonder why He is letting some things happen in my life. I went to church and took my three kids the last eight years of my marriage, without my husband and through the separation. Everything seems to be going my husband's way. My husband, Joe, would hit my oldest son and tell him he was stupid. He was verbally abusive to all three kids and me. It looks like he is going to get temporary custody of the children because no one will listen to me. God knows all that has happened and I don't understand why he would let my children go through this.

Ellie had not yet taken a more comprehensive view about domestic violence and religion. She questions, but remains relatively inactive. Loraine, an Apostolic woman, wrote this:

One week prior to my severe beating, I told a friend if God does not take me out of this situation soon, I am not going to be able to keep going on. I prayed over and over every day, asking God to take the burden and the whole situation off my shoulders. I felt that God was not listening to me because the abuse—instead of things changing, things became worse. I really felt like giving up on prayers. Right when I couldn't take anymore, God took me out of the situation. I was put on a plane, sent to people I did not know, left my home, children, job, etc. I finally had the strength from out of nowhere to leave the abuse. God answers our prayers in his own precious time, not in our time. So now, I continue to give all to him and wait for his answer or what will be sent to me next.

Loraine believes experience has changed her, but she has not changed enough to reorder her life. She waits passively for God to direct her. Neither Ellie nor Loraine have a convincing local theology yet or even a convincing social view of domestic violence. There is no sense of reckoning with social, economic, or political matters. Ellie is thwarted; Loraine is unmotivated. They wait for things to happen instead of making things happen. Ellie does seek out the shelter, but Loraine seems to get there by magic. And both women are still vulnerable to violence.

In this study I have tried to capture one strand of language change (that is, religious) when battered women heal; yet, not every woman heals and not everyone heals in the way I have described. Not every woman benefits from shelter life in the same way. Some women change, but not when they live in the shelter. Other women change, but they would not attribute the change to language dynamics or the shelter experience. Some change, but not in a healing or healthy direction. Finally, some women come and go from the shelter without significant change. The possibilities are many. When women do not heal, however, there may be common reasons or patterns. These concern the individual, the residents, or the shelter as an institution. I will briefly touch on some possibilities.

Individual Circumstances

Psychological states may prevent significant personal change. A woman may be too traumatized, overwhelmed, depressed, or fatigued. Most communal activity is voluntary and some women do not engage in it. Reasons vary.

Many women leave the shelter without serious transformation. They go to families or friends where they participate in familiar social and religious practices. Other women return to their partners. They do not see the emotional advantage of change even if they understand the political arguments for it. Many women simply are afraid of their abusers or their churches. Change jeopardizes the fragile balances of power in relationships and they do not want to imperil the few resources they access in those relationships. In short, they see survival as a matter of accommodation rather than transformation.

Undoubtedly, some women do not see the shelter as a safe place to disclose facts or feelings. They forgo the chance to talk, thus learn, with others. Some women have no, little, or different religious backgrounds. They sit silently, not wishing to offend or change. Some women resist social explanations for domestic violence; instead, they think they just got a bad partner. Next time, they hope to select a more compassionate partner or they want to change their current partners, not themselves. Women may use the shelter in their struggle for power with their partners. They do not seriously think about domestic violence because they do not believe they are victims of it even if they have physical or emotional injuries.

Individual women may not change because of medical, physiological, or situational reasons. They may be in withdrawal from drugs/alcohol or impacted by physical injury. They may be physically or mentally ill or challenged. There are myriad reasons why women do not change: Some may be very good and convincing indeed.

Resident Dynamics

Sometimes shelter women show no signs of change. Resident interaction is a reason. Sometimes cliques or factions form. Races and ages conflict; personalities clash. A woman is stigmatized and shunned. Ultimately, there may be insurmountable conflict. In any of these scenarios, the formation of community is thwarted—not surprising because tensions run high in the shelter, the stresses are enormous, and activities to siphon them off are few and far between.

Children and views about child-rearing are frequent sources of interpersonal conflict. Difficulties stemming from slim resources—sometimes as minor as access to clothes donations or bus tokens—result in conflict and dispute. The conflict sweeps beyond dyad and triad boundaries to affect house dynamics.

Incredibly, there may be no one in the shelter to provide enthusiasm, direction, or guidance for change. For whatever reason, the residents, the staff, or volunteers at any one time may be relatively uncommunicative or unresourceful. This happens particularly around holidays when residents are unhappy to be at the shelter. There is little incentive to develop relations because they are desperate to find a place to stay—anywhere besides a shelter during a holiday. Relatedly, the rapid turnover in residents may also be relevant. Generally, women are allowed to stay for six weeks; yet, sustained talk may be necessary for authentic change. Change is hard to maintain without extended relationships. This is an argument for more transitional programs.

These are only some of the reasons that dynamics may be thwarted or spoilt between interlocutors. As with ordinary conversationalists anywhere, there can be numerous obstacles to healthful communication. Given their history and their stresses, it is remarkable battered women communicate as well as they do.

Shelter Issues

Ironically, the shelter may inadvertently prevent the changes it seeks in battered women. It is often understaffed, the workers underpaid, overworked, and unhappy. Resource cuts eliminate staff, programs suffer, community-building opportunities are lost. Consequently, fewer viable conceptual alternatives are available. The shelter women may have to organize their own interaction. Of course, this happens and, women being as resourceful as they are, it can happen very well indeed. There are other reasons the shelter may inhibit transformation. As I argued in chapter 2, some factors as subtle as architectural design have significant impact on interaction. On the other hand, shelter rules and regulations can thwart a recalcitrant woman from change. Women are not infrequently sent away for infractions. The shelter can significantly constrain healing.

In summary, there are many reasons shelter women may not change. These are related to individuals, the dynamics between residents, the institution, or a combination of these reasons. For any one of these reasons, or for reasons unknowable to us, a woman may be "bracketing" or avoiding personal growth either through or beyond the development of local theology. Finally, it must be acknowledged that linguistic performance is not a guarantee of authentic or long-term change. Still, when linguistic change occurs, there is reason for hope.

RETHINKING THE PROBLEM OF EVIL: FURTHER EVIDENCE OF NEW THEOLOGY

Before I conclude this chapter, I would like to visit briefly a few themes that arise around particularly late Phase Two and Phase Three battered women's notions of suffering and evil.[15] These are themes that arise about some of the basic traditional terms in theodicy: evil, sin, suffering, grace, salvation/redemption, and relations with God/Other. They further suggest local theology.

In most religious traditions, *evil* is viewed as the opposite or absence of good. Traditionally, men have located the cause or origin of evil in women.

For particularly Phase Three women, evil is primarily located in systems that allow women to be harmed or to go without justice, for example, the legal, political, or religious systems. Evil is the ensuing violation of the well-being of women and their children. After anger against partners subsides, women see the factors like the inefficacy of the law enforcement, judicial, and penal systems that allow men to hurt women with impunity. By extension, they criticize cultural institutions, including religious ones, for creating a climate in which it is possible to hurt women without censure. The mixing of secular social work language with the women's religious language facilitates the shift.

For particularly Phase Three battered women, *sin* is epitomized by a violation of individual or communal well-being and it originates in systems whose activities lead to domestic violence. Actions are interrelated and thus no one person or event is completely removed from others or another. Abusers come to be seen as men who make poor decisions about relationships, but they learned it from dysfunctional birth family relations, social institutions, and other culture-shapers, including churches. In the logic of many African American women, societal racism leads to individual frustration that then leads to poor choices within domestic partnerships. No excuse is made for the batterers, but a shelter woman who has been in dialogue with staff members and informed residents and volunteers, for example, can see the interrelationship between such factors.

In traditional theology, *grace* is understood as God's mercy for humans in their sinfulness. Except for early Phase One shelter women, most shelter women do not see themselves as fundamentally sinful—thus deserving of their woes. As they learn about the dynamics of domestic violence, they reject the name-calling and bodily harm doled out by abusers. While acknowledging some denominational differences, I believe many battered women see grace as arising in connection with other people; that is, grace is not simply God's divine power to forgive and transform, but their own relational openness in the context of family, particularly children, and community that redeems. This belief may come from the experience of being called out of shame and isolation by other women in the shelter in the process of healing. For example, as Tina and Rita's words in an earlier section suggest, there seems to be no, few, or permeable boundaries between the sacred and the ordinary. Battered women also find solace in one another—an opportunity they were denied before their escape from their partners. Their appreciation for one another as companions on the road to freedom is remarkable—a noticeable feature of community talk.

Suffering is a part of everyday life for battered women and, to some degree, all women. In traditional theology, suffering derives from sin. In many battered women's view suffering is immediate, male originating, and (for many Phase Three women) not related to the women's behavior. They learn that male violence is nearly always random. Women's broken bones and hearts, bruised flesh and feeling, carry the weight of evidence here. When they talk to other battered women, they learn that explanations based on individual sinfulness do not make sense.

With respect to *salvation or redemption*: In traditional theology, the unique role of Jesus is emphasized in the workings of salvation. Jesus frees us from evil through his death and resurrection. However, in the throes of a dual system of belief—a belief system composed of both traditional and alternative ideas—some (particularly Phase Three) women at the shelter seem to believe that salvation/redemption means righting relations so that women and their children obtain safety and peace. To illustrate: Most battered women rethink the meaning and composition of family to be safe. Salvation is being realized as they enter the shelter and as their new life unfolds. There is generally much praise and thanksgiving. There is hope for the new relations with children and other women though there is usually little interest in relations with men. If there is talk about relationships with men, it is not romanticized or idealized talk. As one battered woman said, "I haven't seen anyone pick up a romance novel here!"

In fact, and finally, *relations with God and others* are desirable if they are characterized by mutuality. Women who are healing see right relationship as characterized by equality of power and responsibility and love that does not oppress or consume. Indeed, the model for right relationship is friendship. For example, when a Phase One woman moves out of the isolation within which her abuser imprisons her, she rediscovers the strength and the joy that comes from finding solace and support in a web of friends, allies, or companions. These opportunities are not always available; instead, many women's needs are subsumed to service to others. Perhaps Mary E. Hunt is right: The opposite of suffering is not pleasure; it's friendship.[16]

The changes are due to the mixing of languages within the shelter. Given these transformations, these manifestations of local theology I, like Kathleen M. Sands, believe it is time "to exorcise the patriarchal language of evil, sin, and suffering and to enlist ideals such as justice in the service of women" (67) or others held captive by unjust systems of domination.

FIVE CRITERIA FOR DISCERNING GENUINE LOCAL THEOLOGY

In *Constructing Local Theologies*, Robert Schreiter offers five criteria to discern the "genuineness" of local theology. First, it should have internal consistency. Second, it should be able to translate into worship. Third, the theological expression should pass muster in terms of "orthopraxis": its consequences should be good and just. Fourth, the theology should be open to critique. Fifth, the theology should positively challenge other churches.

Does the theological expression of women meet these criteria? Many professional theologians might not consider the language of shelter women as local theology. After all, the shelter is not a regional unit though it does reflect regional language practices. It is not a religious unity though it does reflect denominational backgrounds of a particular class, race, and regional mix of women. It is not a cultural setting in which theological expression is officially encouraged though suffering often invokes spontaneous theological expression.

From the theologian's standpoint, shelter women's language may qualify relatively on the grounds of the second (that is, translatable to worship), third (that is, orthopraxis), fourth (that is, open to criticism), and fifth (that is, strength) criteria. Within this local manifestation, the ideas women have about God do have viable strength, openness to criticism, and empowering results. The women's God-talk, in fact, is worship—acts of testifying and witnessing. The language of the shelter women does not have internal consistency—Schreiter's first criterion—because it is evolving. It is fragmented and inconsistent. It is the very aligning and colliding dialogic nature of language that offers the possibility of new formations at all. Thus shelter women's language reflects nascent local theology if consideration is given to matters of form—the crux of Schreiter's first criterion.

The problems with local theology? It is selective, argues Patrick Bascio, and others note that it does not systematically address all theological issues.[17] Then there is the question of form. Theology is dominated by scholarly forms. Currently, however, questions of agency, authority, and form are being reconsidered. In *Models of Contextual Theology*, Bevans allows even dance and other art forms as legitimate vehicles for theology. Within such a scope, battered women's conversational fragments would qualify. Of course, shelter women themselves do not characterize their talk as theology. Instead, they see it as acts of "witnessing" or "testifying." For them, it is worship or preaching. Consider Sabrina's words: "Women can preach the word of God. We can preach the Word of God by discussion. It's not a theological discussion. If you speak in his name, you are preaching the Word of God. We are doing it right now. It's the Holy Spirit." For me, Sabrina's and other women's language is truly nascent local theology: the beginnings of authentic social and theological change through language as action.

CONCLUSION: LOCAL THEOLOGY AS SOCIAL CHANGE

In Christianity, salvation is change. It means deliverance from evil into a new reality. Does this happen for Vanessa, Chloe, Tina, Lisa, and Rita? Escape from a partner who uses patriarchal religion to justify his abuse is deliverance paradoxically sustained by a different, deeper faith. Most importantly, local theology is evidence of social change: an essential point given that many activists think battered women are too traumatized for street action or political work.

Models are analytical tools used to produce rational and systematic observations. They cannot completely capture the linguistic, social, and psychological complexities of the healing processes of battered women. Some last thoughts about the women's language:

The contextualizing is the healing. A battered woman begins to heal as she contextualizes her story. She casts the unhappy events in narrative form and critiques them through theological language (or another discourse with affective components). The details entail the historical, social, economic, political, and theological. As she provides or is provided with these details, she moves out of the silence and isolation of the initial stage of healing, she works with the anger and sorrow of the second phase of healing, and she develops a sense of interconnection and the need for action of the last phase of healing. Abusers decontextualize scripture to gain power; together, the women recontextualize.

The sense of interconnection is the theological change. When women contextualize, they see similarities in their stories. Situating oneself in context means mapping out relations. Women connect and, by mixing of ideas, jointly develop new ideas about God and relationship. Abuse is disconnection; healing is reconnection. In theological terms, the discourse used by so many battered women *is* the new theology.

The theological change is the political action. Since the development of speech act theory, linguists commonly refer to words as action. The development of concepts of more equity for women in their families and faith communities is the ideological shift necessary to fuel further social action.

The long and short: Battered women share their stories of suffering. Their lived experience and shared knowledge uncovers problems with the usual recourses for relief: church and scripture. They imagine new language, new relationships, and new theology. Healing happens. Women resist, even faithful ones.

CONCLUSION

"Take Me to My Sister's House"

My best friend here is someone who is always there for me no matter what. When I'm in trouble, she's there to help me out. She doesn't care if she gets into trouble to help me. She's like a sister to me.

—Lia

For battered women, the problem of evil is a concrete problem, not an abstract theological one. They suffer from bruises and broken bones. They suffer from the loss of income, housing, transportation, food, furniture, and clothing. Sometimes they have had to leave behind their children. Battered women suffer from anxiety, fear, anger, loneliness, and depression. Even in the relative safety of the shelter, they often are concerned for their very lives:

JANEY: I'm scared if I walk out these doors, I might not have my life.

ALMA: I don't want to be another woman who was put in her grave by her husband. I don't want to walk down the street and have him kill me.

Women like Janey and Alma know they will continue to suffer—almost always materially or economically, sometimes physically, spiritually, and psychologically—even as they slowly heal from the trauma and pain inflicted by violent partners. As Lynette starkly puts it: "I'm going to suffer. I'll suffer even after today." The reality of systemic oppression is not beyond the ken of shelter women. It is a rare woman who passes through the Women's House who does not know she is suffering from a pervasive sexism in her personal relationship with her abuser and in society. She may not understand all the ways the social organization of values, beliefs, and activities—that is, language and culture—cause sexism, but she knows women suffer from it.

Most women will readily acknowledge that the patriarchal church is integrally involved in the problem. They know by lived experience within their family, social, and faith communities that men in a male-dominated society often use religion to manipulate and ultimately harm women. Most battered women do not have naïve attitudes about the problem of evil or simple faith solutions to their problems. Marnay, a resident, puts her faith in perspective. "What's keeping me going? My family and friends and the support I get from the shelter. Working everyday. Medication I'm on. My personal relationship with God." She knows she will have to work for herself and with other women to cope with her crisis—no matter what her faith community has to say about the relationship of God to evil and suffering.

Still the women persist faithfully. Maxine says it simply in her declaration to the men in her life: "To all the men I loved: God loved me more." To survive, women like Maxine and the many other women whose voices fill the pages of this book rely strongly on their faith. But often enough it is their own situated articulation of faith shaped within a new local context—the conversation of shelter life and the immediate concerns of their crisis. Not infrequently, the women resist strongly traditional sexist formulations of their faith or their suffering. They are able to integrate new concepts carved out of collectively shaped stories of trauma and abuse. Indeed, the argument writ short of this study has been that, despite the harmful patriarchal nature of their religion, shelter women sustain their faith. At best, their theologies are made more subtle and less sexist by the sharing of stories. The dialogic processes of language—the mixing, juxtaposing, reinventing of meaning— create new vision and sometimes social change. At the very least, most women help one another begin to heal by talking about the issues that matter to them: suffering, family, God, and faith. Sometimes critical questions arise. Witness another brief example of the process in the following conversation as the women help one another work out new ideas, the makings of newly situated theodicy or theology:

DELISE: It took me six years to figure out I didn't have to suffer. I suffered! I felt like it was my fault.

LYNETTE: You felt guilty.

DELISE: Suffering is pain and I am so sick of pain. They say time heals all wounds. I've accepted pain don't leave overnight. I'm tired of suffering. Sometimes I'm making myself suffer because it tends to make me feel sorry for him. He done me wrong and I shouldn't feel sorry for him. But I do. But I will never ever ever ever go through this again.

STELLA: He's gonna make it all right. The Father above. You have suffered enough. He's gonna make it right.

DELISE: Well, I don't know who it is, but it's some being I met from above. It gave me strength whatever it is. . . . A strong, determined feeling. I don't want to suffer anymore. It is done, done, done. [My abuser] took kindness for weakness. That's what's wrong. People take kindness for a weakness.

STELLA: It's not your battle. It's His. He'll help from above.

DELISE: No one can change the situation or make the suffering disappear. You have to do it yourself. No one can get you out of it. You have to do it. But I always say, someone else's situation might be worser, way worser than yours. Someone can help, but I'm doing this by myself. I put my foot forward. I said, "No more! I said, "This is the lowest I could go!" I've never been in this situation in my life. I had things good all my life. But now I'm making a change. The power has come to me. I will never be like this again. Never.

In this short conversation, Stella encourages Delise to see that she can be inspired by faith to leave a seemingly hopeless domestic situation. Delise agrees that she is helped by a kind of faith she cannot unambiguously define, but she invites Stella to see that a woman ought not to wait in attitudes of theological or social passivity for God to change her situation. Delise may have assistance from a non-gendered "being" above, but it was her social intercourse with other people that helps her to see what she needs to do. Notice that, while she defers to the *strength* and *power* she receives supernaturally, she emphasizes the action of speaking to others: *I said, I always say.* . . . She knows she must move into more active modes of healing, growing, changing. God helps, but she is putting her "foot forward." Notice too that "the power" is expressed in non-gendered terms.

This conversation does not demonstrate new theology, but it prefigures one. It prefigures a new religious language tempered by social language and lived experience. One day Stella, who holds more traditional religious views, may speak it. With Delise as interlocutor, she is participating in a system that entails it. With some prompting by Delise, Stella at least concedes that God helps; God does not simply make everything all right. This is an ideological shift. One day, Delise may reinflect her utterances to recognize how a political "sisterhood"—here, the shelter as an institution and as a community of women— did indeed help her out of her situation. She put her foot forward because of her access to women who help women by living a more politically aware life— in this case, made manifest by the shelter as a material location and an ideological space where using violence to control others is not acceptable.

In short, the main argument of this study has been that the juxtaposing of ideas, the give and take of different thoughts, notions, opinions, stimulates women to develop new stories, new visions, new articulations. In linguistic terms, this is an ordinary systemic function of language diversity or "heteroglossia," as Bakhtin puts it. Referring to the macrolevel of language use, Bakhtin says, you may recall: ". . . 'languages' of heteroglossia intersect each other in a variety of ways, forming new socially typifying "languages."[1] Such a dynamic happens, my study seeks to show, on the microlevel, as women talk to one another. Indeed, the women themselves have good metacognition, that is, a good sense of the value of shared stories. Comments such as these are typical in the shelter:

STELLA: If you sit up there and learn about a mother who has lost her children, then my heart is going to bleed. Because I know how I would feel if I lost my children. You should all have bleeding hearts! Listen to one another.

MELODY: This beautiful day was filled with noticing my surroundings and the people around me. Women filled with pain joined together by different problems, insecurities, dreams of a better way of life. Having a stranger full of conversation on religion, hope, fear, happiness. Suddenly I realized I spent too much time worrying, fearing failure and loneliness. I'm not alone, not now nor was I ever. Thank you stranger and protected environment.

ALLYSA: Talking about it helps. Talking about it in a group like this helps.

BERNIE: You talk about your troubles and everything and the women explain to you.

Stella, Melody, Allysa, and Bernie know—in some sense—that healing is a social process. They know, by experience, that they need other people with whom to share stories. This is why Earlin, a shelter resident, is so distressed by what her abuser forces her to do when she is speaking with her lifelong confidant: "When you talk to your sister, he goes, 'Hang up now, hang up now.' Sometimes he cuts me off. I tell my sister, 'I have to make dinner now,' so I can hang up. I have to lie to my sister." And this is why Lia, whose words appear at the beginning of this chapter, is so delighted with a newfound shelter companion. She says, "My best friend here is someone who is always there for me no matter what. When I'm in trouble, she's there to help me out. She doesn't care if she gets into trouble to help me. She's like a sister to me." Lia found a friend who listens deeply and responds despite personal cost. This is compassion born of shared struggle, shared stories, and shared vision.

Hopefully, in the safety of the shelter, women will come to healthier shared articulations and thus contribute to healthier socially typifying languages about theological and social issues. One dynamic in this linguistic equation is that in forming a new religious imagination, shelter women are sometimes able to develop a new social imagination—and vice versa. By integrating new social concepts about domestic violence and sexism into their cognitive (thus linguistic) repertoire, shelter women are sometimes able to articulate a new religious imagination. Indeed, the two ideological strands are unavoidably inseparable and inevitably woven together in the personal and the social consciousness. For example, inspired by the staff, volunteers, or residents, some women who see themselves as "religious" though not as "feminist" begin to verbalize more progressive or feminist leanings. Witness these short stretches of speech that indicate new movements of mind:

SONJA: Since I have been here my ideas about women have changed. I look at the world in a different way. Women are beautiful. Now I see beauty in all of a woman. I feel happy about my own self. I see the women here and I am awed at their strength. To be strong enough to put themselves in this situation. Strong enough to want to try anew. . . . I am beginning to notice things in terms of women. I used to think masculine because I live in masculine conditions. Now I struggle to educate myself and other people about women's ways.

BESS: Women together is the power, the only power we have—women together.

These statements indicate a transformed social consciousness and they undercut any traditional notions of womanhood offered by religion. Such vision is threatening to the current organization of culture and many of its churches.

LANGUAGE UNIVERSALS OR SITUATED EXPERIENCE?

My intention, in sharing the words of shelter women, has been to describe in ethnographic terms the culture of one shelter for battered women in an urban area in the upper South. One might convincingly argue against extrapolating from this study to another context. Katie Geneva Cannon, a womanist theologian, notes that suffering is a "normal state of affairs" for black women.[2] Some womanist scholars argue that black women and white women do not even suffer in the same way.[3]

These views pose provocative questions about the universality of suffering. Surely the experience of battery, if not its attendant suffering, depends on multiple and complex factors. Theologian M. Shawn Copeland points out, however, that although womanist theology remembers and retells stories of suffering, it does not spiritualize suffering.[4] That is, it does not make suffering a virtue that African American women seek and sanctify as a unique feature of their relationship with God. African American scholar Gloria Wade-Gayles, in an anthology celebrating the wide diversity of African American women's spiritualities asserts that spirituality (in distinction to institutionally learned senses of religiosity) cannot be ascribed to race and gender; instead, Wade-Gayles draws our attention to the range of ways African American women witness for the Spirit.[5] Of the ambiguity of spirituality, she writes:

> Like the wind, it cannot be seen, and yet, like the wind, it is surely there, and we bear witness to its presence, its power. We cannot hold it in our hands and put it on a scale, but we feel the force of its influence in our lives. We cannot hear it, but we hear ourselves speaking and singing and testifying because it moves, inspires, and directs us to do so.[6]

Through speech, song, and other forms of testimony, shelter women free conceptual space for the imagination, thus the potential to move and change one another. This ability to transform one another is the common phenomenon—intrinsic to other language situations. Language promises it; indeed, it is what is universal to other communities and contexts—the dynamic, the potential, of change itself.

There is more to bear in mind. Certainly, the experience of battered African American women and white women is not homogenous. Yet, as Wade-Gayle's words would suggest, neither is the experience of all African American women, all white women, or all women who belong to the religious affiliations or denominations described here. The local context gives shape to the meaning of domestic violence, as do sociological variables such as race/ethnicity, class, education, religion, sexual orientation, dis/ability, age, and a host of other factors. Each situation gives rise to different considerations, different concerns, and different implications for appropriate intervention.

Still the diverse women in this study fashion a contextually sensitive community language. I suggest that, despite the context-bound nature of the ethnographic enterprise and its object of study, there are general findings or features of this study that safely cross the community boundaries. Indeed, contemporary feminist linguists know from the study of gender and language differences that it is not productive to look for absolute features or language universals to which exceptions cannot be found; it is more productive to look for language tendencies that may be variously revealed in different communities.[7] Readers must critically discern which facets of the findings of this study have significance or applicability to their own locations, settings, or stances.

This being said, this study suggests that battered women may use certain genres and conversational strategies to heal. They share features of a healing process constituted by at least three basic nonlinear or recursive phases or tendencies: a phase of isolation and silence, a phase of lamentation and anger, and a phase solidarity and action. Undergirding these phases—which are precipitated by crisis—is a tendency to reevaluate basic beliefs, values, and other cultural practices. Religious belief in particular undergoes scrutiny. Indeed, this scrutiny may be a common denominator for many survivors of domestic violence in a changing cultural climate in which violence against women has become increasingly unacceptable. Regardless of whether a woman regularly practices her faith, religious ideology inundates culture. Even agnostics and atheists move through an atmosphere heavily saturated with religious ideology or social ideology. Since the threads of ideology are not easily disentangled and since they are fundamentally related, one ideology affects another. And language being the active, dialogic process that it is, women's difference and diversity is mutually influential. In a very real sense, the newly forged interconnections *are* the healing. Healing is not a state, but a set of new possibilities, concepts, and relations. Healing is a social process. It is a function of relationship, a rearrangement of self and other in society as a result of new ways of thinking and being. Women affect one another through the use of language, storytelling, and imaginative recreation or invention. They invent new ways of looking at the world, sometimes more healthy or wholesome ways. This innovation entails their religious imagination, yearnings, and longings and, as a result, battered women sometimes alter their ways of speaking about God, faith, spirituality, scripture, and religious institutions.

The details of these processes certainly vary across circumstances, communities, and cultures. But I believe it is safe to assume that many battered women have a tendency to travel through this sort of general healing trajectory. Whether such change is reinforced or sustained over the long term or is undercut and dispersed by opposition is a vital question open to debate and further inquiry. Clearly, lasting change is a matter of sustaining and encouraging further new relations and the concepts that are possible because of them. Of course, the patriarchal church has not rushed to incorporate in its structure or tenets the longings and visions of women. Rather, it makes use of women who are willing to support its status quo and punishes by exclusion or by conferring stigma upon women who are not. The threat of such eventualities coerces many battered women to return to their abusers. Some faith communities, for example, do not support the break-up of families when marriage counseling is available (even if marriage counseling is not supported by domestic violence experts because it has proven ineffective). Meanwhile, some battered women cannot withstand disapproval or exclusion by their faith communities: They would rather endure the suffering of domestic violence while they hope and pray that their partners change. Their new visions and relations, made possible by the temporary relief of a shelter stay, may collapse. In any case, battered women are not likely to witness the behavioral conversion of their partners to nonviolence.

In my experience, however, shelter women themselves are interested in sharing their stories with others in order not only to pursue their own healing, but also to educate others about the suffering of domestic violence. They hope others will not go through the same suffering as they have had to endure. In light of my own transformative years in the shelter, I believe that scholars and educators should listen more deeply to them. In this way we help to transform their witness into social action, their spirituality into politics. We contribute to healing as a social process that includes action for change. These are some possible meanings of our interconnectedness with victims of domestic violence. We become interdeterminative, mutually influential, the cocreators of social change.

A CHALLENGE TO SOCIAL CHANGE EDUCATORS

In the ways we are able, we are called to accompany battered women. There are different ways and means to do so. Theologians and pastoral care workers might pay particular attention to a basic uncomfortable message battered women share: Patriarchal systems, such as the institutional church, greatly contribute to their suffering. This is an assertion seemingly too simple for longtime or committed feminists to hear. It is a deceptively simple. Contrary to what church workers often believe, battered women are not typically angry with God whom they most often view as "on their side" in domestic struggles and violence. They are angry at the patriarchy and its manifestations. Further, women at the grassroots are increasingly aware and angry at the role the church as a patriarchal institution plays in their oppression. When church workers do not take cognizance of this simple truth, when they misname the actual source of women's anger, they contribute to the complicity of the institutional church in remittable suffering by making it invisible or by diminishing its role. Christianity—with its patriarchal structures and selective use of scriptural language, through its control of members, representatives, and spokespersons—is being called to see the problem of suffering through the eyes of ordinary women. Battered women repeatedly report that their abusers use the authority of the church and scripture to justify gender inequality and violence. Christian spokespersons diminish this critique by translating it in to the age-old problem of theodicy and its struggle to explain unmerited evil in traditional ways, as if all victims of unmerited evil would say: "I am angry at God for my undeserved suffering." Church spokespersons diminish the problem by letting God "stand in" as the recipient of anger instead of their churches and church structures. This strategy, intentional or otherwise, diminishes the truth about the suppression of women by the patriarchal church.

Naturally, then, many battered women see patriarchal religion as integrally involved in the violence against them. Such ideas are not merely the theories of academic or professional feminists. They are criticisms made by many faithful women at the grassroots—even at the conservative Holiness/Sanctified and fundamentalist/evangelical grassroots. Christianity is being called by battered women to confront and redress its own role in their victimization.

American women in general are pushing the boundaries of theological thought as, in local contexts, they struggle to make sense of situations of sexism, violence, or simply social change. They are creating examples of Bakhtin's "new socially typifying languages" that increasingly are rejecting patriarchal modes of traditional religious thought while still dealing with the complexities of gender socialization and differentiation. Mary Farrell Bednarowski points out, in *The Religious Imagination of American Women*, that women in the many religious traditions are beginning to write about not only how their traditions have hurt them, but also how they are working to heal these traditions and how they find healing within themselves "often on their own terms."[8] Not only scholars and writers are involved in this process, however. As we have seen, women at the grassroots level are thoroughly involved in these salvific activities. Evidence of this shows up regularly in conversation, in interviews, in therapeutic discourse—that is, in oral genres not likely to make their way to publication or other significant public venues.

Kathleen M. Sands, in *Escape from Paradise: Evil and Tragedy in Feminist Theology*, argues "women of color and women of the two-thirds world are infusing Christianity with liberative meaning."[9] Like Emilie Townes and other scholars (often from the margins themselves and whose work was introduced in chapter 4), Sands recognizes contributions from the disenfranchised or marginalized. Yet many scholars write expositions substantiated with the voices of only academically educated women, for example, feminist theologians and ministers. Of course, these are significant articulations in academic and professional discourse for, as Bednarowski points out, ". . . women's narratives and interpretations of their experiences have almost never been publicly incorporated into the theologies and institutional structures of religious communities . . . and when they are, major symbols, rituals, stories, teachings, and manifestations of authority begin to take different shape."[10]

Yet the voices of ordinary and marginalized women are almost never incorporated into the language of theologians or other academics and professionals and are not often incorporated into the language of the feminists among them. Battered women do not speak for themselves in the fora of these professionals. They are not often offered the access or the authority to speak for themselves as subjects. Increasingly, however, as domestic violence becomes more visible in the public sphere, they at least are being noticed—that is, they are being commented on as the objects of scholarly attention. It would be beneficial to amend this state of affairs. Women struggling to recover from situations of trauma and suffering, such as in the Women's House, are prophetic witnesses with their lived experience of the relationship between religion and domestic violence. My relationship with shelter women made clear to me that they are often willing and ready to speak out—and, as we know, the act of speaking is itself healing.

Though mostly still invisible or ignored, domestic violence and other situations of sexism, discrimination, and other acts of gender violence are the ordinary everyday experience of women and girl children throughout the world. Battered women have extraordinary things to say about the relationship of God, faith, and religion to this existential and political fact. When battered women learn through their lived experience that there are new ways to view suffering and evil in which they are not the scapegoat, the violated or inferior other, they have powerful words to share. Like prophets, they rake through the ordinary to make extraordinary proclamations. Their articulations may be ambiguous, sometimes tense with contradiction and conflict, but as Bednarowski points out, the ambivalence of contemporary American women's religious thought—as women simultaneously express "creative attachment" and negative critique—can be viewed as a new religious virtue.[11] In the words of the present study, shelter women devise "local theologies" to account for their lived and shared experience, and these new situated articulations are healing—for themselves, other women, and someday perhaps the institutions they implicate. In short, we might better attend to the suffering of individual victims and survivors. Though significant social change begins at the grassroots, their voices must be raised up to those in power in both the institutional church and academia before there is a chance of institutional change.

Of course, victims of violence against women cannot wait for the institutional church to address how—to name just a few examples—exclusive language use, the selective citation of scripture, or the limitations of the roles and rights of women in churches harms everyone. In seeking relief from their suffering, battered women encounter more than pastoral care workers (and, of course, they would not typically encounter a theologian unless she or he sought out battered women—a circumstance that should speak to theologians.). A minority of trauma victims, approximately 25 percent, seeks help from the other care giving professions.[12] Thus social workers or other health care givers have a responsibility to learn from shelter women.

The contours of this ethnography were suggested by my observation that battered women speak about their faith almost unremittingly. It is a near constant under all the other vital talk about violence, about safety and recovery, about housing, jobs, transportation, and so forth. Most social workers in the shelter shy away from or dismiss the faith language of battered women because it is not the accepted language of their professions. Some, of course, are empathetic and responsive. The battered women's movement in general has negatively critiqued—and rightly so—the role of religion in women's mistreatment. Incensed residents once told me that the staff had forbidden them to bring their Bibles to the first-floor general living area where women and their children congregate to talk or to watch television. The staff, perhaps recognizing the ramifications of civil and human rights violations within the shelter, refused to confirm this story with me. Later I once again saw women with their Bibles on the first floor. Apart from the legal issues, this is simply a disconcerting situation in its revelation of the profound disrespect of some social workers in the shelter for women's faith lives.[13]

Given that their faith is so significant to many battered women, and given that it is so integral to their recovery, it seems social workers and other health care providers might be more respectful and responsive to battered women's language about God. While they may not be able or willing to engage theologically with their clients, they might recognize the ways in which the many languages we speak interact, intermix, and become mutually influential. Instead of dismissing or denigrating women's God-talk, they might more productively engage it, adding ideas, questioning and clarifying issues, and contributing what they know about the relationship between domestic violence and religion, both positive and negative. A woman in crisis may not immediately respond, but she may respond at some point in her journey. New information may be integrated within her worldview. At the very least, the interconnections that a woman in crisis cocreates with sympathetic interlocutors are essential to her well-being and recovery.

Social workers and other health care providers cannot be pastoral care givers. But they can respond to battered women in their wholeness as physical, emotional, and spiritual beings. To do so, they need to be more strategically or creatively responsive to women's religious language. For example, shelter administration or staff might look for ways to interconnect with faith communities that do recognize the relationship between patriarchy and violence, that do unmask religious obstacles to a battered woman's recovery, that do see the potential for an altered spiritual renewal. Sheltered women often cannot immediately return to their own churches due to the lack of transportation or safety issues. But shelters might make available to residents connections with more progressive churches, religious women, or ministers/

clergy who understand and deal with the dynamics of domestic violence and specifically the role of religion in it. Not any church will do—only a progressive church that recognizes the expertise of the battered women's movement in dealing with domestic violence and that recognizes how traditional church ideologies are ultimately harmful for women and girl children.

In earlier days, shelters tried to hire staff who were survivors of domestic violence and who could thus demonstrate women's empowerment to others. Today such practices are not as pertinent to shelters functioning under social work models. These shelters prefer to hire women with university degrees, not women whose credentials are the lived experience of domestic violence. Yet the practice of staffing shelters with former victims is one that may be expedient to the goal of conversation as healing. Former victims may know or speak the language of the local religious culture. They are likely to appreciate the importance of women's faith when they are in crisis. They may be more willing to testify to the harmfulness of patriarchal practices while, at the same time, giving witness to the benefits of healthier spirituality or more progressive religious practices.

I have noticed over the years that shelter women are most receptive to staff who recognize the difficulty of recovery and healing, who recognize and respond to the many complexities of leaving an abuser and reestablishing oneself in the community, not staff who prioritize shelter policies and social order, feminist explanations of domestic violence, or who have lock-step notions of recovery and a woman's transition back into the community. That is, the most helpful staff members are those who respond to women on an individual basis. This means being able to encounter and respond to victims with compassion—an acceptance of where women are in their affective, including religious, lives and an ability to move forward from that place. This is not to say, however, that staff members who have not been former victims cannot be empathetic and effective advocates. I suggest only that the language of social work—ironically enough given its Christian reformist origins[14]—does not easily lend itself to faith perspectives. Yet, those of us who encounter battered women might make an effort to be more receptive to their language, including their religious language.

Healing, of course, is not confined to the province of social work or health care relationships. Battered and abused women are present among us all. Teachers may contribute to personal and social healing. Typically, for example, as women's or gender studies teachers, we encourage our students to activism by showing them their commonalties with other women. In our classes, we try to show them that the "personal is political," that is, that many of the struggles our students face in their individual lives are of the same fabric as the struggles women face everywhere because of sexism and its interstructuring with racism, classism, ageism, ableism, and so forth. We hope that, by the end of the semester, we will have moved at least some students—with our readings and class discussions—to engage in campus or community activities that contribute to the ongoing struggle for women's human rights. In short, the method we usually follow is this: We try to show students that the commonalties and unities between women everywhere ought to lead to our concerted action for social change.

This may be the wrong starting point. This starting point—the commonalties and unities—might more effectively be conceptualized as the end goal. The unfamiliarity, the tension and dissonance of meeting battered women—women who are much like, but often much unlike them—may be more productive of the kinds of affective, action-oriented learning we desire for our students. Certainly, it is more realistic. The forming of alliances for broad-based activism is a matter of eliciting relationships between unlikely groups of people—that is, across university, community, and cultural divides. An effective pedagogy for social activism is a matter of transforming the relationships between diverse groups of people who at least temporarily come together at a point of common interest—here, the human rights of women. It means initiating and, finally, transforming an unlikely set of relationships that women can access to effect authentic, democratic social change. To achieve this, women's studies teachers might initiate such alliances for their students through service learning or action research[15] opportunities for them in shelters or other places involved in women's crisis intervention rather than simply hoping to spark intellectual insight solely through traditional textbook learning.

The experience tends to be mutually beneficial. It benefits the shelter and the teacher and it benefits the residents and the students. To residents, students provide direct services through activities such as watching their children, assisting them with house chores, helping them with resumes and, in other ways, providing assistance and companionship. To the shelter staff, students provide services such as secretarial assistance, cleaning and donation sorting, yard work, and so forth. Throughout the semester, however, much deeper mutual giving and learning can happen.

Throughout these activities there is an opportunity for shared storytelling. Whether in group session or more casual exchanges, the sharing of stories avails opportunities for residents and students to listen deeply to one another, to see their commonalties and differences, and to at least temporarily support each other as they learn new strategies for personal and social change. Collective storytelling helps women sort out more viable ideas regarding the causes and meaning of suffering, the frequent role of misapplied or misogynist scripture in abusive situations, and the importance of helping one another and women they may never meet in the common struggle for human dignity, for women's greater freedom and independence. Within the context of deep and collective listening, residents are able to rehearse the dynamics of their abusive relationships, to analyze them with sympathetic, knowledgeable others, and to imagine new, different, more healthy futures for themselves and their children. Indeed, it is part of the healing process to be able to transform personal suffering into energy for voluntarily chosen political ends for the good of the greater human community. When they publicly speak about their experiences, many battered women are able to deeply move other people and thus invite human transformation. I know because it happened to me and it happens with regularity to my students.

To illustrate my point, I offer this: After a semester-long service learning experience, one of my students, Carrie, wrote this journal passage:

> Jebba spoke of having a gun pulled on her head, how many times her life has been threatened. . . . How do you turn down the pleading man in front of you when you so desperately want to believe he has a deep love for you? How can you stop the cycle of violence when you see so few options for yourself? You have been isolated from your friends and family. You don't have an income. He has humiliated you and cut you down so often, diminished your sense of independence and of making choices regularly so you feel you have very few options. Jebba went on to say that sometimes it even feels like you really don't have any options. She also went into how after awhile you feel like you have a certain dependence on him and can't imagine living without him. But, one day, she said you begin to see things more clearly [. . .] and you leave. [. . .] Jebba talked about how much happier she was now, away from her abuser, and in such a caring community. This brought up what some of the women described as one of the most special things about the shelter—the solidarity of the community of women there. Being with women who have experienced so many of the same fears and feelings and situations and sharing each other's stories has a tremendous effect. . . . I love to think about this nurturing, empowering atmosphere of women building each other up, of listening, of sharing, of caring. Tonight has had a powerful effect on me.

I am not convinced Carrie could have experienced this profound affective learning about violence against women without her exchanges with Jebba, that is, by way of textbook or classroom information only. Consequently I believe teachers, particularly women's studies teachers, might consider ways to transform their pedagogies to effect such interactions. Classroom visits by survivors, opportunities for service learning, and action research initiatives are among the obvious means.

To know how shelter women try to talk through suffering can be especially useful for social change educators and their students, theologians and pastoral care providers, social workers, health care providers, and others who are trying to facilitate the healing process. This presents a challenge to critically engaged linguists and ethnographers of communication. Linguists, to my knowledge, have not been drawn to the topic of domestic violence; yet, their analytical skills would yield forth valuable information—both theoretical and practical.

Practically, there are many issues not broached here about which reflections accessible to a general audience would be helpful. For example, how are the psychological characteristics of battered women, such as the tendency to self-blame or withdraw, reinforced by not simply sexist society, but the people they encounter as they contemplate decisions about leaving or returning to abusers? Studies of victims' interactions with service and health care providers from a linguistic perspective would contribute greatly. There also are longitudinal questions: What kinds of language practices contribute to long-term change? What happens to the language practices, the alternative worldviews, of battered women when they leave the shelter and enter different communities of practice? Do women and men recover from trauma in the same way? How is the answer to this last question perceived or managed by the people with whom victims have social exchange? How does sexual orientation, as a sociological factor, influence access to personal and social support and thus the healing process? What other sociological factors not typically heeded, besides religious orientation and practice, call for consideration?

These questions are grounded in theoretical issues about which language scholars have interest. The tendency in sociolinguistics to consider sociological factors as static is giving way to the realization that language-users shift meaning-making practices as they move from speech community to speech community. The significant question is: How do people negotiate meaning in and across the specific communities of practice to which they belong?[16] My study tries to ascertain discursive dynamics between shelter women with respect to religious outlook. Other language studies on how language shifts as rhetorical or local context shifts would be immensely useful. The shelter situation is an interesting one for linguists because it is a highly liminal situation in which typical power variables are fluid, disturbed, and open to challenge; that is, women are not hierarchically subservient within the shelter to male domination, at least not in a typical face-to-face way (although they certainly are influenced by internalized oppression and external factors). Shelter women's identity is unstable, vulnerable, unfixed, changeable. Their identity, including gender identity (and religious identity as my study shows) is being reconstituted and reinvented as community members interact. In truth, every language user's identity is being constantly constituted as they interact, moving from speech situation to speech situation. However, the trauma level of shelter residents is high and thus it highlights—brings out of the shadows by its very dynamism—the nature of the fluidity of identity. I find the notion of parallel discursive systems—that is, the phenomena of simultaneously operative discourse or conceptual systems—enormously interesting, especially in view of the dearth of material on long-term individual and social language change.

The fluidity of language in liminal situations can be profitably studied from different theoretical stances. I have primarily chosen the scholarship of M. M. Bakhtin (recall, for example, the introduction and especially chapters 8 and 9), to inform my analysis. The intersection of different social languages, the function of ambiguity and contradiction, the change of language in periods of (here personal, for Bakhtin, social) upheaval have proven useful lenses for analysis. Yet there are other theoretical beginning points and much left to study. The debates on women's language certainly are not over and language scholars approach those debates from various theoretical and thematic stances. For example, the issue of gender and language cooperativeness, specifically the belief that women are more conversationally cooperative, still surfaces in scholarly and especially popular literature. It is commonly proposed that relational or connection-oriented language is a feature of middle-class white women's language.[17] Cooperative, connection-oriented language—the kind of language typically associated with feminine language or with women, of course, is widely evaluated as powerless language. In this study, however, the cooperation between shelter women of different race, religion, and so forth lead to new imaginings, new visions, new worldviews—and thus, I would argue, is powerful language. Situationally, at least, it leads to new ideological reflection. African American women are often at the forefront as they give testimony, witness, and praise.

In any case, more sensitive listening attention would be most welcome by women such as the generous and courageous women whose voices echo in these pages. May we all contribute to finding ways to accompany them as they struggle to move on in their journeys to safety and well-being. May we all find ways to mend the human community. About such a daunting project we might be as optimistic as Nell, a shelter woman, who one day said to me with a glint of satisfaction in her eyes: "Everyone here is losing a little suffering. Little by little, we are losing our suffering."

NOTES

INTRODUCTION

1. The Women's House is a pseudonym for the shelter. All names used in this study are likewise pseudonymous to protect confidentiality. The women's words are used with permission.

2. The shelter is operated by the YWCA, a national network of educational and health facilities funded by a variety of federal, state, and local sources. See chapter 2.

3. M. M. Bakhtin, *The Dialogic Imagination*, 276.

4. Ibid., 279.

5. Bakhtin, "The Problem of Speech Genres," 93.

6. Bakhtin, *The Dialogic Imagination*, 291.

7. Sandra M. Schneiders, *Beyond Patching: Faith and Feminism in the Catholic Church* (Mahwah, N.J.: Paulist Press, 1991), 32–33.

8. The typology is based on the work of Kristine M. Rankka in *Women and the Value of Suffering*.

9. Soelle, *Suffering*, chapter 3, 61–86.

10. I intend the term "local theology" to capture the notion that local people, rather than theologians, ministers, priests, or other pastoral care workers, are the primary shapers of theological responses to the problems of everyday lives. See chapter 9.

11. George Spindler and Louise Spindler, *Interpretive Ethnography of Education* (Hillsdale, N.J.: Lawrence Erlbaum Press, 1987), 17.

12. A subculture is "any self-identified group of people—who share language, stories, rituals, behaviors, and values," a group defined by geography, ethnicity, behaviors, interests. See Elizabeth Chiseri-Strater and Bonnie Stone Sunstein, *Field Working: Reading and Writing Research* (Upper Saddle River, N.J.: Prentice Hall, 1997), 5. Survivors at the shelter may be defined as a specific subculture in the upper South.

13. See Clifford Geertz, *The Interpretation of Cultures*, 5.

14. Kathleen M. Sands, *Escape from Paradise*, 65.

CHAPTER 1

1. There has not been, however, a good understanding of how self-defense factors into woman-perpetrated violence or how male multiple aggression patterns change the outcomes of violence. Women suffer graver injuries so the meaning of female and male violence is different. See Murray A. Straus and Richard J. Gelles, *National Family Violence Survey* and Ronet Bachman and Linda E. Saltzman, *Violence Against Women: Estimates from the Redesigned Survey.*

2. Yet women are more likely to seek out medical rather than mental health services to deal with domestic violence. See Soraya M. Coley and Joyce O. Beckett, "Black Battered Women: A Review of the Empirical Literature," *Journal of Counseling and Development* 66.6 (February 1988): 268.

3. For these and further feminist perspectives on the meanings of violence to battered women, see R. Emerson Dobash and Russell P. Dobash, *Violence Against Wives: A Case Against the Patriarchy* (New York: Free Press, 1979); Kersti Yllo and Michele Bograd, *Feminist Perspectives on Wife Abuse* (Newbury Park, Calif.: Sage, 1988); and Mildred D. Pagelow, *Woman-Battering: Victims and Their Experiences* (Beverly Hills, Calif.: Sage, 1981). On the cycle and escalation of violence, see Lenore Walker, *The Battered Woman* (New York: Harper, 1979).

4. See C. Doran, "Family Violence," in *Dictionary of Pastoral Care and Counseling,* ed. Rodney J. Hunter, (Nashville: Abingdon, 1990), 426–29.

5. I will not be explicitly concerned, in this study, with instances of violence between homosexual partners, between siblings and relatives, and by women against men.

6. The following information can be found in Jana L. Jasinski and Glenda Kaufman Kantor, "Dynamics and Risk Factors in Partner Violence," in *Partner Violence*; eds. Jana L. Jasinski and Linda M. Williams; Bachman and Saltzman, *Violence Against Women: Estimates from the Redesigned Survey*; A. L. Kellerman and J. A. Mercy, "Men, Women, and Murder: Gender-Specific Differences in Rates of Fatal Violence and Victimization," *Journal of Trauma* 33.1 (1992): 1–5; and Jan E. Stets and Murray A. Straus, "Gender Differences in Reporting of Marital Violence and Its Medical and Psychological Consequences," in *Physical Violence in American Families,* eds. Murray A. Straus and Richard J. Gelles, 151–65.

7. This is a finding of the Johns Hopkins School of Public Health and the Center for Health and Gender Equity. See "Women Abused Worldwide," *Off Our Backs* (February 2000): 4, which cites the figure from the Feminist Majority Website at *http://feminist.org/news.*

8. See Judith McFarlane, Pam Willson, Dorothy Lemmey, and Ann Malecha, "Women Filing Assault Charges on an Intimate Partner," *Violence Against Women* 6.4 (April 2000): 397.

9. Donna E. Shalala, "Domestic Terrorism: An Unacknowledged Epidemic," *Vital Speeches of the Day,* vol. LX. 15 (May 15, 1994): 450.

10. Some locales have mandatory arrests policies if there is evidence of physical abuse; others have preferred arrest policies. The shelter is located in an area with a preferred arrest policy. The women complain that police often arrest them instead of the abusers.

11. Recent information is posted by the United States Department of Justice at *http://www.ojp.usdoj.gov/bjs/pub/press/fvvc.pr*. This information was accessed on June 11, 1998. Other primary sources of information are the *National Family Violence Survey* and the *National Crime Victimization Survey*. See Bachman and Saltzman, 1995.

12. See Carol J. Adams and Marsha Engle-Rowbottom, "A Commentary on Violence Against Women and Children in Rural Areas," in Marie M. Fortune, *Violence in the Family: A Workshop Curriculum for Clergy and Other Helpers* (Cleveland: Pilgrim Press, 1991), 163–71.

13. This information was posted by the United States Department of Justice, Bureau of Justice Statistics, at *http://www.ojp.usdoj.gov/bjs/pub/press/femvied.pr* on June 6, 1998.

14. Coley and Beckett, 269.

15. Coley and Beckett, 268. On race and domestic violence, see Beth E. Richie, "Battered Black Women: A Challenge for the Black Community," in *Words of Fire: An Anthology of African-American Feminist Thought*, ed. Beverly Guy-Sheftall (New York: New Press, 1995); Patricia Brownell, "Multicultural Practice and Domestic Violence," in *Multicultural Perspectives in Working with Families*, ed. Elaine P. Congress (New York: Springer, 1997), 217–35; Delores S. Williams, "A Womanist Perspective on Sin," in *A Troubling in My Soul*, ed. Emilie M. Townes, 130–49; and Mary Alice Saunders-Robinson, "Black Women Who Are Battered," 86–92, and "Battered Women: An African American Perspective," *The ABNF* (Association of Black Nursing Faculty) *Journal*. (Fall 1991): 81–84. The United States Department of Justice reports on race/ethnicity and domestic violence.

16. Gerald David Jaynes and Robin M. Williams Jr., eds. *A Common Destiny: Blacks and American Society* (Washington, DC: National Academy Press, 1989), 529.

17. See Margaret Abraham, "Ethnicity, Gender, and Marital Violence: South Asian Women's Organizations in the United States," *Gender and Society* 9.4 (August 1995): 450–68.

18. See Laura Ann McCloskey, "Socioeconomic and Coercive Power within the Family," *Gender and Society* 10.4 (August 1996): 449–63.

19. McCloskey, "Socioeconomic and Coercive Power," 458.

20. Noted in Neil Websdale and Meda Chesney-Lind, "Men Victimizing Women and Children: Doing Violence to Women/Research Synthesis on the Victimization of Women," in *Masculinities and Violence*, ed. Lee H. Bowker (Thousand Oaks: Sage, 1998), 57. The original citation is Kersti Yllo and Murray Straus, "Patriarchy and Violence Against Wives: The Impact of Structural and Normative Factors," *Journal of International and Comparative Social Welfare* 1 (1984): 1–13.

21. Linda Gordon, *Heroes of Their Own Lives*, 2–3.

22. See Carl A. Bersani and Huey-Tsyh Chen, "Sociological Perspectives in Family Violence," in *Handbook of Family Violence*, eds. Vincent. B. Van Hasselt, Randell L. Morrison, Alan S. Bellack, and Michel Hersen (New York: Plenum, 1988), 57–86.

23. Kristin L. Anderson, "Gender, Status, and Domestic Violence: An Integration of Feminist and Family Violence Approaches," *Journal of Marriage and the Family* 59 (August 1997): 655–69.

24. R. Emerson Dobash and Russell P. Dobash, "Violence against Women," in *Gender Violence: Interdisciplinary Perspectives*, eds. Laura L. O'Toole and Jessica R. Schiffman (New York: New York University Press, 1997), 268.

25. Gordon, *Heroes of Their Own Lives*, 3.

26. Patrick C. McKenry, Teresa W. Julian, and Stephen M. Gavazzi offer an integrated approach in "Toward a Biopsychosocial Model of Domestic Violence," *Journal of Marriage and the Family* 57 (May 1995): 307–20.

27. For a discussion of the research, see Frank A. Elliott, "Neurological Factors," in *Handbook of Family Violence*, eds. Vincent B. Van Hasselt, et al., 359–82.

28. Richard J. Gelles, "Through a Sociological Lens: Social Structure and Family Violence," in *Current Controversies on Family Violence*, eds. Richard J. Gelles and Donileen R. Loseke, 41. However, Patrick C. McKenry, Teresa W. Julian, and Stephen M. Gavazzi in "Toward a Biopsychosocial Model of Domestic Violence," *Journal of Marriage and the Family* 57 (May 1995): 307–20, argue that integrationist/interdisciplinary approaches are now the dominant models receiving federal funding.

29. Linda Gordon, "More than Victims: Battered Women, the Sydrome Society, and the Law." *The Nation* (24 March 1997): 26. For another historical view, see Elizabeth Pleck, *Domestic Tyranny*, 1987.

30. Marilyn French, "Fifteenth-century Feminism." *The Nation* 264.25 (30 June 1997): 24.

31. See Walker, *The Battered Woman*.

32. For more, see Walker, chapter 2, 42–54.

33. For example, Phyllis B. Frank and Gail Kadison Golden, "Blaming by Naming: Battered Women and the Epidemic of Codependence," *Social Work* 37.1 (January 1992): 5–6.

34. Jan E. Stets and Murray A. Straus, "Gender Differences," 151–65.

35. Ohio State Medical Association, *Ohio Physicians' Domestic Violence Prevention Project: Trust Talk* (Columbus: Ohio Department of Human Services and the Ohio State Medical Association, 1993), 1.

CHAPTER 2

1. Noelie Maria Rodriquez, "A Successful Feminist Shelter: A Case Study of the Family Crisis Shelter in Hawaii," *The Journal of Applied Behavioral Science* 24.3 (August 1988): 237.

2. YWCA *Women's Shelter Resident Agreement of Stay* form.

3. Sarah Heath, "Negotiating White Womanhood," 86–110. The YWCA was segregated.

4. Federal, state, and local politics influence policy decisions as well. Grants and donations depend on officeholders and the general political climate.

5. See Ben J. Refuerzo and Stephen Verderber, "Effects of Personal Status and Patterns of Use on Residential Satisfaction in Shelters for Victims of Domestic Violence," *Environment and Behavior* 21.4 (July 1989): 413–34.

6. Angela Browne and Kirk R. Williams, "Exploring the Effect of Resource Availability and Likelihood of Female-Precipitated Homicides," *Law and Society Review* 23.1 (1989): 75–94.

7. The shelter's Director of Program Resources provided these figures.

8. Categories do not address abuse by coworkers, relatives, or same-sex partners.

9. *The Federal Register* 65.31 (February 15, 2000), 7555–57.

10. Many poverty-level families are headed by women fleeing domestic violence.

11. Researchers continually note the correlation. See Dorothy Ayers Counts, "Female Suicide and Wife Abuse: A Cross-Cultural Perspective," *Suicide and Life-Threatening Behavior* 17 (Fall 1987): 194–204. On connections between trauma and other self-destructive behaviors (substance abuse, self-mutilation, eating disorders, suicide, et cetera), see Bessel A. van der Kolk, "A Complexity of Adaptation to Trauma: Self-Regulation, Stimulus Discrimination, and Characterological Development," in *Traumatic Stress*, eds. Bessel A. van der Kolk, Alexander C. McFarlane, Lars Weisaeth, 182–213.

12. Stets and Straus, "Gender Differences," 151–65.

13. Carole Warshaw, "Limitations of the Medical Model in the Care of Battered Women," *Gender & Society* 3.4 (December 1989): 506–07.

14. See Lesley Doyal, *What Makes Women Sick: Gender and the Political Economy of Health* (New Brunswick, N.J.: Rutgers University Press, 1995), 55–56.

15. Deborah Belle, "Inequality and Mental Health: Low Income and Minority Women," in *Women and Mental Health Policy*, ed. Lenore E. Walker (Beverly Hills: Sage, 1984), 135–50. This quote is from 145. See also Jennifer Bernard, "Homosociality and Female Depression," *Journal of Social Issues* 32.4 (1976): 213–38.

16. Jeffrey L. Edleson, "Problems Associated with Children's Witnessing of Domestic Violence," 10 December 2000 (INTERNET) *http://www.vaw.umn.edu/Vawnet/witness/htm*.

17. D. A. Wolfe, L. Zak, S. Wilson, and P. Jaffe, "Child Witnesses to Violence between Parents: Critical Issues in Behavioral and Social Adjustment," *Journal of Abnormal Child Psychology* 53 (1985): 657–65.

18. Daphne Blunt Bugental, in "Communication in Abusive Relationships," *American Behavioral Scientist* 36.3 (January 1993): 288–308, discusses "counter-power" in which people in authority (particularly those who operate out of "threat-oriented" worldviews, such as battered women) perceive their subordinates as more powerful than they are in fact.

19. See Kathryn M. Neckerman, "The Emergence of 'Underclass' Family Patterns, 1900–1940," in *The "Underclass" Debate*, ed. Michael B. Katz (Princeton, N.J.: 1993), 194–219.

20. Both statistics and Walker's 1984 study are cited by Fortune, *Violence in the Family: A Workshop Curriculum for Clergy and Other Helpers*, 112.

21. See, for example, Carol S. Wharton, "Splintered Visions: Staff/Client Disjunctions and Their Consequences for Human Service Organizations," *Journal of Contemporary Ethnography* 18.1 (April 1989): 50–71; Jillian Ridington, "The Transition Process: A Feminist Environment as Reconstitutive Milieu," *Victimology: An International Journal* 2.3–4 (1977–78): 563–75; Noelie Maria Rodriquez, "A Successful Feminist Shelter": 237, and "Transcending Bureaucracy: Feminist Politics at a Shelter for Battered Women," *Gender & Society* 2.2 (June 1988): 214–27; and Kathleen J. Ferraro, "Negotiating Trouble in a Battered Women's Shelter," *Urban Life* 12.3 (October 1983): 287–306.

22. See Neckerman, "The Emergence of 'Underclass' Family Patterns," especially 202 and 219.

23. Unfortunately, shelter workers and volunteers are also discouraged from becoming friends with residents outside the shelter or after they leave the system for "confidentiality" reasons.

24. See Lori Beaman-Hall and Nancy Nason-Clark, "Partners or Protagonists? The Transition House Movement and Conservative Churches," *Affilia* 12.2 (Summer 1997): 176–96.

25. See, for example, Harold W. Neighbors, Karin A. Elliott, and Larry M. Gant, "Self-Help and Black Americans," (189–217), Barry Checkoway, Mark A. Chesler, and Stephen Blum, "Self-Care, Self-Help, and Community Care for Health" (277–300), and Mark A. Chesler, "The Dangers of Self-Help Groups," (301–24) in *Working with Self-Help*, ed. Thomas J. Powell (Silver Spring, Md.: National Association of Social Workers Press, 1990).

26. *YWCA Women's Shelter Resident Agreement of Stay.*

27. *Communication Tips for Parents and Kids.*

28. *To All Residents With Children.*

29. *YWCA Battered Women Shelter Clarification of Shelter Rules Regarding Children* and the *Resident Agreement of Stay.*

30. *Resident Agreement of Stay.*

31. Linda Mills, "Empowering Battered Women Transnationally: The Case for Postmodern Interventions," *Social Work* 41.3 (May 1996): 266.

32. Heath, "Negotiating White Womanhood," 89.

CHAPTER 3

1. David B. Morris, *The Culture of Pain* (Berkeley: University of California Press, 1991), 3.

2. Doyle, *What Makes Women Sick,* 55.

3. Deeply humiliated by sexual assault, women rarely speak of it. See Dee L. R. Graham with Edna I. Rawlings and Roberta K. Rigsby, *Loving to Survive: Sexual Terror, Men's Violence, and Women's Lives* (New York: New York University Press, 1994), 73–76.

4. Michael P. Johnson, "Patriarchal Terrorism and Common Couple Violence: Two Forms of Violence against Women," *Journal of Marriage and the Family* 57 (May 1995): 283–94. I do not agree with Johnson that common couple violence and patriarchal terrorism are two distinctly different types of violence. Intimate violence is used to control women and is thus part of the problem of the patriarchy.

5. Ibid., 290.

6. Judith Lewis Herman, *Trauma and Recovery,* 175. Some scholars do conflate physical pain and suffering. See, for example, Harold Schweizer's *Suffering and the Remedy of Art* (Albany: State University of New York Press, 1997). Curiously, Schweizer argues only that one should give witness to the language of suffering (19–20); that is, he does not give emphasis to social action or accompanying the sufferer. In a more delicate analysis, Herman argues that the witness-therapist provides language to the victim who has no words (175).

7. Morris, *The Culture of Pain,* 3.

8. I do not dispute the phrase "survivors of domestic violence." I agree with its usage to emphasize the courage of women who endure or escape partner violence; however, the phrase does diminish existential facts. I use the term "battered women" to bring women's physical suffering to the forefront. I agree that, in some contexts, its usage may diminish attention to the strength and resistance of women who do endure and survive male violence.

9. See, for example, Diana Russell's sociological study on sexual violence, *Sexual Exploitation: Rape, Child Abuse, and Sexual Harassment* (Beverly Hills, Calif.: Sage, 1984).

10. Morris, *The Culture of Pain*, 20, 104.

11. Ibid., 198–99.

12. In this regard, their accounts are also characterized by translation processes. But unlike battered women, medical personnel appear to deflect or ignore issues of agency or causation. In their accounts, they describe wounds inflicted as if by no agent. The women most often specify agency—their partner and his weapons. Some states or locales have laws stipulating that domestic violence cases must be reported to authorities by medical personnel; however, doctors and nurses—in perhaps unconscious collaboration with embarrassed or ashamed battered women or in attempts to be efficient—may not follow through on these laws.

13. Warshaw, Carole. "Limitations of the Medical Model in the Care of Battered Women," *Gender & Society* 3.4 (December 1989): 506–17.

14. Scarry works with the metaphors of weapons and wounds. See *The Body in Pain*, 11–19.

15. According to attorneys Daniel G. Atkins and John S. Whitelaw ("Turning the Tables on Women: Removal of Children from Victims of Domestic Violence," *Clearinghouse Review* [Special Issue, 1996]: 261–72): "The reported case law generally reflects courts' eagerness to find a child neglected or to terminate the mother's parental rights in cases where she is the victim of domestic violence" (263). They quote the Vermont Supreme Court affirming a trial court's termination of a mother's parental rights: "The [trial] courts findings and conclusion are substantiated by testimony regarding father's abuse towards mother, mother's resulting physical injuries, and her inability to make protecting her children a priority over her relationship with her husband" (263). Atkins and Whitelaw also argue there is an increasing judicial willingness to turn the "battered woman's syndrome" against women in child neglect/abuse contexts. They cite case law in which, for example, the Nebraska Supreme Court found that the "learned helplessness" of the battered women's syndrome "affects a woman's ability to protect her children . . ." (265).

16. Herman, *Trauma and Recovery*, 165.

17. Readers may remember that Mary's point was articulated earlier by Marilyn Frye in "In and Out of Harm's Way: Arrogance and Love," *The Politics of Reality: Essays in Feminist Theory* (Freedom, Calif.: Crossing, 1983), 52–83.

18. See, for example, Ann Callender's *Pathways through Pain* (Cleveland: Pilgrim, 1999). Although she deals with nature-caused chronic pain, Callender perpetuates other woman-damaging ideologies and ideas, including this notion, for example: "Given the fact that we are all inadequately mothered to some degree, all of us possesses a greater or lesser capacity for masochistic behaviours as adults" (72).

Callender approvingly quotes St. Paul, "suffering produces endurance, and endurance produces character" (Romans 5:4) (129), and admiringly quotes Thomas à Kempis (fifteenth-century canon), "you will progress [spiritually] in proportion as you do violence to yourself" (31).

19. For a succinct, primary text treatment of the early Christian Fathers' thoughts on women and the female body, see *Woman Defamed and Woman Defended: An Anthology of Medieval Text,* ed. Alcuin Blamires (Oxford: Clarendon, 1992).

20. I do not doubt psychologists who believe that denial and avoidance behaviors may help a victim cope with trauma in small doses while she strengthens herself in recovery. See Janoff-Bulman, *Shattered Assumptions,* 96–101.

21. Herman cites an interview with Terence Keane that stresses the importance of the victims' full recall of bodily sensations in *Trauma and Recovery,* 177.

22. See, for example: Herman, *Trauma and Recovery;* Salter, *Transforming Trauma,* Janoff-Bulman, *Shattered Assumptions;* and Pennebaker, *Opening Up.* Pennebaker provides empirical data on the physical and emotional healing effects of writing about trauma.

23. Only 25 percent of trauma victims get help from mental health care professionals. See Ronnie Janoff-Bulman, *Shattered Assumptions,* 161. For this section, I also learned particularly from: Herman's *Trauma and Recovery,* Salter's *Transforming Trauma;* and van der Kolk's *Traumatic Stress.*

24. American Psychiatric Association, *DSM-III-R,* 1987: 250.

25. See Herman, *Trauma and Recovery,* 9, and Janoff-Bulman, *Shattered Assumptions,* 53.

26. Stets and Straus, "Gender Differences," 151–65.

27. E. Stark and A. Flitcraft, "Spouse Abuse," in *Violence in America: A Public Health Approach,* eds. Mark L. Rosenberg and Mary Ann Fenley (New York: Oxford University Press, 1991), 123–57.

28. Not all shelter women suffer from post-traumatic stress disorder. The psychological threshold of tolerance varies. Some women leave before extreme violence occurs. The American Psychiatric Association rules out "marital conflict" as an "out-of-the-ordinary" crisis, but what women consider "conflict" or "violence" surely involves differences.

29. The disorder is in the *DSM-III-R* (1987) and not in the original version (1980).

30. Herman acknowledges the function of the hyper-aroused sympathetic nervous system, particularly the rush of adrenaline, the narrow focusing of attention, and other alterations of ordinary perception in making trauma victims impervious to pain in *Trauma and Recovery,* 34. In the forthcoming account, Mary recalls the adrenaline rush.

31. To name a few: Herman, Kearney, Salter, Janoff-Bulman, and Pennebaker.

32. Herman notes the occurrence of another possibility: the victims' dialectic of processes of alternatively numbing and experiencing trauma. See *Trauma and Recovery,* 47.

33. See Dori Laub, "Bearing Witness or the Vicissitudes of Listening," *Testimony: Crises of Witnessing in Literature, Psychoanalysis, and History,* eds. Shoshana Felman and Dori Laub (New York: Routledge, 1992), 57.

34. Bessel van der Kolk, "The Trauma Spectrum: The Interaction of Biological and Social Events in the Genesis of the Trauma Response," *Journal of Traumatic Stress* 1 (1988): 273–90. The study is cited in Herman, *Trauma and Recovery*, 39.

35. Many studies link domestic violence to depression and suicide. For example, see Robert Desjarlais, Leon Eisenberg, Byron Good, and Arthur Kleinman, *World Mental Health* (New York: Oxford, 1995), 192–95. Desjarlais et al. discuss the social origins of women's psychological and psychiatric distress globally. They link long-term depression with physical ailments or generally poorer physical health. Ruth L. Fischbach and Barbara Herbert argue that: "Gender-based violence, only recently emerging as a pervasive global issue, contributes significantly to preventable morbidity and mortality for women across diverse cultures" (1161). See "Domestic Violence and Mental Health: Correlates and Conundrums Within and Across Cultures," *Social Science and Medicine* 45.8 (1997): 1161–76. Kearney, in *Understanding Women's Recovery from Illness and Trauma*, 18, notes the interconnection of domestic violence and women's health conditions.

36. Eric J. Cassell, "Pain and Suffering," in *Encyclopedia of Bioethics*, vol. 4, ed. Warren Thomas Reich (New York: Macmillan, 1995), 1899, and cited in Rankka, *Women and the Value of Suffering*, 27.

37. See Soelle, *Suffering*, 1975.

38. Simone Weil, *Waiting for God*, trans. Emma Crauford (New York: Harper and Rowe, 1951).

39. Chronic pain eludes medical researchers; yet, it also has psychological, affective dimensions. See "Suffering in Chronic Illness," in Eric J. Cassell's *The Nature of Suffering*, 48–65.

40. Cassell, "Pain and Suffering," 1899.

41. Kenneth Surin, in *Theology and the Problem of Evil* (Oxford: Basil Blackwell, 1986), 114–15, notes the totality of suffering in his discussion of theodicies.

42. Arthur Kleinman, *The Illness Narratives: Suffering, Healing, and the Human Condition* (New York: Basic Books, 1988), 18–19, 233.

43. Schweizer, *Suffering and the Remedy of Art*, 11–22.

44. Frequently they do recognize traditional theologies/theodicies as problematic.

45. Herman, *Trauma and Recovery*, 73

CHAPTER 4

1. The women are predominately Christian, mostly fundamentalist/evangelical or Holiness/Sanctified, but there is diversity across and within denominations. Their current practices, church attendance, prayer rituals, and so forth, are also diverse.

2. Geertz, *The Interpretation of Cultures*, 103. In "Religion as a Cultural System" (87–125), he notes that the meaning (not the cause) of suffering is the important issue.

3. The logical arguments explore the idea of an all-perfect, all-knowing, all-powerful God and the fact of evil. The epistemic arguments explore the subjective probabilities that an all-perfect, all-knowing, all-powerful God exists in view of the fact of intense instances of suffering. That is, the first type of argument is logical,

deductive, or a priori; the second type of argument is empirical, probabilistic, or a posteriori. See Michael L. Peterson, ed., *The Problem of Evil* (Notre Dame, Ind.: University of Notre Dame Press, 1992) and Daniel Howard-Snyder, ed., *The Evidential Argument from Evil* (Bloomington: Indiana University Press, 1996).

4. See Brennan R. Hill, Paul Knitter, and William Madges, *Faith, Religion, and Theology* (Mystic, Conn.: Twenty-Third Publications, 1990; sixth printing, 1995), 326–28.

5. See Alfred North Whitehead, *Process and Reality: An Essay in Cosmology*, corrected ed., edited by David Ray Griffin and Donald W. Sherburne (New York: Free Press, 1978) and Charles Hartshorne, *A Natural Theology for Our Time* (La Salle, Ill.: Open Court, 1967).

6. Lucien Richard, *What Are They Saying About the Theology of Suffering?* (New York: Paulist Press, 1992), 329–30.

7. Kenneth Surin, "The Problem of Evil," *Blackwell Encyclopedia of Modern Christian Thought*, ed. Alister E. McGrath (Cambridge: Blackwell, 1993), 194.

8. Madges in *Faith, Religion, and Theology*, 331.

9. Soelle, *Suffering*, 1975. See also Lucien Richard, "Suffering from a Feminist Perspective: Dorothy Soelle," in *What Are They Saying About the Theology of Suffering?*, 73–88.

10. Soelle, "God and Her Friends," in *The Window of Vulnerability: A Political Spirituality* (Minneapolis: Fortress Press, 1990).

11. Soelle, *Suffering*, 11. See also Eric Cassell, "Pain and Suffering," 1897–1905. Cassell defines physical pain and suffering as socially constructed. Physical pain involves a psychological component that can be affected by perceptions or social interactions.

12. Weil, Simone. 1951. *Waiting for God*. Trans. Emma Craufurd (New York: Putnam).

13. Soelle, *Suffering*, 12–13.

14. Elizabeth A. Johnson, *She Who Is*, 268–71.

15. For feminist theologians on violence against women, see Mananzan, et al., eds., *Women Resisting Violence*, 1996; Adams and Fortune, eds., *Violence against Women and Children*, 1995; and Annie Imbens and Ineke Jonker, *Christianity and Incest* (Kent, Great Britain: Burns and Oakes, 1985; second ed. 1992). For womanist views, see Renita J. Weems, *Battered Love: Marriage, Sex, and Violence in the Hebrew Prophets* (Minneapolis: Fortress Press, 1995); and Townes, ed., *A Troubling in My Soul*, 1993.

16. Fortune, "The Transformation of Suffering," in *Violence against Women and Children*, 86.

17. Other theologians and pastoral care workers discuss battered women's tendency to blame God. See Joy M. K. Bussert, *Battered Women: From a Theology of Suffering to an Ethic of Empowerment* (New York: DMNA/LCA, 1986), especially 63–66, and James Leehan, *Defiant Hope: Spirituality for Survivors of Family Abuse* (Louisville: Westminster/John Knox Press, 1993), especially chapter 7.

18. See Brenda E. Brasher, *Godly Women*, 54. No fundamentalist woman in her sociological study blamed God for her troubles and no woman blamed herself or society. Herein lies a major difference in the attitudes of our participants. Initially battered women do blame themselves and, as they gain critical awareness, they blame society for their suffering.

19. A Catholic male pastoral care worker told me that an advocated pedagogy in pastoral counseling is to encourage people to express their anger against God as a means to healing and recovery. The entry on "family violence" in the *Dictionary of Pastoral Care and Counseling* (Nashville: Abingdon Press: 1990), 426–29, encourages a "church response" which, in my view, is dangerous. It advocates drug/alcohol treatment even before the address of physical violence and it advocates family counseling, a recourse roundly rejected by most domestic violence experts.

20. Imbens and Jonker, *Christianity and Incest*, 33. See also Barbara W. Snow and Geraldine G. Hanni, "Counseling the Adult Survivor of Child Sexual Abuse: Concepts and Cautions for the Clergy," in *Abuse and Religion: When Praying Isn't Enough*, eds. Anne L. Horton and Judith A. Williamson (Lexington, Mass.: Heath, 1988), 161.

21. Refer to Beth E. Richie, "Battered Black Women: A Challenge for the Black Community," in *Words of Fire*, ed. Guy-Sheftall, 400–01.

22. Gary L. Fowler, "The Residential Distribution of Urban Appalachians," in *The Invisible Minority: Urban Appalachians*, eds. William W. Philliber and Clyde B. McCoy with Harry C. Dillingham (Lexington: University of Kentucky Press, 1981), 79–94.

23. Most women attend racially segregated churches.

24. Geertz, *The Interpretation of Cultures*, 123.

25. Jaynes, Gerald Davis and Robin M. Williams, Jr., eds. *A Common Destiny: Blacks and American Society* (Washington, DC: National Academy Press, 1989), 176.

26. J. Milton Yinger, "Black Americans and Predominantly White Churches," a paper prepared for the Committee on the Status of Black Americans, National Research Council, Washington DC, 1986, 4, cited in *A Common Destiny*, eds., Jaynes and Williams, Jr., 94.

27. *A Common Destiny*, 174. In this study, I classify Pentecostal and Apostolic churches as Sanctified/Holiness. This includes the Church of God and the Church of God in Christ.

28. The shelter does not keep records of religious affiliation. These are estimates based on participant observation and the demographic data from neighborhood surveys undertaken by researchers of urban Appalachians represented in *The Invisible Minority*, eds. Philliber and McCoy with Harry C. Dillingham. See also John D. Photiadis, ed. *Religion in Appalachia: Theological, Social, and Psychological Dimensions and Correlates.* (Center for Extension and Continuing Education, Division of Social and Economic Development, Office of Research and Development: West Virginia University, n.d.); and Howard Dorgan, *In the Hands of a Happy God: The "No-Hellers" of Central Appalachia* (Knoxville: University of Tennessee Press, 1997); *The Airwaves of Zion: Radio and Religion in Appalachia* (Knoxville: University of Tennessee Press, 1993); *The Old Regular Baptists of Central Appalachia: Brothers and Sisters in Hope* (Knoxville: University of Tennessee Press, 1989); and *Giving Glory to God in Appalachia: Worship Practices of Six Baptist Subdenominations* (Knoxville: University of Tennessee Press, 1987).

29. For a useful survey, see Rosemary Skinner Keller and Rosemary Radford Ruether, eds., *In Our Own Voices: Four Centuries of American Women's Religious Writing* (San Francisco: Harper, 1995). Chapters 4 and 5 concern black women and Evangelical

women respectively. See also Shawn M. Copeland, "Wading Through Many Sorrows: Toward a Theology of Suffering in Womanist Perspective," in A Troubling in My Soul, ed. Townes, 109–29; Jacquelyn Grant, White Women's Christ and Black Women's Jesus: Feminist Christology and Womanist Response (Atlanta: Scholars Press, 1989); and "Womanist Jesus and the Mutual Struggle for Liberation," in The Recovery of Black Presence, eds. Randall C. Bailey and Jacquelyn Grant (Nashville: Abingdon Press, 1995), 129–42; Diana L. Hayes, And Still We Rise: An Introduction to Black Liberation Theology (New York: Paulist Press, 1996); Deborah James, "A Good Catholic Woman: Reflections on Conflict and Continuity in the Nineties," in My Soul Is a Witness: African-American Women's Spirituality, ed. Gloria Wade-Gayles (Boston: Beacon Press, 1995), 234–40; Emilie M. Townes, In a Blaze of Glory: Womanist Spirituality as Social Witness (Nashville: Abingdon Press, 1995); Townes, ed., A Troubling in My Soul, and Wade-Gayles, ed. My Soul Is a Witness.

30. Emilie M. Townes, "Black Women: From Slavery to Womanist Liberation," In Our Own Voices, 160.

31. Relevant is a schema of the distinct worldviews of the black and white communities. See Cassandra Hoffman-Mason and Rosie P. Bingham, "Developing a Sensitivity for Culture and Ethnicity in Family Violence," in Abuse and Religion, eds. Horton and Williamson, 138–43.

32. See Grant, White Women's Christ and Black Women's Jesus, chapter 7.

33. See Townes, In a Blaze of Glory, 163; Delores S. Williams, "A Womanist Perspective on Sin," in A Troubling in my Soul, ed. Townes, 130–49; Grant, White Women's Christ and Black Women's Jesus, 138.

34. Townes, In a Blaze of Glory, 25.

35. See Wade-Gayles, ed., My Soul Is a Witness, 2.

36. I use the names "Holiness" and "Sanctified" to refer to a number of churches also known as Pentecostal, Apostolic, and Wesleyan Methodist. For discussion of the complex origins of the many Sanctified churches in the United States, see Cheryl J. Sander's Saints in Exile, 1996. Sometimes I use the name "Evangelical" to refer to fundamentalist churches. Most times, I use a slash to group, but designate the terms. My divisions here between black women and white Holiness Appalachian women can be misleading. Some African American women in the shelter have Appalachian roots and many African American women were raised in or now belong to the Sanctified Church. My divisions are an attempt to manage the major divisions in ethnic self-identity and (oftentimes even mixed) religious backgrounds.

37. In Saints in Exile, Sanders argues that ecstatic behaviors originated in African traditional religious practices and were imitated by whites. The Sanctified Church is related to three distinct traditions: African religion, white "protest" Protestantism, and Haitian vaudou (3).

38. The information here has been gathered from shelter women and augmented by reference to: Sanders, Saints in Exile, 1996; Encyclopedia of American Religions: Religious Creeds, vol. 1., ed. J. Gordon Melton (Detroit: Gale Research, 1988), 283; Cheryl Townsend Gilkes, "Together and in Harness: Women's Traditions in the Sanctified Church," 223–44; and In Our Own Voices, 1995.

39. Sanders, Saints in Exile, 57.

40. "Summary Statement of Belief," The National Association of Holiness Churches, *Encyclopedia of American Religions*, 327.

41. Refer to Pearl Williams-Jones, "A Minority Report: Black Pentecostal Women," *Spirit* 1.2 (1977): 31–44, cited in Sanders, *Saints in Exile*, 32–34. The black sanctified church moved away from its original tendency to gender equality. For similar arguments about white Holiness/Pentecostalism, see R. M. Riss, "The Role of Women," in *Dictionary of Pentecostal and Charismatic Movements*, eds. Stanley M. Burgess and Patrick H. Alexander (Grand Rapids, Mich.: Zondervan, 1988), 893–99, and Timothy C. Morgan, "The Stained-Glass Ceiling," *Christianity Today* 38.6 (May 16, 1994): 52. Explanations include: less urgency about the Second Coming, a reaction to feminism, and the influence of conservatives.

42. Elaine J. Lawless, "Not So Different a Story After All," 41–52.

43. *Encyclopedia of American Religions*, 572.

44. *Battle for the Minds*, eds. Steven Lipscomb and Anthony Sherin (Los Angeles: Battle for the Minds, 1997), explores tensions within the Southern Baptist Convention on women's roles.

45. Victor Witter Turner, *The Anthropology of Performance*, (New York: PAJ Publications, 1986), 494.

46. See Catherine C. Kroeger and James R. Beck, *Women, Abuse, and the Bible: How Scripture Can Be Used to Hurt or Heal* (Grand Rapids, Mich.: Baker Books, 1996) and Nancy A. Hardesty, "Evangelical Women," in *In Our Own Voices*, eds. Keller and Ruether, 209–45.

47. In *Godly Women*, Brasher argues female enclaves empower and disempower. See 168.

CHAPTER 5

1. The typology is based on the work of Rankka in *Women and the Value of Suffering*.

2. See Troy D. Abell, "The Holiness Pentecostal Experience in Southern Appalachia," in *Religion in Appalachia*, ed. John D. Photiadis, 79–101, especially 97.

3. A reader may categorize some statements differently if we focus on different utterances. Women blend or shift theodicies, the subject of upcoming chapters. Here I do not mean to suggest that particular women adhere to only one theodicy; on the contrary, a particular statement, uttered in a particular context, evidences shades of at least one type of theodicy.

CHAPTER 6

1. As I discussed in chapter 5, battered women do not refer to their explanations for suffering as "theodicy;" yet, they have religiously grounded explanations to which they subscribe.

2. Hayes, *And Still We Rise*, 69.

3. I treat specific aspects of this question extensively in other chapters.

4. Refer to chapter 2 for an extended discussion.

5. When Christian commentators argue this point, they are displacing or evading the fundamental role of patriarchal religion in the dynamics of woman abuse.

6. This woman was referring to her feelings about trying to find a place to live, applying for social services, dealing with shelter life, and suffering the loss of her relationship.

7. I do not claim that no woman is ever angry with God, but the typical pattern of response is anger at abusers, then conditions and institutions that aid and abet the abuse of women.

8. I will deal with the process of healing more fully in the next chapter. Here I address healing in the context of the issues already raised.

9. I am referring to cultural feminism in the theories of scholars such as M. F. Belenky, N. R. Goldberg, and J. M. Taurel in *Women's Ways of Knowing* (New York: Basic Books, 1986) and Deborah Tannen in *You Just Don't Understand: Women and Men in Conversation* (New York: Morrow, 1990). The basic idea is that women use language in distinct ways. For Belenky et al., the emphasis is on cognitive and psychological processes, an idea largely discarded in contemporary feminist linguistics.

CHAPTER 7

1. I have changed the times and frequency of meetings, but I began going in May of 1992. The location of our group has changed from a dining room, to a conference room, to a sitting room with couches. The first location, then the last, were most amenable to our conversation. See Pennebaker's remarks about settings and self-disclosure in *Opening Up*, 181–87. He believes that unique settings, dark lighting, emotional arousal, and an accepting audience facilitate self-disclosure. These are features of our sessions.

2. In *Trauma and Recovery* Herman notes other types of traumatic events, including domestic violence. See 9.

3. Ibid., 207. Contrarily, in the storytelling circle at the Women's House, many women address the religious significance of their suffering.

4. See, for example, Allan Stoekl, "Elaine Scarry's *The Body in Pain*, Paul Bove's *Intellectuals in Power*; The Pain of Being an Intellectual" in *Southern Humanities Review* 22.1 (1988): 49–62, especially 58.

5. Trudy Mills, "The Assault on the Self: Stages in Coping with Battering Husbands," *Qualitative Sociology* 8.2 (Summer 1985): 103–23.

6. Pamela Cooper-White, "An Emperor Without Clothes: The Church's Views about the Treatment of Domestic Violence," *Pastoral Psychology* 45.1 (1996): 3–20. See also *Cry of Tamar: Violence against Women and the Church's Response* (Minneapolis: Fortress Press, 1995). Cooper-White is a pastoral care worker and clinical social worker.

7. Cooper-White, "An Emperor Without Clothes," 10.

8. Gordon, *Heroes of Their Own Lives*, 5.

9. Cooper-White, "An Emperor Without Clothes," 13, and Fortune, "Forgiveness: The Last Step," in *Violence against Women and Children*, eds. Adams and Fortune, 201–06.

10. See Fortune, "Forgiveness: The Last Step," 201.

11. Such an emphasis is more fitting to the healing of battered women than, for example, that of another pastoral care worker, Ron Roth, who advocates a healing schema of five stages: awakening, purification, illumination, dark night of the soul, and divine union. This traditional, religiously based, and mystical schema focuses intensely on the individual and neglects almost entirely the social context of suffering. See Ron Roth with Peter Occhiogrosso, *Prayer and the Five Stages of Healing* (Carlsbad, Calif.: Hay House, 1999).

12. See Elisabeth Schussler Fiorenza, "Ties That Bind: Domestic Violence Against Women" in *Women Resisting Violence,* eds. Mary John Mananzan, et al., 39–55; Townes, ed., *A Troubling in My Soul*; and Lisa Sowle Cahill, *Sex, Gender, and Christian Ethics* (Cambridge: Cambridge University Press, 1996).

13. Elizabeth A. Johnson, *She Who Is*.

14. Fortune, "The Transformation of Suffering," 85–91. Fortune's analysis is not applicable to the majority of shelter women I have met. In a helpful conversation, a friend suggested to me that child incest victims might be more apt to blame God, particularly when they are recounting past incidents or feelings. Once women analyze their material situations, they are less inclined to blame a transcendent God and more inclined to ascribe blame where it more logically belongs: the abuser, their sociocultural status, and their economic situation.

15. Soelle, *Suffering*. See chapter 3, "Suffering and Language," particularly 73.

16. Soelle is influenced by philosopher Simone Weil, especially in her development of the notion of "affliction." See Weil's *Waiting for God*, particularly 122.

17. At the same time, Soelle recognizes the phase of "numb pain" as a feature of society in which workers are alienated from one another, God, and their labor. See *Suffering*, 71.

18. Refer to Soelle, *Suffering*, 76.

19. Gustavo Gutierrez, *On Job: God-Talk and the Suffering of the Innocent* (Maryknoll, N.Y.: Orbis, 1988). See chapter 4, especially 30.

20. Soelle, *Suffering*, 78. The result of prayer depends on the nature of the God to whom people pray, Soelle notes on 77.

21. Again, this is not to say that Phase Three language persists indefinitely. It does not persist indefinitely even for those of us who are not in crisis. The argument is simply that Phase Three survivors have become capable of realistic, but hopeful language.

22. Soelle, *Suffering*, 72 and 77 respectively. Soelle, interestingly, is familiar with Basil Bernstein whose work on language and class, and the concepts of elaborated and restricted codes, is classic. See *Class, Codes and Control* (London: Routledge and Kegan Paul, 1971). Soelle diminishes the importance of elaborated codes for solidarity and change.

CHAPTER 8

1. By "storytelling" I do not mean to suggest that the women narrate stories with a typical structure that involves, for example, an introduction, building climax, and resolution. I use this term in a very general sense to denote conversations, both spontaneous and more structured, in which the women share autobiographical details,

that is, their life stories. They tell stories, for example, of their upbringing, marriage, and abuse.

2. Refer to Anne Balsamo, *Technologies of the Gendered Body: Reading Cyborg Women* (Durham: Duke University Press, 1996); Donna J. Haraway, "A Cyborg Manifesto: Science, Technology, and Socialist-Feminism in the Late Twentieth Century," in *Simians, Cyborgs, and Women: The Reinvention of Nature* (New York: Routledge, 1991); speech genres in Bakhtin, *Speech Genres and Other Late Essays*; linguistic creativity in Volosinov, *Marxism and the Philosophy of Language*. See also Teresa de Lauretis, *Technologies of Gender: Essays on Theory, Film, and Fiction* (Bloomington: Indiana University Press, 1987) and "The Violence of Rhetoric: Considerations on Representation and Gender," in *The Violence of Representation: Literature and the History of Violence*, eds. Nancy Armstrong and Leonard Tennenhouse (New York: Routledge, 1989), 239–58.

3. See Chapter 3 and note especially Townes, *In a Blaze of Glory*, and Townes, ed., *A Troubling in My Soul*; Bendroth, *Fundamentalism and Gender*; and Gilkes, " 'Together and in Harness,' " 223–44.

4. I will not analyze the language for denominational distinctions: I consider religious language generally. The two denominations currently treat gender in similar ways. See chapter 3. I will not focus on markers for race/ethnicity, although African American and white battered women often face different struggles and speak accordingly.

5. *The Oxford Companion to the English Language*, ed. Tom McArthur (Oxford: Oxford University Press, 1992), 489–90.

6. Bakhtin, *The Dialogic Imagination*, 265.

7. Ibid., 279.

8. Ibid., 291.

9. Volosinov, *Marxism and the Philosophy of Language*, 23. Scholars believe Volosinov and Bakhtin may be the same author. Volosinov refers to societal change, but I argue from the assumption that this applies to individual change as well.

10. Refer to Peter L. Berger, *The Sacred Canopy; Elements of a Sociological Theory of Religion* (Garden City, N.Y.: Doubleday, 1969), 18–21, 32. Short-term language change is evident within this conversation, but there is no way to prove long-term change in this study.

11. I offer not quantitative, statistically significant data; rather, I offer ethnographically gathered qualitative evidence to substantiate my sense of shelter experience.

12. See Penelope Brown for a good articulation of such a position in "How and Why Are Women More Polite: Some Evidence from a Mayan Community," in *Language and Gender*, ed. Jennifer Coates (Oxford: Blackwell, 1998), 81–99, especially 97. I have also benefited from the work of other feminist linguists, especially Penelope Eckert and Sally McConnell-Ginet, who argue for ethnographic and other interdisciplinary studies to further our understanding of social, cultural, and language universals—all with the understanding that we will never arrive at "a detailed theory of the general principles and parameters of gender and language interactions." Instead we hope to "get a grip on the ranges of human language, thought, and social life" (454). See their essay: "Think Practically and Look Locally:

Language and Gender as Community-Based Practice, in *The Women and Language Debate*, 432–60.

CHAPTER 9

1. A positive dynamic is not guaranteed: Regressive movement is possible.

2. In "Contextual Theology," in *Dictionary of Mission: Theology, History, Perspectives*, eds. Karl Muller, S.V.D., Theo Sundermeier, Stephen B. Bevans, S.V.D., and Richard H. Bliese (Maryknoll, New York: Orbis, 1997), 82–87, Hans Waldenfels, S.J. makes a distinction between contextual perspectives such as liberation theology, black theology, et cetera, and local theologies such as African theology, Latin American liberation theology, et cetera (86). I prefer "local theology."

3. William A. Dyrness, *Invitation to Cross-Cultural Theology: Case Studies in Vernacular Theologies* (Grand Rapids, Mich.: Zondervan, 1992), 16.

4. Ibid., 32.

5. Waldenfels, S.J., "Contextual Theology," *Dictionary of Mission*, 84.

6. Dyrness, *Invitation to Cross-Cultural Theology*, 31.

7. Waldenfels, S.J., "Contextual Theology," *Dictionary of Mission*, 84.

8. In *Feet-on-the-Ground Theology* (Maryknoll, N.Y.: Orbis, 1987), Clodovis Boff calls the process "homemade theology" and the participants the "collective intellectual." (119–20).

9. Robert J. Schreiter, *Constructing Local Theologies*. See also Schreiter's *The New Catholicity*.

10. Genesis 3:16 reads: "To the woman he [God] said, 'I will greatly multiply your pain in childbearing; in pain you shall bring forth children, yet your desire shall be for your husband, and he shall rule over you." *The New Oxford Annotated Bible*, Revised Standard Version, ed. Herbert G. May and Bruce M. Metzger (New York: Oxford University Press, 1973).

11. Stephen B. Bevans, S.V.D., discusses five models in *Models of Contextual Theology* and an additional model in "Taking Culture Seriously in Religious Education," *The Catholic World* (September–October 1994): 236–40.

12. The semiotic model describes Schreiter's "contextual" model. See Richard N. Longenecker, *New Wine into Fresh Wineskins: Contextualizing the Early Christian Confessions* (Peabody, Mass.: Hendrickson, 1999), 147.

13. I will not deal extensively with theodicy, but it shifts when informed by lived experience.

14. Mary Ann Hinsdale, et al., *It Comes from the People*, 211.

15. For this section, I consulted Letty M. Russell and J. Shannon Clarkson, *Dictionary of Feminist Theologies* (Louisville: Westminster John Knox Press, 1996); Gerald O'Collins, S.J., and Edward G. Farrugia, S.J., *A Concise Dictionary of Theology* (New York: Paulist, 1991); and Van A. Harvey, *A Handbook of Theological Terms* (New York: MacMillan, 1964).

16. Mary E. Hunt, *Fierce Tenderness: A Feminist Theology of Friendship* (New York: Crossroad, 1991), 129.

17. Patrick Bascio, *The Failure of White Theology: A Black Theological Perspective* (New York: Peter Lang, 1994), 37.

CONCLUSION

1. Bakhtin, *The Dialogic Imagination*, 291.

2. Katie Geneva Cannon, "Black Women's Stories and Moral Wisdom," in *In Our Own Voices*, eds. Keller and Ruether, 195.

3. See Deborah Hines, "Racism Breeds Stereotypes," *The Witness* 65 (February 1982): 7, cited in Grant, *White Women's Christ and Black Women's Jesus*, 201; and see also Audre Lorde, *Sister Outsider: Essays and Speeches* (New York: Crossing Press, 1984), 67, cited in Grant, 171. In *The Nation* (11 August 1997: 2), Kathy Rodgers makes a similar point from a secular point of view, citing Catherine T. Kenney and Karen R. Brown's *Report from the Front Lines: The Impact of Violence on Poor Women* (New York: National Organization of Women Legal Defense and Education Fund, 1996).

4. See Copeland, "Wading Through Many Sorrows," in *A Troubling in My Soul*, ed. Townes, 123.

5. Wade-Gayles, ed., *My Soul Is a Witness*, 6. My inclination is to agree with her. Likewise, I tend to agree with Soelle in *Suffering*, Scarry in *The Body in Pain*, and Herman in *Trauma and Recovery*. These three scholars argue that suffering cannot be articulated in its most acute phase. It follows that, only after it has moved out of its most acute phase, can suffering be articulated from the various standpoints of race, class, and gender.

6. Wade-Gayles, ed., *My Soul Is a Witness*, 2.

7. For a brief but clear discussion of gender and language universals, see Janet Holmes, "Women's Talk: The Question of Sociolinguistic Universals," in *Language and Gender*, ed. Jennifer Coates, 461–83.

8. Mary Farrell Bednarowski, *The Religious Imagination of American Women* (Bloomington: Indiana University Press, 1999), 153.

9. Sands, *Escape from Paradise*, 59.

10. Bednarowski, *The Religious Imagination*, 16.

11. Ibid., 17.

12. Janoff-Bulman, *Shattered Assumptions*, 161.

13. An overly enthusiastic resident may have annoyed staff and residents with her witness; however, the staff's solution—banning Bibles from public space—was not appropriate.

14. See chapter 2 on the history of the shelter.

15. In action research all participants—teacher-researchers, community members, clients, students, and so forth—work together on an agreed upon project that leads to a particular end goal, such as useful information or tangible products. There are various types of action research, but generally it involves community-university collaboration. The community's rather than the researchers' interests are the starting point. Action research represents a democratic thrust in pedagogy by recognizing the value of including all participants in the generation of useful knowledge regarding major social, political, economic, and cultural problems. It is not research on people; it is research for people. The term "action" indicates a systemic effort to contribute to social change. For a basic introduction, see Ernest T. Stringer, *Action Research: A Handbook for Practitioners* (Thousand Oaks, Calif.: Sage Publications, 1996). Service

learning, by contrast, integrates classroom and experiential learning by sending students into the community to perform service. Students do not research for the site and the agency participates only indirectly in the curriculum. See Joseph A. Erickson and Jeffrey B. Anderson, eds., *Learning With the Community: Concepts and Models for Service-Learning in Teacher Education* (Washington, D.C.: AAHE, 1997).

16. See Eckert and McConnell-Ginet's, "Think Practically," 432–60.

17. There are many examples in Coates, ed., *Language and Gender*. For a contrastive view, see Eckert and McConnell-Ginet's, "Think Practically," 441.

Selected Bibliography

Adams, Carol J., and Marie M. Fortune, eds. 1995. *Violence against Women and Children: A Christian Theological Sourcebook*. New York: Continuum.

Bachman, Ronet, and Linda E. Saltzman. 1995. *Violence Against Women: Estimates from the Redesigned Survey*. Washington, D.C.: U.S. Department of Justice, Office of Justice Programs, Bureau of Justice Statistics.

Bakhtin, M. M. 1981. *The Dialogic Imagination*. Edited by Michael Holquist and translated by Michael Holquist and Caryl Emerson. Austin: University of Texas Press.

———. 1986. "The Problem of Speech Genres." Edited by Caryl Emerson and Michael Holquist. In *Speech Genres and Other Late Essays*. Translated by Vern W. McGee. Austin: University of Texas Press. 60–102.

Bendroth, Margaret Lamberts. 1993. *Fundamentalism and Gender, 1875 to the Present*. New Haven: Yale University Press.

Bevans, Stephen B., S.V.D. 1992. *Models of Contextual Theology*. Maryknoll, N.Y.: Orbis.

Brasher, Brenda E. 1998. *Godly Women: Fundamentalism and Female Power*. New Brunswick, N.J.: Rutgers University Press.

Cassell, Eric J. 1991. *The Nature of Suffering and the Goals of Medicine*. New York: Oxford.

Coates, Jennifer, ed. 1998. *Language and Gender*. Oxford: Blackwell.

Cooper-White, Pamela. 1995. *Cry of Tamar: Violence against Women and the Church's Response*. Minneapolis: Fortress Press.

Dayton, Donald W., and Robert K. Johnston, eds. 1991. *The Variety of American Evangelicalism*. Knoxville: University of Tennessee Press.

Diagnostic and Statistical Manual of Mental Disorders: DSM-IV. 1994. Washington, D.C.: American Psychiatric Association.

Dobash, R. Emerson, and Russell P. Dobash. 1992. *Women, Violence, and Social Change*. New York: Routledge.

Eckert, Penelope, and Sally McConnell-Ginet. 1994. "Think Practically and Look Locally: Language and Gender as Community-Based Practice." In *The Women and Language Debate*. Edited by Camille Roman, Suzanne Juhasz, and Cristanne Miller. New Brunswick, N.J.: Rutgers University Press. 432–60.

Geertz, Clifford. 1983. *Local Knowledge: Further Essays in Interpretive Anthropology*. New York: Basic Books.

———. 1973. *The Interpretation of Cultures*. New York: Basic Books.

Gelles, Richard J., and Clair Pedrick Cornell. 1990. *Intimate Violence in Families*. London: Sage.

Gelles, Richard J., and Donileen R. Loseke. 1993. *Current Controversies on Family Violence*. Newbury Park: Sage.

Gilkes, Cheryl Townsend. 1990. " 'Together and in Harness': Women's Traditions in the Sanctified Church." In *Black Women in America: Social Science Perspectives*. Edited by Micheline R. Malson, Elisabeth Mudimbe-Boyi, Jean F. O'Barr, and Mary Wyer. Chicago: University of Chicago Press. 223–44.

Gordon, Linda. 1988. *Heroes of Their Own Lives: The Politics and History of Family Violence*. New York: Penguin.

Grant, Jacquelyn. 1989. *White Women's Christ and Black Women's Jesus: Feminist Christology and Womanist Response*. Atlanta: Scholars Press.

Griffith, R. Marie. 1997. *God's Daughters: Evangelical Women and the Power of Submission*. Berkeley: University of California Press.

Guy-Sheftall, Beverly, ed. 1995. *Words of Fire: An Anthology of African American Feminist Thought*. New York: New York Press.

Hardesty, Nancy A. 1995. "Evangelical Women." In *In Our Own Voices: Four Centuries of American Women's Religious Writing*. Edited by Rosemary Skinner Keller and Rosemary Radford Ruether. San Francisco: Harper. 209–45.

Hayes, Diana L. 1996. *And Still We Rise: An Introduction to Black Liberation Theology*. New York: Paulist Press.

Heath, Sarah. 1997. "Negotiating White Womanhood: The Cincinnati YWCA and White Wage-Earning Women, 1918–1929." In *Men and Women Adrift: The YMCA and the YWCA in the City*. Edited by Nina Mjagkij and Margaret Spratt. New York: New York University Press. 86–110.

Herman, Judith Lewis. 1992. *Trauma and Recovery*. New York: Basic Books.

Hinsdale, Mary Ann, Helen Lewis, and S. Maxine Waller. 1995. *It Comes from the People: Community Development and Local Theology*. Philadelphia: Temple University Press.

Holmes, Janet. 1998. "Women's Talk: The Question of Sociolinguistic Universals." In *Language and Gender*. Edited by Jennifer Coates. Oxford: Blackwell. 461–83.

Janoff-Bulman, Ronnie. 1992. *Shattered Assumptions: Towards a New Psychology of Trauma*. New York: Free Press.

Jasinski, Jana L., and Linda M. Williams, eds. 1998. *Partner Violence: A Comprehensive Review of 20 Years of Research*. Thousand Oaks: Sage.

Johnson, Elizabeth A. 1992. *She Who Is: The Mystery of God in Feminist Discourse*. New York: Crossroad.

Kearney, Margaret H. 1999. *Understanding Women's Recovery from Illness and Trauma*. Thousand Oaks: Sage.

Lawless, Elaine J. 1993. "Not So Different a Story After All: Pentecostal Women in the Pulpit." In *Women's Leadership in Marginal Religions: Explorations Outside the Mainstream*. Edited by Catherine Wessinger. Chicago: University of Illinois Press. 41–52.

Mananzan, Mary John, Mercy Amba Oduyoye, Elsa Tamez, Shannon J. Clarkson, Mary C. Grey, and Letty M. Russell, eds. 1996. *Women Resisting Violence: Spirituality for Life*. Maryknoll, N.Y.: Orbis.

Mjagkij, Nina, and Margaret Spratt, eds. 1997. *Men and Women Adrift: The YMCA and the YWCA in the City*. New York: New York University Press.

Morris, David B. 1991. *The Culture of Pain*. Berkeley: University of California Press.

Pennebaker, James W. 1990. *Opening Up: The Healing Power of Confiding in Others*. New York: William Morrow.

Pleck, Elizabeth. 1987. *Domestic Tyranny: The Making of American Policy Against Family Violence from Colonial Times to the Present*. New York: Oxford.

Rankka, Kristine M. 1998. *Women and the Value of Suffering: An Aw(e)ful Rowing Toward God*. Collegeville, Minn.: Liturgical Press.

Roman, Camille, Suzanne Juhasz, and Cristanne Miller, eds. 1994. *The Women and Language Debate*. New Brunswick, N.J.: Rutgers University Press.

Salter, Anna C. 1995. *Transforming Trauma*. Thousand Oaks: Sage.

Sanders, Cheryl J. 1996. *Saints in Exile: The Holiness-Pentecostal Experience in African and American Religion and Culture*. New York: Oxford.

Sands, Kathleen M. 1994. *Escape from Paradise: Evil and Tragedy in Feminist Theology*. Minneapolis: Fortress Press.

Saunders-Robinson, Mary Alice. 1993. "Black Women Who Are Battered: Between a Rock and a Hard Place." In *River of Tears: The Politics of Black Women's Health*. Edited by Delores P. Aldridge and La Francis Rogers-Rose. Norfolk, Virginia: Traces Institute Publications. 86–92.

Scarry, Elaine. 1985. *The Body in Pain: The Making and Unmaking of the World*. New York: Oxford University Press.

Schneiders, Sandra. 1991. *Beyond Patching: Faith and Feminism in the Catholic Church*. Mahway, N.J.: Paulist Press.

Schreiter, Robert J. 1985. *Constructing Local Theologies*. Maryknoll, N.Y.: Orbis.

————. 1997. *The New Catholicity: Theology Between the Global and the Local*. Maryknoll, N.Y.: Orbis.

Soelle, Dorothee. 1975. *Suffering*. Translated by Everett R. Katlin. Philadelphia: Fortress Press.

Straus, Murray A., and Richard J. Gelles, eds. 1990. *Physical Violence in American Families: Risk Factors and Adaption to Violence in 8,145 Families*. New Brunswick, N.J.: Transaction.

Straus, Murray A., and Richard J. Gelles. 1992. *National Family Violence Survey*. Los Altos, Calif.: Sociometrics Corporation, American Family Data Archive.

Townes, Emilie M., ed. 1993. *A Troubling in My Soul: Womanist Perspectives on Evil and Suffering*. Maryknoll, N.Y.: Orbis.

van der Kolk, Bessel A., Alexander C. McFarlane, and Lars Weisaeth, eds. 1996. *Traumatic Stress: The Effects of Overwhelming Experience on Mind, Body, and Society*. New York: Guilford.

Volosinov, V. N. 1986. *Marxism and the Philosophy of Language*. 1973. Translated by Ladislav Matejka and I. R. Titunik. Cambridge: Harvard University Press.

Wade-Gayles, Gloria, ed. 1995. *My Soul Is a Witness: African-American Women's Spirituality*. Boston: Beacon Press.

Walker, Lenore E. 1979. *The Battered Woman*. New York: Harper & Row.

ADDITIONAL REFERENCES CITED IN TEXT OR NOTES NOT INCLUDED
IN SELECTED BIBLIOGRAPHY.

Abell, Troy D. n.d. "The Holiness Pentecostal Experience in Southern Appalachia."
In *Religion in Appalachia: Theological, Social and Psychological Dimensions and Correlates*. Edited by John D. Photiadis. West Virginia Morgantown: West Virginia University Press. 79–101.

Abraham, Margaret. 1995 "Ethnicity, Gender, and Marital Violence: South Asian Women's Organizations in the United States," *Gender and Society* 9.4 (August): 450–468.

Adams, Carol J. and Marsha Engle-Rowbottom. 1991. "A Commentary on Violence Against Women and Children in Rural Areas." In *Violence in the Family: A Workshop for Clergy and Other Helpers*. Edited by Marie M. Fortune. Cleveland: Pilgrim Press. 163–171.

Anderson, Kristin L. 1997. "Gender, Status, and Domestic Violence: An Integration of Feminist and Family Violence Approaches." *Journal of Marriage and the Family* 59 (August): 655–669.

Atkins, Daniel G. and John S. Whitelaw. 1996. "Turning the Tables on Women: Removal of Children from Victims of Domestic Violence," *Clearinghouse Review* (Special Issue): 261–272.

Bakhtin, M. M. 1986. *Speech Genres and Other Late Essays*. Edited by Caryl Emerson and Michael Holquist. Translated by Vern W. McGee. Austin: University of Texas Press.

Balsamo, Anne. 1996. *Technologies of the Gendered Body: Reading Cyborg Women*. Durham: Duke University Press.

Bascio, Patrick. 1994. *The Failure of White Theology: A Black Theological Perspective*. New York: Peter Lang.

Beaman-Hall, Lori and Nancy Nason-Clark. 1997. "Partners or Protagonists? The Transition House Movement and Conservative Churches." *Affilia* 12.2 (Summer): 176–196.

Bednarowski, Mary Farrell. 1999. *The Religious Imagination of American Women*. Bloomington: Indiana University Press.

Belenky, M. F., Goldberg, N. R., and J. M. Taurel. 1986. *Women's Ways of Knowing*. New York: Basic.

Belle, Deborah. 1984. "Inequality and Mental Health: Low Income and Minority Women." In *Women and Mental Health Policy*. Edited by Lenore E. Walker. Beverly Hills: Sage. 135–150.

Berger, Peter L. 1969. *The Sacred Canopy: Elements of a Sociological Theory of Religion*. Garden City, N.Y.: Doubleday.

Bernard, Jennifer. 1976. "Homosociality and Female Depression," *Journal of Social Issues* 32.4: 213–238.

Bernstein, Basil B. 1971. *Class, Codes and Control*. London: Routledge and Kegan Paul.

Bersani, Carl A. and Huey-Tsyh Chen. 1988. "Sociological Perspectives in Family Violence." In *Handbook of Family Violence*. Edited by Van Hasselt, Vincent B., Morrison Randell L., Bellack, Alan S. and Michel Hersen. New York: Plenum. 57–86.

Bevans, Stephen, SVD. 1999. "Living between Gospel and Context: Models for a Missional Church in North America." In *Confident Witness—Changing World: Rediscovering the Gospel in North America*. Edited by Craig Van Gelder. Grand Rapids: Eerdsmans. 141–154.

———. 1994. "Taking Culture Seriously in Religious Education." *The Catholic World*. (September–October): 236–240.

Blamires, Alcuin, ed. 1992. *Woman Defamed and Woman Defended: An Anthology of Medieval Texts*. Oxford: Clarendon.

Boff, Clodovis. 1987. *Feet-on-the-Ground Theology*. Maryknoll, N.Y.: Orbis.

Brown, Penelope. 1998. "How and Why Are Women More Polite: Some Evidence from a Mayan Community." In *Language and Gender*. Edited by Jennifer Coates. Oxford: Blackwell. 81–99.

Browne, Angela and Kirk R. Williams. 1989. "Exploring the Effect of Resource Availability and Likelihood of Female-Precipitated Homicides." *Law and Society Review* 23.1: 75–94.

Brownell, Patricia. 1997."Multicultural Practice and Domestic Violence." In *Multicultural Perspectives in Working With Families*. Edited by Elaine P. Congress. New York: Springer. 217–235.

Bugental, Daphne Blunt. 1993. "Communication in Abusive Relationships," *American Behavioral Scientist* 36.3 (January): 288–308.

Bussert, Joy M. K. 1986. *Battered Women: From a Theology of Suffering to an Ethic of Empowerment*. New York: DMNA/LCA.

Cahill, Lisa Sowle. 1996. *Sex, Gender, and Christian Ethics*. Cambridge: Cambridge University Press.

Callender, Ann. 1999. *Pathways Through Pain*. Cleveland: Pilgrim.

Cannon, Katie Geneva. 1995. "Black Women's Stories and Moral Wisdom." In *In Our Own Voices: Four Centuries of American Women's Religious Writing*. Edited by Rosemary Skinner Keller and Rosemary Radford Ruether. San Francisco: Harper. 193–196.

Cassell, Eric J. 1995. "Pain and Suffering." In *Encyclopedia of Bioethics*, Vol. 4. Edited by Warren Thomas Reich. New York: Macmillan. 1897–1905.

Checkoway, Barry, Chesler, Mark A., and Stephen Blum. 1990. "Self-Care, Self-Help, and Community Care for Health." In *Working with Self-Help*. Edited by Thomas J. Powell. Silver Spring, Md.: National Association of Social Workers Press. 277–300.

Chesler, Mark A. 1990. "The Dangers of Self-Help Groups." In *Working with Self-Help*. Edited by Thomas J. Powell. Silver Spring, Md.: National Association of Social Workers Press. 301–324.

Chiseri-Strater, Elizabeth and Bonnie Stone Sunstein. 1997. *Field Working: Reading and Writing Research*. Upper Saddle River, N.J.: Prentice Hall.

Coates, Jennifer, ed. 1998. *Language and Gender*. Oxford: Blackwell.

Coley, Soraya M. and Joyce O. Beckett. 1988. "Black Battered Women: A Review of the Empirical Literature." *Journal of Counseling and Development* 66.6 (February): 266–270.

Cooper-White, Pamela. 1996. "An Emperor Without Clothes: The Church's Views About the Treatment of Domestic Violence." *Pastoral Psychology* 45.1. 3–20.

Copeland, Shawn M. 1993. "Wading Through Many Sorrows: Toward a Theology of Suffering in Womanist Perspective." In *A Troubling in my Soul: Womanist*

Perspectives on Evil and Suffering. Edited by Emilie M. Townes. Maryknoll, N.Y.: Orbis. 109–129.

Counts, Dorothy Ayers. 1987. "Female Suicide and Wife Abuse: A Cross-Cultural Perspective." *Suicide and Life Threatening Behavior* 17.3 (Fall): 194–204.

de Lauretis, Teresa. 1989. "The Violence of Rhetoric: Considerations on Representation and Gender." In *The Violence of Representation: Literature and the History of Violence.* Edited by Nancy Armstrong and Leonard Tennenhouse. New York: Routledge. 239–258.

———. 1987. *Technologies of Gender: Essays on Theory, Film, and Fiction.* Bloomington: Indiana University Press.

Desjarlais, Robert, Eisenberg, Leon, Good, Bryon and Arthur Kleinman. 1995. *World Mental Heath.* New York: Oxford University Press.

Diagnostic and Statistical Manual of Mental Disorders: DSM-III-R. 1987. Washington, D.C.: American Psychiatric Association.

Diagnostic and Statistical Manual of Mental Disorders: DSM-IV. 1994. Washington, D.C.: American Psychiatric Association.

Dictionary of Feminist Theologies. 1996. Edited by Letty M. Russell and J. Shannon Clarkson. Louisville: Westminster John Knox Press.

Dictionary of Pastoral Care and Counseling. 1990. Edited by Rodney J. Hunter, Nashville: Abingdon Press.

Dobash, R. Emerson and Russell P. Dobash. 1979. *Violence Against Wives: A Case Against the Patriarchy.* New York: Free Press.

———. 1997. "Violence Against Women." In *Gender Violence: Interdisciplinary Perspectives.* Edited by Laura L. O'Toole and Jessica R. Schiffman. New York: New York University Press. 266–278.

Doran, C. 1990. "Family Violence." In *Dictionary of Pastoral Care and Counseling.* Edited by Rodney J. Hunter. Nashville: Abingdon Press. 426–429.

Dorgan, Howard. 1997. *In the Hands of a Happy God: The "No-Hellers" of Central Appalachia.* Knoxville: University of Tennessee Press.

———. 1993. *The Airwaves of Zion: Radio and Religion in Appalachia.* Knoxville: University of Tennessee Press.

———. 1989. *The Old Regular Baptists of Central Appalachia: Brothers and Sisters in Hope.* Knoxville: University of Tennessee Press.

———. 1987. *Giving Glory to God in Appalachia: Worship Practices of Six Baptist Subdenominations.* Knoxville: University of Tennessee Press.

Doyle, Lesley. 1995. *What Makes Women Sick: Gender and the Political Economy of Health.* New Brunswick, N.J.: Rutgers University Press.

Dyrness, William A. 1992. *Invitation to Cross-Cultural Theology: Case Studies in Vernacular Theologies.* Grand Rapids, MI: Zondervan.

Edleson, Jeffrey L. 2000. "Problems Associated with Children's Witnessing of Domestic Violence," (10 December) INTERNET: Available World Wide Web. http://www.vaw.umn.edu/Vawnet/witness/htm.

Elliott, Frank A. 1988. "Neurological Factors." In *Handbook of Family Violence.* Edited by Vincent B. Van Hasselt, Randell L. Morrison, Alan S. Bellack, and Michel Hersen. New York: Plenum. 359–382.

———. 1997. "More than Victims: Battered Women, the Syndrome Society, and the Law." *The Nation* (24 March): 25–28.

Erickson, Joseph A. and Jeffrey B. Anderson, eds. 1997. *Learning With the Community: Concepts and Models for Service-Learning in Teacher Education.* Washington, D.C.: AAHE.

Farley, Wendy. 1990. *Tragic Vision and Divine Compassion: A Contemporary Theodicy.* Louisville: John Knox Press.

Federal Register 65.31. 2000. "Annual Update of the HHS Poverty Guidelines." Washington, D.C.: Department of Health and Human Services (February 15): 7555–7557.

Ferraro, Kathleen J. 1983. "Negotiating Trouble in a Battered Women's Shelter." *Urban Life* 12.3 (October): 287–306.

Fiorenza, Elisabeth Schussler. 1996. "Ties That Bind: Domestic Violence Against Women." In *Women Resisting Violence: Spirituality for Life.* Edited by Mary John Mananzan, Mercy Amba Oduyoye, Elsa Tamez, J. Shannon Clarkson, Mary C. Grey, and Letty M. Russell. Maryknoll, N.Y.: Orbis. 39–55.

Fischbach, Ruth L. and Barbara Herbert. 1997. "Domestic Violence and Mental Health: Correlates and Conundrums Within and Across Cultures." *Social Science and Medicine* 45.8: 1161–1176.

Fortune, Marie, M. 1995. "The Transformation of Suffering: A Theological and Biblical Perspective." In *Violence against Women and Children: A Christian Theological Sourcebook.* Edited by Carol J. Adams and Marie M. Fortune. New York: Continuum. 85–91.

———. 1991. *Violence in the Family: A Workshop Curriculum for Clergy and Other Helpers.* (Revised edition of *Family Violence,* 1980.) Cleveland: Pilgrim Press.

———. 1995. "Forgiveness: The Last Step." In *Violence Against Women and Children: A Christian Theological Sourcebook.* Edited by Carol J. Adams and Marie M. Fortune. New York: Continuum. 201–206.

Fowler, Gary L. 1981. "The Residential Distribution of Urban Appalachians." In *The Invisible Minority: Urban Appalachians.* Edited by William W. Philliber and Clyde B. McCoy with Harry C. Dillingham. Lexington: University of Kentucky Press. 79–94.

Frank, Phyllis B. and Gail Kadison Golden. 1992. "Blaming by Naming: Battered Women and the Epidemic of Codependence." *Social Work* 37.1 (January): 5–6.

French, Marilyn. 1997. "Fifteenth-century Feminism." *The Nation* 264.25 (30 June): 24.

Frye, Marilyn. 1983. "In and Out of Harm's Way: Arrogance and Love." *The Politics of Reality: Essays in Feminist Theory.* Freedom, Calif.: Crossing. 52–83.

Graham, Dee L. R., Rawlings, Edna I. and Roberta K. Rigsby. 1994. *Loving to Survive: Sexual Terror, Men's Violence, and Women's Lives.* New York: New York University Press.

Grant, Jacquelyn. 1995. "Womanist Jesus and the Mutual Struggle for Liberation." *The Recovery of Black Presence.* Eds. Randall C. Bailey and Jacquelyn Grant. Nashville: Abingdon Press. 129–142.

Gutierrez, Gustavo. 1988. *On Job: God-Talk and the Suffering of the Innocent.* Maryknoll, N.Y.: Orbis.

Haraway, Donna J. 1991. "A Cyborg Manifesto: Science, Technology, and Socialist-Feminism in the Late Twentieth Century," *Simians, Cyborgs, and Women: The Reinvention of Nature* New York: Routledge.

Hartshorne, Charles. 1967. *A Natural Theology for Our Time*. La Salle, IL: Open Court.

Harvey, Van A. 1964. *A Handbook of Theological Terms*. New York: MacMillan.

Hill, Brennan, Knitter, Paul, and William Madges. 1990. (Sixth printing 1995). *Faith, Religion, and Theology*. Mystic, Conn.: Twenty-Third Publications.

Hines, Deborah. 1982. "Racism Breeds Stereotypes." *The Witness* 65 (February), 7.

Hoffman-Mason, Cassandra and Rosie P. Bingham. 1988. "Developing a Sensitivity for Culture and Ethnicity in Family Violence." Eds. Anne L. Horton and Judith A. Williamson. *Abuse and Religion: When Praying Isn't Enough*. Lexington, Mass.: Heath. 138–143.

Holmes, Janet. 1998. "Women's Talk: The Question of Sociolinguistic Universals." In *Language and Gender*. Edited by Jennifer Coates. Oxford: Blackwell. 461–483.

Howard-Synder, Daniel, ed. 1996. *The Evidential Argument from Evil*. Bloomington: Indiana University Press.

Hunt, Mary E. 1991. *Fierce Tenderness: A Feminist Theology of Friendship*. New York: Crossroad.

Imbens, Annie and Ineke Jonker. 1992. *Christianity and Incest*. [English translation of *Godsdienst en incest: De Horstink i.s.m. de Vereniging tegen Seksuele Kindermishandeling binnen het Gezin*, Amsterdam: Uitgeverij An Dekker, 1985.) Kent, Great Britain: Burns and Oakes.

James, Deborah. 1995. "A Good Catholic Woman: Reflections on Conflict and Continuity in the Nineties." In *My Soul is a Witness : African-American Women's Spirituality*. Edited by Dolores Wade-Gayles. Boston: Beacon Press. 234–240.

Jasinski, Jana L. and Glenda Kaufman Kantor. 1998. "Dynamics and Risk Factors in Partner Violence." In *Partner Violence: A Comprehensive Review of 20 Years of Research*. Edited by Jana L. Jasinski and Linda M. Williams. Thousand Oaks, Calif.: Sage. 1–43.

Jaynes, Gerald David and Robin M. Williams, Jr., eds. 1989. *A Common Destiny: Blacks and American Society*. Washington, D.C.: National Academy Press.

Johns Hopkins School of Public Health and the Center for Health and Gender Equity. 2000. "Women Abused Worldwide." *Off Our Backs* (February): 4.

Johnson, Michael P. 1995. "Patriarchal Terrorism and Common Couple Violence: Two Forms of Violence Against Women." *Journal of Marriage and the Family* 57 (May): 283–294.

Keller, Rosemary Skinner and Rosemary Radford Ruether. 1995. *In Our Own Voices: Four Centuries of American Women's Religious Writing*. San Francisco: Harper.

Kellerman, Arthur L. and James A. Mercy. 1992. "Men, Women, and Murder: Gender-Specific Differences in Rates of Fatal Violence and Victimization." *Journal of Trauma* 33.1: 1–5.

Kenney, Catherine T. and Karen R. Brown. 1996. *Report From the Front Lines: The Impact of Violence on Poor Women*. New York: National Organization of Women Legal Defense and Education Fund.

Kleinman, Arthur. 1988. *The Illness Narratives: Suffering, Healing, and the Human Condition*. New York: Basic Books.

Kroeger, Catherine Clark and James R. Beck. 1996. *Women, Abuse, and the Bible: How Scripture Can Be Used to Hurt or Heal*. Grand Rapids, Mich.: Baker Books.

Laub, Dori. 1992. "Bearing Witness or Vicissitudes of Listening." In *Testimony: Crises of Witnessing in Literature, Psychoanalysis, and History*. Edited by Shoshana Felman and Dori Laub. New York: Routledge. 57–74.

Leehan, James. 1993. *Defiant Hope: Spirituality for Survivors of Domestic Violence*. Louisville: Westminster/John Knox Press.

Lipscomb, Steven and Anthony Sherin, eds. 1997. *Battle for the Minds*. [videorecording]. Los Angeles: Battle for the Minds.

Longenecker, Richard N. 1999. *New Wine into Fresh Wineskins: Contextualizing the Early Christian Confessions*. Peabody, Mass.: Hendrickson.

Lorde, Audre. 1984. *Sister Outsider: Essays and Speeches*. New York: Crossing Press.

McCloskey, Laura Ann. 1996. "Socioeconomic and Coercive Power within the Family." *Gender and Society* 10.4 (August): 449–463.

McFarlane, Judith, Willson, Pam, Lemmey, Dorothy, and Ann Malecha. 2000. "Women Filing Assault Charges on an Intimate Partner." *Violence Against Women* 6.4 (April): 396–408.

McKenry, Patrick C., Julian, Teresa W., and Stephen M. Gavazzi. 1995. "Toward a Biopsychosocial Model of Domestic Violence." *Journal of Marriage and the Family* 57 (May): 307–320.

Melton, J. Gordon, ed. 1988. "Summary Statement of Belief." In *Encyclopedia of America Religions: Religious Creeds*. Vol. 1. The National Association of Holiness Churches. Detroit: Gale Research. 327.

Mills, Linda. 1996. "Empowering Battered Women Transnationally: The Case for Postmodern Interventions." *Social Work* 41.3 (May): 261–268.

Mills, Trudy. 1985. "The Assault on the Self: Stages in Coping with Battering Husbands." *Qualitative Sociology* 8.2 (Summer): 103–123.

Morgan, Timothy C. 1994. "The Stained-Glass Ceiling." *Christianity Today* 38.6 (May 16): 52.

Neckerman, Kathryn M. 1993. "The Emergence of 'Underclass' Family Patterns, 1900–1940." In *The "Underclass" Debate: Views From History*. Edited by Michael B. Katz. Princeton: Princeton University Press. 194–219.

Neighbors, Harold W., Elliott, Karin A., and Larry M. Gant. 1990. "Self-Help and Black Americans." In *Working with Self-Help*. Edited by Thomas J. Powell. Silver Spring, Md.: National Association of Social Workers Press. 189–217.

O'Collins, SJ, Gerald and Edward G. Farrugia, SJ. 1991. *A Concise Dictionary of Theology*. New York: Paulist Press.

Ohio State Medical Association. 1993. *Ohio Physicians' Domestic Violence Prevention Project: Trust Talk*. Columbus: Ohio Department of Human Services and the Ohio State Medical Association.

The Oxford Companion to the English Language. 1992. Edited by Tom McArthur. Oxford: Oxford University Press.

Pagelow, Mildred D. 1981. *Woman-Battering: Victims and Their Experiences*. Beverly Hills: Sage.

Peterson, Michael L., ed. 1992. *The Problem of Evil*. Notre Dame: University of Notre Dame Press.

Philliber William W., and Clyde B. McCoy with Harry C. Dillingham, eds. 1981. *The Invisible Minority: Urban Appalachians*. Lexington: University of Kentucky Press.

Photiadis, John D., ed. n.d. *Religion in Appalachia: Theological, Social, and Psychological Dimensions and Correlates.* Center for Extension and Continuing Education, Division of Social and Economic Development, Office of Research and Development: West Virginia University.

Refuerzo, Ben J. and Stephen Verderber. 1989. "Effects of Personal Status and Patterns of Use on Residential Satisfaction in Shelters for Victims of Domestic Violence." *Environment and Behavior* 21.4 (July): 413–434.

Richard, Lucien. 1992. *What are They Saying about the Theology of Suffering?* New York: Paulist Press.

Richie, Beth E. 1995. "Battered Black Women: A Challenge for the Black Community." In *Words of Fire: An Anthology of African-American Feminist Thought.* Edited by Beverly Guy-Sheftall. New York: New Press. 398–404.

———. 1991. "Battered Women: An African American Perspective." *The ABNF* (Association of Black Nursing Faculty) *Journal* (Fall): 81–84.

Ridington, Jillian. 1977–8. "The Transition Process: A Feminist Environment as Reconstitutive Milieu." *Victimology: An International Journal* 2.3–4: 563–575.

Riss, R. M. 1988. "The Role of Women." *Dictionary of Pentecostal and Charismatic Movements.* Eds. Stanley M. Burgess and Patrick H. Alexander. Grand Rapids: Zondervan. 893–899.

Rodgers, Kathy. 1997. *The Nation.* (11 August). 2.

Rodriquez, Noelie Maria. 1988. "A Successful Feminist Shelter: A Case Study of the Family Crisis Shelter in Hawaii." *The Journal of Applied Behavioral Science* 24.3 (August): 235–250.

———. 1988. "Transcending Bureaucracy: Feminist Politics at a Shelter for Battered Women." *Gender … Society* 2.2 (June): 214–227

Roth, Ron with Peter Occhiogrosso. 1999. *Prayer and the Five Stages of Healing.* Carlsbad, Calif.: Hay House.

Russell, Diana. 1984. *Sexual Exploitation: Rape, Child Abuse, and Sexual Harassment.* Beverly Hills: Sage.

Schweizer, Harold. 1997. *Suffering and the Remedy of Art.* Albany: State University of New York Press.

Shalala, Donna E. 1994. "Domestic Terrorism: An Unacknowledged Epidemic." *Vital Speeches of the Day.* Vol. LX. 15 (May 15): 450–453.

Snow, Barbara W. and Geraldine G. Hanni. 1988. "Counseling the Adult Survivor of Child Sexual Abuse: Concepts and Cautions for the Clergy." In *Abuse and Religion: When Praying Isn't Enough.* Edited by Anne L. Horton and Judith A. Williamson. Lexington, Mass.: Heath. 157–163.

Soelle, Dorothee. 1990. *The Window of Vulnerability. A Political Spirituality.* Translated by Linda M. Maloney. Minneapolis: Fortress.

Spindler, George and Louise Spindler. 1987. *Interpretive Ethnography of Education: At Home and Abroad.* Hillsdale, N.J.: Lawrence Erlbaum.

Stark, Evan and Anne H. Flitcraft. 1991. "Spouse Abuse." In *Violence in America: A Public Health Approach.* Edited by Mark L. Rosenberg and Mary Ann Fenley. New York: Oxford University Press. 123–157.

Stets, Jan E. and Murray A. Straus. 1990. "Gender Differences in Reporting of Marital Violence and Its Medical and Psychological Consequences." In *Physical Violence in American Families: Risk Factors and Adaptations to Violence in 8,145 Families.* Edited by Murray A. Straus and Richard J. Gelles. New Brunswick, N.J.: Transaction, 151–165.

Stoekl, Allan. 1988. "Elaine Scarry's *The Body in Pain,* Paul Bove's *Intellectuals in Power*; The Pain of Being an Intellectual." *Southern Humanities Review* 22.1. 49–62.

Stringer, Ernest T. 1996. *Action Research: A Handbook for Practitioners.* Thousand Oaks, Calif.: Sage.

Surin, Kenneth. 1986. *Theology and the Problem of Evil.* Oxford: Basil Blackwell.

———. 1993. "The Problem of Evil." In *Blackwell Encyclopedia of Modern Christian Thought.* Edited by Alister E. McGrath. Cambridge: Blackwell. 194.

Tannen, Deborah. 1990. *You Just Don't Understand: Women and Men in Conversation.* New York: Morrow.

Townes, Emilie M. 1995"Black Women: From Slavery to Womanist Liberation." Eds. Rosemary Skinner Keller and Rosemary Radford Ruether. *In Our Own Voices: Four Centuries of American Women's Religious Writing.* San Francisco: Harper. 155–205.

———. 1995. *In A Blaze of Glory: Womanist Spirituality as Social Witness.* Nashville: Abingdon Press.

Turner, Victor. 1986. *The Anthropology of Performance.* New York: PAJ Publications.

van der Kolk, Bessel. 1988. "The Trauma Spectrum: The Interaction of Biological and Social Events in the Genesis of the Trauma Response," *Journal of Traumatic Stress* 1: 273–90.

Waldenfels, SJ., Hans. 1997. "Contextual Theology." *Dictionary of Mission: Theology, History, Perspectives.* Eds. Karl Muller, SVD, Theo Sundermeier, Stephen B. Bevans, SVD, and Richard H. Bliese. Maryknoll, N.Y.: Orbis. 82–87.

Warshaw, Carole. 1989. "Limitations of the Medical Model in the Care of Battered Women," *Gender ... Society* 3.4 (December): 506–517.

Websdale, Neil and Meda Chesney-Lind. 1998. "Men Victimizing Women and Children: Doing Violence to Women/Research Synthesis on the Victimization of Women." In *Masculinities and Violence.* Edited by Lee H. Bowker. Thousand Oakes, Calif.: Sage).

Weems, Renita J. 1995. *Battered Love: Marriage, Sex, and Violence in the Hebrew Prophets.* Minneapolis: Fortress Press.

Weil, Simone. *Waiting for God.* 1951. Translated by Emma Crauford. New York: Harper and Rowe.

Wharton, Carol S. 1989. "Splintered Visions: Staff/Client Disjunctions and Their Consequences for Human Service Organizations." *Journal of Contemporary Ethnography* 18.1 (April): 50–71.

Whitehead, Alfred North. 1978. *Process and Reality: An Essay in Cosmology,* corrected edition. Edited by David Ray Griffin and Donald W. Sherburne. New York: Free Press.

Williams, Delores S. 1993. "A Womanist Perspective on Sin." In *A Troubling in my Soul: Womanist Perspectives on Evil and Suffering.* Edited by Emilie M. Townes. Maryknoll, N.Y.: Orbis. 130–149.

———. 1996. "A Complexity of Adaptation to Trauma: Self-Regulation, Stimulus Discrimination, and Characterological Development." In *Traumatic Stress: The*

Effects of Overwhelming Experience on Mind, Body, and Society. Edited by Bessel A. Van der Kolk, Alexander C. McFarlane, Lars Weisaeth. New York: Guilford. 182–213.

Williams-Jones, Pearl. 1977. "A Minority Report: Black Pentecostal Women," *Spirit* 1.2. 31–44.

Wolfe, D. A., Zak, L., Wilson, S., and P. Jaffe. 1985. "Child Witnesses to Violence between Parents: Critical Issues in Behavioral and Social Adjustment," *Journal of Abnormal Child Psychology* 53: 657–665.

Yinger, J. Milton. 1986. "Black Americans and Predominantly White Churches." Paper prepared for the Committee on the Status of Black Americans, National Research Council, Washington D.C. 36–7.

Yllo, Kersti and Michele Bograd. 1988. *Feminist Perspectives on Wife Abuse.* Newbury Park, Calif.: Sage.

Yllo, Kersti and Murray Straus. 1984. "Patriarchy and Violence Against Wives: The Impact of Structural and Normative Factors." *Journal of International and Comparative Social Welfare* 1: 1–13.

Author Index

Adam (of Genesis), 4; and Eve, 98, 116, 135–37
Aquinas, St., 9, 82
Atkins, Daniel G., 239 n15
Augustine, St., 9, 82

Bachman, Ronet, 234 n1
Bakhtin, M. M., 4–6, 168, 173, 220, 225, 232
Bascio, Patrick, 214
Bednarowski, Mary Farrell, 225
Belenky, M. F., 246 n9
Belle, Deborah, 35
Bernstein, Basil, 247 n22
Bevans, Stephen, 193–94, 200, 214
Brasher, Brenda E., 242 n18
Brown, Penelope, 248 n12
Bugental, Daphne Blunt, 237 n18

Cahil, Lisa Sowle, 153–54
Callender, Ann, 239 n18
Camus, Albert, 9, 82
Cannon, Katie Geneva, 221
Cassell, Eric, 8, 56, 70, 242 n11
Copeland, M. Shawn, 221

Desjarlais, Robert, 241, n35
Dostoevsky, Fyodor, 9, 82
Dyrness, William, 186

Eckert, Penelope, 248 n12
Eisenberg, Leon, 241 n35
Eve (of Genesis), 65, 191

Farley, Wendy, 84
Fiorenza, Elisabeth Schussler, 153–54
Fortune, Marie M., 9, 11, 81, 86, 146–48, 152–55, 162, 163, 247 n14
Fowler, Gary L., 90

Gavazzi, Stephen M., 236 n28
Geertz, Clifford, 12, 82, 91, 241 n2
Gelles, Richard J., 24, 233 n1
Gilkes, Cheryl Townsend, 95
Goldberg, N. R., 246 n9
Good, Byron, 241, n35
Gordon, Linda, 23–25, 152
Grant, Jacquelyn, 94, 115

Hartshorne, Charles, 83
Hayes, Diana L., 121
Heath, Sarah, 50
Herman, Judith Lewis, 8, 11, 54, 63, 66, 77, 146–48, 153–55, 162–63
Hinsdale, Mary Ann, 199
Howard-Synder, Daniel, 242 n3
Hume, 9, 82
Hunt, Mary E., 213

Imbens, Annie, 87

Janoff-Bulman, Ronnie, 66–67, 70
Job, 9, 82, 110–11, 117, 133, 159
Johnson, Elizabeth A., 9, 81, 85–86, 153–54
Johnson, Michael P., 54, 238 n4

265

SUBJECT INDEX

---

abuse, 33, 35; 80; childhood 146; economic 17; emotional 1, 3 17; kinds of, 15–18, 53–55; mental 17; physical 1, 3, 17; sexual 1; social, 156; structural, 156; unreckoned dimensions of, 163

action research, 229, 231, 250 n15

affliction, 70, 84, 108

African-American (women), 2, 34, 39, 87, 199, 221, 232

age, 7, 21, 34, 322; language deriving from, 81

agency, 52, 57–60, 105, 149, 152–53, 239 n12; losing, 157; no agency, 57; batterer's agency, 149

agnostics, 223

all-female enclaves, 99

American Psychiatric Association, 66–67

anointing, 95

apathy, 63

Apostolic tradition, 138, 206; and women, 208

Appalachian, 1, 2, 21, 34, 87, 90, 99, 199, 243 n28

atheists, 223

atonement, 96, 98, 115

avoidance (as coping strategy), 68–69

Baptist, 80, 92, 128–29, 136, 140, 182, 201, 207

battered woman's syndrome, 239 n15

battered women, critical capabilities of, 88; as identity group, 8; and physical health, 18, 70, 241 n35; terminology for, 26, 55, 239 n8

battery, meanings of, 91

bible church (*see also* Baptist), 97

biological distress, 57

black churches, 9, 90–95

body language, 59, 64

Catholic, 7, 65, 80, 91–92, 103, 117, 139, 207

childcare, 39, 42, 156

child-rearing (conflict about), 210

children, abuse of, 160; aggression in, 36; assaulted by abusers, 54; discipline of, 47; and guilt, 150; in the shelter, 33, 35–36, 42

Church of God in Christ, 92

church, (role of), 6, 153, 224–26; evading, 246 n5

church attendance, 102, 125–26

church mothers, 130

church reform, 153

class, 2, 3, 21, 91, 222; conflicts, 33; discrimination, 44; language deriving from 81, 247 n22; middle-class women, 28, middle-class staff, 39; and religious affiliation, 89–92; and suffering, 250 n5; and tensions from, 51

classism, 88